The ESSENTIAL PHONICS TOOLKIT

The ESSENTIAL PHONICS TOOLKIT

KATIE WHITEHEAD

1 Oliver's Yard
55 City Road
London EC1Y 1SP

2455 Teller Road
Thousand Oaks
California 91320

Unit No 323-333, Third Floor, F-Block
International Trade Tower
Nehru Place, New Delhi – 110 019

8 Marina View Suite 43-053
Asia Square Tower 1
Singapore 018960

Editor: Amy Thornton
Assistant editor: Harry Dixon
Production editor: Ian Antcliff
Cover design: Wendy Scott
Typeset by: C&M Digitals (P) Ltd, Chennai, India
Printed in the UK by Bell and Bain Ltd, Glasgow
BB0354178

Library of Congress Control Number: Available

British Library Cataloguing in Publication data

A catalogue record for this book is available from the British Library

ISBN 978-1-5296-8345-5
ISBN 978-1-5296-8344-8 (pbk)

CONTENTS

Acknowledgements   vii
About the author   ix

 1 Introduction   1

 2 Preparing children for phonics   13

 3 Starting school   39

 4 Introducing letters and sounds   57

 5 Blending to read   75

 6 Segmenting to spell   93

 7 Digraphs and trigraphs   107

 8 Moving on from CVC words   121

 9 Reading longer words   135

10 High-frequency words   147

11 Learning to read and spell more complex words   159

12 Year 1 Phonics Screening Check   187

13 Developing a love of reading   201

14 What does an effective phonics lesson look like?   211

15 Ofsted inspections and reading deep dives   221

References   231
Index   235

ACKNOWLEDGEMENTS

Thank you to Delayna, Harry and the team at Sage Publishing for reaching out and making my dream a reality.

To my Ashmead School family for their support, encouragement, time and flexibility over the last 15 years, all of which has enabled me to follow my passion for leading and teaching phonics. There really is no better place to work.

A huge thanks to all the teachers, collaborators, parents and children who have engaged with my Phonics Family Instagram and Facebook pages – without your following this book would not have been possible.

And to my boys. Rob, Thomas, Xander and Miles – my inspiration and motivation. Love you x

ABOUT THE AUTHOR

Katie's undergraduate degree was a BSc Psychology at the University of Sussex where, in her final year, she specialised in Psychology in Education and the Psychology of Language Development. Her dissertation focused on how early print exposure impacted on later comprehension and this is where her interest in teaching literacy started.

In 2005 she studied for an Early Years PGCE at the University of Cambridge. The course developed her passion for teaching young children and began a desire to promote learning through play.

Katie has now been teaching for 19 years and has led a large Reception department, Year 1 team and been instrumental in whole-school phonics development in a large primary school in this time, delivered CPD to internal and external staff, provided training to ITT students and achieved an NPQLL.

She is a Mum to three young boys which has given her the chance to put phonics into action at home and since 2020 has shared thousands of fun and practical literacy activities on her highly successful Phonics Family social media pages.

1
INTRODUCTION

The English language is a complex beast. Its origin is Germanic, brought over to England by the Anglo-Saxons, and over hundreds of years it has Greek, Latin and French influences (Figure 1.1). There are silent letters, irregular spellings and words that have hung on to their original form. For example, the silent 'b' in the word 'doubt' was added by writers in the late fifteenth and sixteenth centuries to help draw a connection to its Latin origin 'dubitare'; the 'b' is actually pronounced in Latin, but silent in its English form. In the word 'climb' the 'b' was originally pronounced by our Old English ancestors but dropped around 1300. The word 'colour', as many of you might know, was adapted from the French word 'couleur'. The English language also experienced what is termed the 'great vowel shift' during the fifteenth century, meaning that the way our vowels sounded changed. This can all make for a pretty tricky language to learn.

Figure 1.1   The influences on the English language over time

As there are some tricky elements to learning the language it can then seem like an absolute minefield to actually teach someone to read it! Teaching children to read through phonics comes with its own baggage. The terminology and jargon involved can seem like a whole new language to learn – phoneme, grapheme, digraph, trigraph, decoding. What does it all mean? You are not only teaching children to read English but also coming to terms with and learning the language involved in teaching it!

All of the above, the complexity of the English language and the terminology involved with phonics, is paired with how crucial it is for children to learn to read and become confident, committed and enthusiastic readers! You are deciphering the black and white marks on this page without really thinking about it. It's automatic, and that's what we want for our children. Research shows that children who become confident in early literacy skills, particularly gaining a wide vocabulary and love of reading, have greater academic success later in life. In comparison, those with low levels of literacy in the early years are more likely to later be excluded from school, suffer with poor physical and mental health, participate in crime (Shinabarger, 2017), misuse medication and have lower-paid jobs, all of which have a huge social and economic cost (Clark and Dugdale, 2008; Mulcahy et al., 2019). In fact, studies show that 57% of adult prisoners in the UK have much lower levels of literacy than the general population and are working at levels below what is expected for an 11-year-old (Ministry of Justice, 2021). The economic cost of illiteracy in the UK is estimated to be around £81 billion per year (Cree et al., 2023).

For children to attain a good level of literacy, to expand their vocabulary and develop a love of reading they must first be proficient in phonics. By teaching children phonics and giving them the opportunity to independently utilise their knowledge and skills, you are providing them with the key to unlock the rest of the curriculum. It is estimated that 85% of the rest of the curriculum involves reading. Reading opens doors. Think about how many times (apart from reading this book) you have read today. Your phone? A social media post? A road sign? A newsletter? An instruction manual? We read for information, for enjoyment, for safety, to learn and to develop. It's a vital skill that needs teaching. It's life changing! It's worrying then that even in developed countries it is estimated that 20–25% of 15-year-olds have yet to achieve the appropriate level of literacy.

The responsibility of teaching a little one to read can therefore be completely overwhelming. It sounds so complicated, yet it is so critical, and needs to be a priority.

I asked a group of primary trainee teachers at the very beginning of their training course what they thought was their biggest hurdle to teaching phonics, and the very large majority responded that they didn't feel confident in their subject knowledge:

It feels like a massive undertaking because it must be done right! Lots of pressure!

I'm worried about saying the sounds wrong

My subject knowledge. I don't know anything about phonics and it's a whole new vocabulary to learn

I lack understanding about the terminology involved and the structure

The comments above are completely understandable for those just starting out on their teaching journey. These trainees, however, will be thrust into teaching phonics at some point during the induction year and, quite rightly, will aim to follow the school's chosen phonics scheme. There will almost certainly be training on how to deliver the adopted published scheme but likely no training about phonics itself. This is where this book can give you a helping hand!

In 2005 when I trained to teach there was no mention of phonics on the course. It was only a couple of years later while teaching in a mixed Reception/Year 1 class that teaching reading via phonics became the focus and we moved away from the 'look and say' or 'my turn, your turn' method of learning to read words. This change in practice is now firmly reflected in the teaching standards: 'If teaching early reading, demonstrate a clear understanding of systematic, synthetic phonics' (Department for Education (DfE), 2011, updated 2021). I would argue that this should go beyond just those 'teaching early reading' and be expanded to all teachers. Those teaching in the older year groups have the responsibility to identify and plug any gaps in reading ability, whether that is gaps in phonic knowledge, fluency, vocabulary or in comprehension, and to do that they need to understand what lies at the foundation of learning to read and what is the most effective way to teach reading.

So, let me get to the point! Why do you need this book?

Its aim is to bridge the gap between an educational text and an activity book. It will be a helping hand that will guide you through the process of teaching young children to read, from developing phonological awareness skills in preschoolers to ultimately encouraging confident, fluent and enthusiastic readers. There will be tips and advice along the way across all the stages of learning to read, targeted multi-sensory activity ideas for each stage, and practical ways to differentiate teaching and support children who are having difficulties. It's ideal for those new to phonics or for those who want to develop their own subject knowledge. I aim to make the mystifying more manageable, break down the barriers of the baffling and ultimately enable you to teach children the skills and knowledge to allow them a swift access to narrative.

THE READING TIMELINE

KEY TERMS

Phonics: a way of learning the sounds that letters, or groups of letters, represent

Synthetic: an approach to teaching reading whereby children are taught to break down words into their individual sounds and then blend these to form words

Systematic: acting according to a progressive plan

Research on how children learn to read has really transformed teaching practice over the last 50 years or so (Figure 1.2). As I mentioned before, when I trained to teach, completing my early years PGCE in 2005, there was no reference to children learning phonics. We learnt about sharing stories, the importance of reading aloud and the benefits of role-play, but nothing on the actual mechanics of teaching a child to read. It was almost as if we were expecting children to just absorb the words and take to reading naturally.

We now know that this is not how it works. Learning to read is not a natural process, it needs to be taught and it needs to be taught in a systematic way (Gotlieb et al., 2022). In order to understand how we have got to this approach, and where we are today in terms of reading instruction, I think it is important to look back on how reading has been taught over the last few decades.

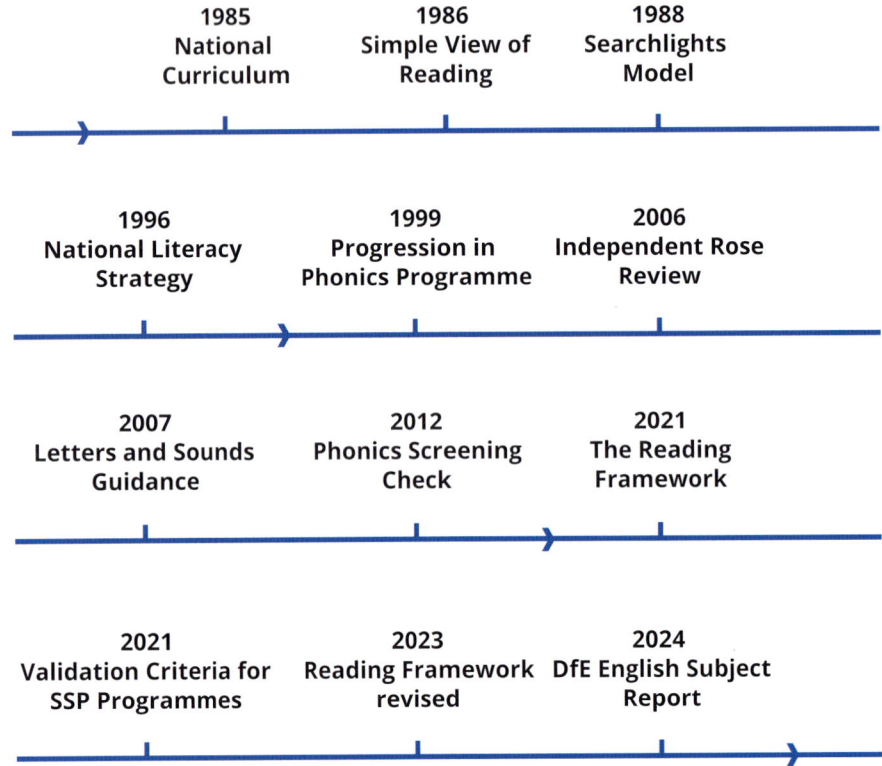

Figure 1.2   Timeline of research and government policies that have influenced the teaching of reading

THE READING WARS

Teaching children to read has historically been a pretty controversial subject, so much so that there is a period during the mid-twentieth century quite often referred to as the 'Reading Wars', where there were two approaches opposed and in conflict about the best way to teach children to read. The synthetic phonics camp encouraged teaching letter–sound correspondence in a systematic way so that children could use this knowledge to blend sounds and read words. On the other side of the fence sat the camp that believed children learn to read via a whole-word method. This approach focuses on the meaning of the words and prompts children to guess unfamiliar words according to the context. Can you guess which side of the fence this book and I sit on? Over the course of several decades the pendulum has swung on both sides of the argument. Quite often, the outcomes of significant research into how best to teach reading can take a long time to filter down and have an impact on policies, curriculum and ultimately classroom practice. Therefore, up until relatively recently this debate still raged on.

THE SEARCHLIGHTS MODEL

Many theoretical models have been proposed to try and put an end to the big debate on how children are taught to read. One of these is the 'searchlights model' (Figure 1.3) which underpinned the approaches to teaching reading within the National Literacy Strategy (1998). This model of reading promotes the idea that learning to read is a very complex issue and that there are multiple influences. Children need knowledge of both grammar and context, word recognition and phonics. The model suggests that children should be encouraged to search for and draw upon the most effective and appropriate aspect every time they read a text. The fact that this model highlights teaching phonics as one of the key components of learning to read has influenced current practice, but it does suggest that each influential factor is independent of others, and if one is taken away then a child can still learn to read, that is to say, a child can still learn to read without any phonics instruction.

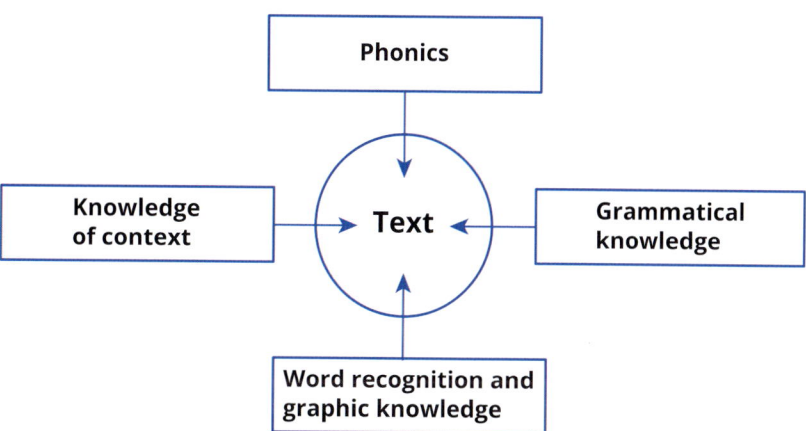

Figure 1.3 The searchlights model showing multiple aspects to learning to read

THE SIMPLE VIEW OF READING

In 1986, during the height of the 'Reading Wars', researchers Gough and Tunmer proposed a different theoretical model (Figure 1.4), one that became embedded in the National Curriculum (Gough and Tunmer, 2013). This model aimed to put an end to the great reading debate. With a background in cognitive research, Gough and Tunmer suggested that reading is a product of both word reading and language comprehension and that these two processes are interlinked. Word reading refers to a child's ability to learn the alphabetic code and use this knowledge to decode words. The other factor is the ability to comprehend what has just been read, and underpinning this is a child's oral language ability. These processes need to come together and be developed to enable children to become proficient and fluent readers. This model was the first step towards teaching children to read via phonics and has been hugely influential in shifting the debate on how reading should be taught. It is represented in a diagram (Figure 1.4) and teachers can use this to plot a pupil's reading skills and knowledge and thereby offer targeted interventions: for example, a child assessed as being in the bottom right quadrant has good language comprehension skills but poor word reading, so needs specific phonics teaching. Quite often children learning English as an additional language may develop the skill of decoding very quickly but need more exposure to vocabulary and comprehension activities so they can understand what they have read. These children would be plotted in the top left quadrant. In an ideal world all children would sit in the top right quadrant. This model was later adopted and had a huge influence on Rose's *Independent Review of the Teaching of Early Reading* (2006) which is discussed in more detail below.

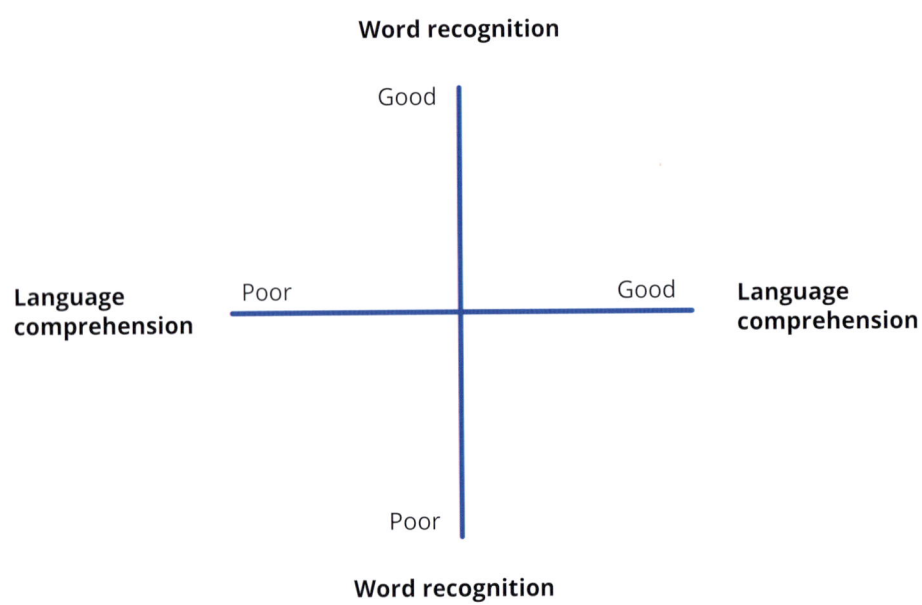

Figure 1.4   The simple view of reading (Gough and Tunmer, 1986)

THE NATIONAL CURRICULUM

In 1985 the *Better Schools* White Paper was published, which pushed for a nationally agreed curriculum. Then in 1987 a consultation document issued by the Department for Education and Science identified key areas that would aim to standardise teaching and assessment across England, ensuring that all children could access a broad and balanced curriculum, setting standards on attainment, improving consistency within the curriculum, and ensuring that the public had a greater awareness and understanding of the importance of schooling. In 1988 Parliament passed the Education Reform Act and the framework for the National Curriculum was set. The framework identified three core subjects, English being one of them. The standardised curriculum was then approved and introduced into primary schools in 1989. Since its introduction it has been reviewed and reformed several times over the years, with a more substantial overhaul in 1995 in response to teachers' complaints regarding testing and assessment.

NATIONAL LITERACY STRATEGY

In 1996 concerns were raised about the poor level of attainment in the core subjects in Key Stage tests, and subsequently two further additions to the National Curriculum were made to support the teaching of English and maths and improve standards and results. The National Literacy Strategy was introduced first in primary schools and then later rolled out into secondary education. The strategy was developed from the requirements of the National Curriculum and based on the 'searchlight model' of reading described above. The strategy highlighted the significance of decoding words and the explicit teaching of phonics to children from the age of 5. It also emphasised the importance of a child's ability to coordinate and utilise other strategies when learning to read (context, knowledge of syntax, making predictions). It was from this that the Literacy Hour was born. A literacy lesson was required to have the following components:

– Phonics and spelling

– Shared text work with an emphasis on reading and writing

– Guided reading

– Independent work

– Plenary

As support for the National Literacy Strategy, *Progression in Phonics* (Department for Education and Employment (DfEE), 1999) was published. This aimed to give teachers a systematic teaching programme and included guidance, training and an accompanying CD-ROM for teachers to develop their subject knowledge and practice. The strategy saw a subsequent rise in standards.

With the introduction of the National Curriculum, National Literacy Strategy and subsequent *Progression in Phonics* guidance, it was clear that the government was responding to current research into how children learn to read and how best to teach them to do so. It was putting phonics up front and centre!

ROSE REVIEW

By 2005 there was a need to raise standards in early literacy skills even further and so the House of Commons Select Committee on Education commissioned the Rose Review (2006). This was to be an independent review of the teaching of early reading with a particular focus on best practice for teaching phonics. The Rose Review drew on evidence from research and practice, and it has consequently been the main catalyst for teaching children to read through a systematic, synthetic phonics (SSP) programme.

As it has such a huge impact on our current policies and practices I think it's necessary to go into a little more detail on what the review concluded and why it is now best practice to teach reading via a systematic, synthetic approach.

Rose published his final report in March 2006, having drawn on sources of information which included evidence from research, consultations with practitioners, and visits to settings. Rose acknowledged that it was the implementation of the National Literacy Strategy that prompted schools to really focus on the way literacy was taught in their settings and to create structured teaching programmes. He further identified four interdependent communication skills of literacy – speaking, listening, reading and writing – and that it was best practice to provide beginner readers with a curriculum that supported these prime skills through a multi-sensory approach. The report also highlighted how reading and writing are interlinked and that the teaching of reading has a big impact on spelling and writing. Rose suggested that the searchlight model needed to be 'reconstructed' as it did not give a big enough emphasis to word recognition as the essential skill in becoming a reader, and that teaching phonics daily would combat this. Through visits to and observations of trainee teaching programmes, Rose suggested that the quality of phonics training needed urgent attention and that practitioners needed to have a more detailed knowledge of phonics and phonics teaching in order to improve standards.

Rose concluded that 'the main ingredients for success in the teaching of beginner readers are: a well-trained teaching workforce, systematic programmes of work that are implemented thoroughly, incisive assessment of teaching and learning, and strong supportive leadership' and that 'high quality phonic work within a language-rich curriculum … gives rise to high standards of reading and writing' (Rose, 2006).

Letters and Sounds Guidance

As a direct result of the Rose Review exposing weaknesses in the searchlight model of learning to read, which was the basis of phonics instruction within the National Literacy Strategy, the Department for Education and Skills (DfES) published the *Letters and Sounds* handbook (DfES, 2007), which gave guidance on teaching phonics using a systematic, synthetic approach. It aimed to also build children's speaking and listening skills and recommended that all children start phonics by the age of 5.

The *Letters and Sounds* handbook broke down the teaching of phonics into phases, which many of the current validated phonics schemes have adopted:

Phase 1: teaching pre-reading skills

Phase 2: introduction of single letters and sounds

Phase 3: teaching digraphs and trigraphs

Phase 4: learning to read polysyllabic words and words that contain adjacent consonants

Phase 5: teaching alternative graphemes and phonemes to those taught in Phases 2 and 3

Up until 2021 many schools throughout England used *Letters and Sounds* as a basis for their phonics teaching. The handbook, however, is guidance and not a full scheme because it did not come with any supplementary resources, such as word cards, grapheme charts or planning.

PHONICS SCREENING CHECK

To continue this sharp focus on synthetic phonics the government introduced the Phonics Screening Check in England during the academic year 2011–2012. This is a statutory assessment administered to children in June of Year 1 and involves them reading a list of 40 words made up of both real words and pseudowords. It is designed to assess children's ability to decode and blend and aims to help identify pupils who may need some extra targeted support. Schools must submit the results to the local authority, but the data are not published or placed in any league tables; they will likely use the data to review their current teaching practice. The national percentage of children achieving the expected level (a pass mark of 32/40) in the check was 80% in 2024, up from 79% in 2023 and almost back to pre-pandemic levels (82% in 2019).

THE READING FRAMEWORK

The Reading Framework, first published in 2021 and revised in 2023, aimed to provide updated guidance and standards for teaching reading in schools and was written to ensure that teaching practice aligns with current educational research, best practice, existing expectations in reading and to ensure that literacy remains at the forefront of children's education. It states that the teaching of reading needs to be a priority. The framework sets out the research underpinning the importance of developing speaking and listening skills, sharing stories, reading aloud, establishing a reading for pleasure culture and the significance of teaching phonics with rigour and fidelity. It outlines best practice criteria for delivering an SSP programme, including the use of matched decodable reading books.

VALIDATION CRITERIA FOR SSP PROGRAMMES

Alongside *The Reading Framework*, in April 2021 the government published core criteria for SSP programmes and began a validation process. SSP programmes wanting to be validated had to apply and prove thorough evidence to the validation board that they met the 16 essential criteria (see below). The process was designed so that schools could select a validated phonics scheme to implement and be sure that they were meeting the criteria for high-quality phonics teaching. Prior to this process many had developed their own programme, often cherry-picking resources and plans from several schemes, based on the *Letters and Sounds* guidance (DfES, 2007). However, the government moved to make phonics teaching more consistent and for a school to have fidelity to one scheme. It is not a statutory requirement to select one of the validated programmes but the school itself would have to show that their phonics instruction was meeting the criteria and their bespoke scheme would more than likely be thoroughly scrutinised during any Ofsted inspection.

The 16 essential criteria outlined by the DfE (2023d) are that a programme should:

- constitute a complete SSP programme providing fidelity to its teaching framework for the duration of the programme

- present systematic synthetic phonic work as the prime approach to decoding print
- enable children to start learning phonic knowledge and skills early in reception, and provide a structured route for most children to meet or exceed the expected standard in the year one phonics screening check and all national curriculum expectations for word reading through decoding by the end of key stage 1
- be designed for daily teaching sessions and teach the main grapheme–phoneme correspondences (GPCs) of English (the alphabetic principle) in a clearly defined, incremental sequence
- begin by introducing a defined group of grapheme-phoneme correspondences that enable children to read and spell many words early on
- progress from simple to more complex phonic knowledge and skills, cumulatively covering all the major grapheme-phoneme correspondences in English
- teach children to read printed words by identifying and blending (synthesising) individual phonemes, from left to right all through the word
- teach them to apply the skill of segmenting spoken words into their constituent phonemes for spelling and that this is the reverse of blending phonemes to read words
- provide the opportunity for them to practise and apply known GPCs for spelling through the dictation of sounds, words and sentences
- ensure they're taught to decode and spell common-exception words (sometimes called 'tricky' words), appropriate to their level of progress in the programme
- provide resources that support the teaching of lowercase and capital letters correctly, with clear start and finish points, and that will move children on by teaching them to write words made up of learned GPCs, followed by simple sentences composed from such words and any common-exception words learned
- be built around direct teaching sessions, with extensive teacher–child interaction and a multi-sensory approach, with guidance on how direct teaching sessions can be adapted for online delivery, either live or recorded
- provide resources to enable teachers to deliver the programme effectively, including sufficient decodable reading material to ensure children can practise by reading texts closely matched to their level of phonic attainment and that do not require them to use alternative strategies to read unknown words
- include guidance and resources to ensure children practise and apply the core phonics they've been taught
- enable their progress to be assessed, and highlight the ways in which the programme meets the needs of those at risk of falling behind, including the lowest-attaining 20%
- provide full guidance for teachers and appropriate programme-specific training, either directly through appointed agents or remotely, with assurances that there is sufficient capacity and those delivering it have both high levels of expertise and relevant experience

THE BUILDING BLOCKS OF READING

Research over many decades has now identified that there are five critical components to becoming a strong reader. I like to think about them as the building blocks of reading. At the foundation lies phonological and phonemic awareness and the essential pre-reading skills that underpin phonics. Once children are confident at word reading they can independently expand their vocabulary, build fluency and develop comprehension; each skill builds upon the previous ones with the ultimate goal to become a confident and enthusiastic reader.

The building blocks are a useful illustration for interventions too. If children are struggling with comprehension, then offer interventions that target fluency. If a child is finding it difficult to read a text with appropriate speed and accuracy, then they need targeted phonics instruction to develop word reading. If a child struggles to decode words, then revert to supporting and developing phonological awareness skills. Like with any child and any area of learning that needs additional support, it's important that gaps in knowledge, skills and understanding are identified, targeted and addressed early so that these gaps do not widen. Every child should be given the opportunity and feel like they can become a reader.

As you read through the book you will climb up the reading pyramid (Figure 1.5). I will talk through how you can support children to develop their phonological awareness; work through, in depth, how to systematically teach children phonics; and discuss how we can encourage fluency and promote a love of reading.

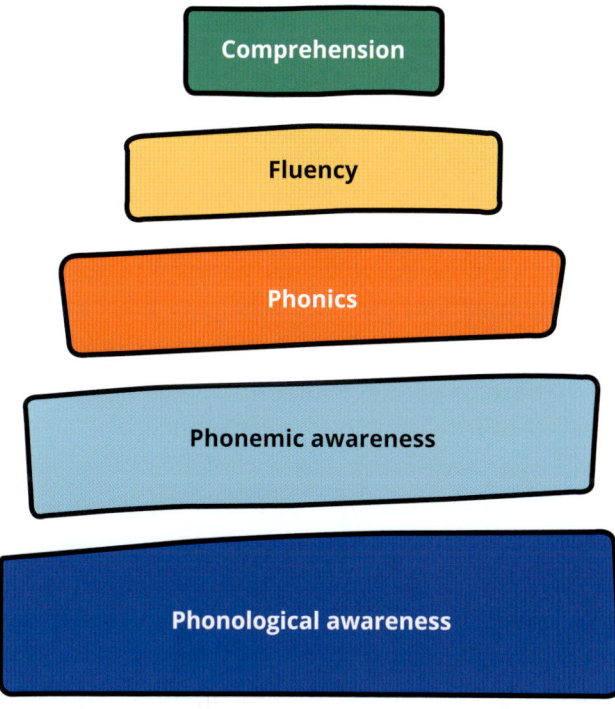

Figure 1.5   The building blocks of reading, showing the five critical components needed to become a successful reader

WHAT IS A MULTI-SENSORY APPROACH TO PHONICS?

As mentioned in the essential criteria above, SSP programmes need to ensure that their approach to teaching is multi-sensory, but what does that mean in practice? Teaching, practice and application activities need to be active, interesting, engaging and motivating but firmly focused on the learning intention. Lessons are planned to engage more than one sense, which can include the use of manipulatives, gestures, visual hooks, reading and writing, and children are given the opportunity to apply their phonic knowledge using movement, interaction and collaboration, not just sitting and listening to the teacher. The phonics lessons themselves remain structured, systematic and predictable to avoid cognitive overload, but children also need to be provided with the opportunity to consolidate their learning with 'hands-on' activities within the classroom provision and across the rest of the curriculum. Multi-sensory reading activates different parts of the brain, affects how we process information and has been found to improve memory performance (Zeynep et al., 2023). Ultimately, the use of multi-sensory phonics means children are much more likely to engage with their learning and retain knowledge. It's in the application that the learning sticks!

> Multi-sensory activities featured strongly in high quality phonic work and often encompassed, variously, simultaneous visual, auditory and kinaesthetic activities involving, for example, physical movement to copy letter shapes and sounds, and manipulate magnetic or other solid letters to build words. (Rose Review, 2006, para. 57, p. 21)

At the end of Chapters 2–12 I share five practical and playful activities that can be incorporated into phonics teaching either one-to-one with a child, within an adult-led small group, or independently chosen during free access to provision. All the activities aim to provide children with the opportunity to apply and consolidate their phonic knowledge and embed learning in a fun and engaging way. There are also useful word banks, checklists, audits or templates at the end of every chapter.

So, I really hope this book does become your essential phonics toolkit! I hope it is an easy manual to lift off the shelf and give you a helping hand as you wade through the terminology and practicalities of teaching your little ones to read, with lots of fun and engaging ways to put phonics teaching into practice. I truly believe that children need to hold phonics in their hands before they hold it in their heads!

IN SUMMARY

- The way we teach children to read has changed over the decades in response to research, influencing government policies at the time, with a frequent pendulum swing between whole-word reading and synthetic phonics.
- The simple view of reading (Gough and Tunmer, 1986) looked to put an end to the 'Reading Wars' and proposed that reading was a result of good language comprehension and word reading.
- The Rose Review (2006) had a huge impact on teaching practice and policies and further embedded phonics as the main route to teaching reading.
- Children are now taught to read using a systematic, synthetic phonics programme.
- There are five main building blocks to becoming a successful reader: phonological awareness, phonemic awareness, phonics, fluency and comprehension.

2
PREPARING CHILDREN FOR PHONICS

Learning to read starts with our eyes closed. (Katie Whitehead)

KEY TERMS

Alliteration: a series of words that begin with the same sound

Auditory: relates to the sense of hearing

Consonant sound: a speech sound that is made by partially or completely blocking air with the lips, teeth, tongue, or throat

Emergent literacy: skills and knowledge that children acquire before being formally taught to read and write

Onset and rime: the onset is the initial phonological unit of a word, and the rime refers to the string of letters that follow

Oral: spoken, as opposed to written

Oral blending: children's ability to listen to the individual sounds within a word and then merge these sounds together to say the word as a whole

Oral segmenting: the ability to listen to a whole word, break it up and say the individual sounds within it

Phoneme: the smallest unit of sound within a word

Phonemic awareness: the ability to break up and manipulate the individual sounds with the spoken word

Phonological awareness: a skill that children develop to recognise and play with the units of sounds within the spoken language

(Continued)

Syllable: a unit of speech sound within a word

Vocabulary: a growing bank of words that students need in order to comprehend texts

Vowel: a speech sound that is made with a fairly open vocal tract

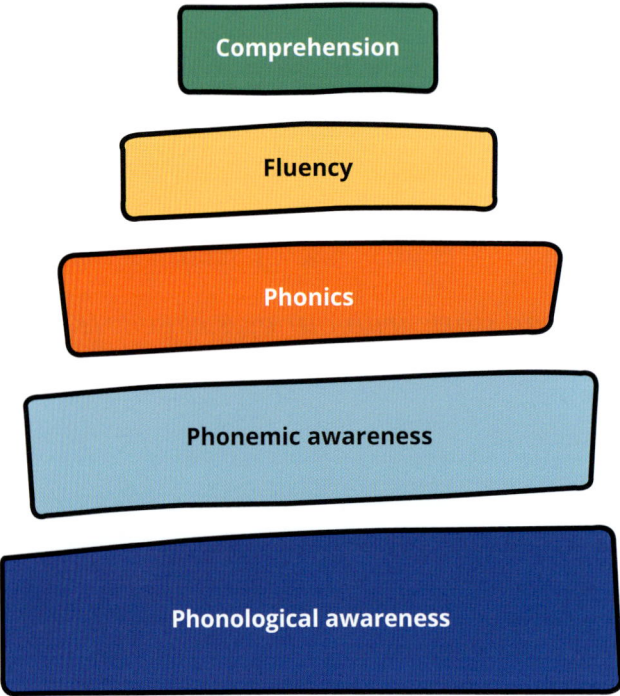

Figure 2.1　The building blocks of reading, showing the five critical components needed to become a successful reader

What do I mean by the quote at the beginning of this chapter? Children's ability to read starts way before they match any letters to their sounds. It starts with children developing vital speaking and listening skills that are fundamental to phonics. If we reference the building blocks of reading from Chapter 1 (see Figure 2.1), the pyramid needs to have a secure foundation for it to remain standing. Likewise, children need to have a solid understanding of the important foundational pre-reading skills as these pave the way for any structured, systematic phonics instruction. But what are the underpinning skills and knowledge that children require before learning to read? How can we encourage emergent literacy? What do we need to provide children to give them the best start to their reading journey?

EMERGENT LITERACY

Reading to children, even before they can understand words, teaches them to associate books with love and affection. (Author unknown)

Emergent literacy includes all the skills and knowledge that children acquire in the early years before they start to be taught formal phonics. More growth happens between the years 0–5 than any other years in a child's life (Whitehead, 2010). These early years are crucial, and the importance of early language skills should not be underestimated as the basis of communicating, reading and writing (DfE, 2023c). In fact, research shows that the soothing, rhythmic sounds of a mother's voice reading a story to their baby in the womb can impact their brain activity, lower foetal heart rate (Voegtline et al., 2013) and improve early literacy skills, indicating that language abilities have their origins before birth (Kisilevsky et al., 2008). A study conducted by the University of Oregon found direct evidence that neural memory traces in the brains of babies were formed by auditory learning prior to birth (Partanen et al., 2013). It's never too early to start promoting key speaking and listening skills!

ACTIVITY 2.1

The Cow Says Moo!

What does knowing that a cow says 'moo' or a sheep says 'baa' have to do with phonics and learning to read? This is a simple activity that you can set up for toddlers to develop the underpinning skills of phonics; using small world role-play will heighten enthusiasm and engagement too! Create a frame to act as a pen for a selection of different farm animals. Now the toddler drives a tractor past the animals, making the animal noise as they reach each one. If you set up a cow, pig and sheep, the child would say 'moo', 'oink' and then 'baa'. What is this teaching them?

1   Matching an object (cow) with an associated sound ('moo') is a prerequisite to learning that symbols (graphemes) have sounds that represent them (phonemes)
2   Children will be saying the sounds from left to right, which reinforces that we read text in this direction and this is exactly what children need to do as they decode a word on a page
3   Isolating sounds in order and manipulating them by changing an animal helps children practise for later segmenting and blending phonemes
4   Physically saying the sounds the animals make means that children are creating different shapes and movements with their mouths which 'trains' the mouth muscles for later more complex speech production

PHONOLOGICAL AWARENESS

Phonological awareness is the foundation upon which all the other layers of literacy are built and is fundamentally the umbrella term for all the speaking and listening skills that children need to acquire prior to learning to read. It encompasses children's understanding that sentences can be broken into words and words can be broken down into syllables. Children will also discover and play with the onset and rime of words. All of these skills require children to listen for and manipulate larger units of sounds within words, which is an essential skill in learning to read.

If children can break up a word into its syllables this means they are more likely to later be able to identify and play with the phonemes within words. If they can match objects that start with the same sound, then they are developing the skill of isolating individual phonemes which will impact their ability to read and write once they start formal phonics instruction. Children need to hone their skill of listening for sounds, starting with larger units of sounds and eventually moving onto the smallest units of sound within a word (phonemes).

There are four key components to phonological awareness, illustrated in Figure 2.2.

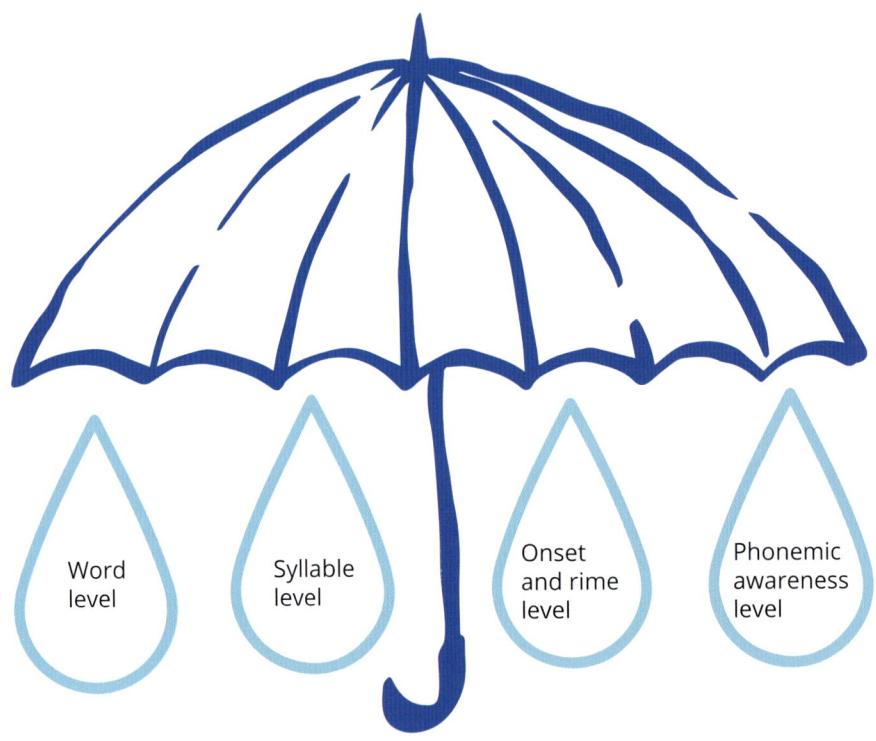

Figure 2.2   The key components of phonological awareness

Word Level

This is the ability to identify individual words within a sentence. Can children repeat back a full sentence to you without missing any words? Can they count the number of words in a sentence? Can they change a word while making the sentence still make sense? Provide children with picture prompts and encourage them to articulate a sentence.

ACTIVITY 2.2

Word Substitution

An activity to help develop children's word level phonological awareness by encouraging children to orally change a word in a sentence each time.

The man is sat on the bus → The man is sat on the train → The girl is sat on the train → The girl is sitting on the train → The boy is sitting on the train → The boy is sitting on the chair

Syllable Level

This requires children to develop the ability to break up words into syllable units; listening for chunks of sounds within a word acts as a good baseline for later breaking up words into their phonemes. Identifying syllable units within words is also a great foundation for later phonics learning when children move on to read longer and more complex words and learn about the different types of syllables, which will aid their spelling. We will go into more depth about this in Chapter 11.

A great place to start is to help children identify the syllables within their name and the names of friends; these are familiar words, and young children are always more motivated when it involves something about themselves!

A syllable always contains one vowel sound:

ant = 1 syllable

spider = 2 syllables

butterfly = 3 syllables

caterpillar = 4 syllables

Tip 2.1   It is important to remember that the length of the word has nothing to do with the number of syllables: 'sat' has one syllable but so does 'straight'.

Below are ten simple and practical ways to help children identify and count syllables:

1   Clapping – first, model clapping the syllables in words. After demonstrating, encourage children to copy and try with other familiar words. You are essentially encouraging children to identify the beats within a word, and this makes it easier to identify and count the syllables. Clapping also adds a physical element so children can *see* the syllables too.
2   Hand under your chin – we produce a vowel sound with our mouths open so, as each syllable contains a vowel sound, place your hand just below your chin and say the word. Your chin will hit your hand for each syllable within the word.
3   Hum the word – encourage children to hum the word. This will make it easier to identify the units of sounds.

4   Robot voice – have children pretend to be a robot and speak in a 'robot voice'. This will force them to slow down when saying words and speak in a robotic manner, meaning they will naturally break up the word into its syllables.

5   Kitchen band – provide children with wooden spoons, pots and pans. They can use them like a set of drums and bang a pot with the wooden spoon for each syllable within a word.

6   Syllable splash – put on your wellies, go outside and jump in the puddles. One jump for every syllable.

7   Making marks – provide children with pencils, pens and paper. Children can make a mark for each syllable in the word. They could draw dots, lines or circles. Once they have finished they can count the number of marks and repeat for other words.

8   Bingo dabbers – bingo dabbers are a great tool to use for any stage of phonics. Children can dab the number of syllables and then count them.

9   Syllable 'I Spy' – instead of the usual initial sound 'I Spy', play with syllables instead. 'I spy an object that is yellow and has three syllables' (sunflower). 'I spy something that has two syllables and it cleans your teeth' (toothbrush).

10 Musical instruments – use musical instruments to create a sound for each syllable within the word.

Example 2.1 shows a few common and familiar words sorted by the number of syllables they contain.

Example 2.1   Words sorted according to number of syllables

1 syllable	2 syllables	3 syllables	4 syllables
cat	dinner	banana	television
bag	breakfast	fantastic	caterpillar
chair	laptop	uniform	alligator
book	toothbrush	crocodile	helicopter
clock	jacket	dinosaur	rhinoceros
bed	sofa	motorbike	watermelon
Mum	table	elephant	avocado
Dad	curtain	umbrella	cauliflower

Onset and Rime Level

The onset of a word is the initial consonant sound that comes before the vowel, and the rime refers to the string of letters that follow. Providing children with the opportunity to practise identifying and playing with the onset and rime within words is an important step to breaking up words into smaller units of sound. Children can also practise sorting pictures and objects by initial sounds, thereby developing their knowledge of alliteration.

ACTIVITY 2.3

Make a Silly Soup to Develop Children's Ability to Recognise Alliteration

One of my favourite alliteration activities is to play a game of 'Silly Soup'. Place out a selection of objects that begin with the same initial sound, a plastic bowl and a wooden spoon. Explain to children that you are going to make some 'silly soup'. They can start stirring the soup and passing the bowl around to all children while you sing the following ditty:

> We're making silly soup,
>
> we'll make it nice and silly!
>
> Put the bowl in the fridge,
>
> and make it nice and chilly!

When you finish singing, ask a child to place one of the objects into the soup, saying the word and emphasising the initial sound as they do. You then repeat until all objects are placed in the bowl. An adult can recap afterwards by pulling out the objects one by one and highlighting and emphasising the matching initial sound. This activity can also be adapted to place objects with the same rime into the bowl instead.

You can organise words according to their rime into what is termed 'word families' (Example 2.2).

Example 2.2 A list of words sorted into word families

at	et	ig	og	ug
bat	bet	big	bog	bug
hat	met	dig	dog	mug
rat	set	pig	log	rug
mat	let	fig	hog	hug
fat	pet	jig	cog	tug
cat	wet	wig		
chat				

When children are struggling to blend all of the phonemes within words they can first attempt to blend the onset and rime as this reduces the amount of sounds they need to merge together to form the word. I'll discuss this further in Chapter 5.

Phonemic Awareness Level

This is the most advanced skill of phonological awareness. Phonemic awareness is the ability to identify the individual phonemes (the smallest unit of sound) within the spoken word and essentially 'play around' with them. Children will practise the skill of oral blending and segmenting. There is no need to look at any words on a page for this; phonemic awareness requires children to use their speaking and listening skills. Can children blend the sounds /s/a/t/ to form the word 'sat'? Can they identify the phonemes within the word 'pen'? Can they listen to an adult say, 'go and get your /c/oa/t/', and retrieve the correct object?

PHONEMIC AWARENESS

Phonemic awareness is the next level in the building blocks to reading and is a fundamental skill for children to become proficient in before they begin to match written letters to sounds and read words on a page. There are six levels of phonemic awareness, illustrated on the ladder in Figure 2.3, in order of difficulty going up the ladder from the easiest to the hardest to master. All the steps on the phonemic awareness ladder involve listening for the phonemes and manipulating them in some way to create new words.

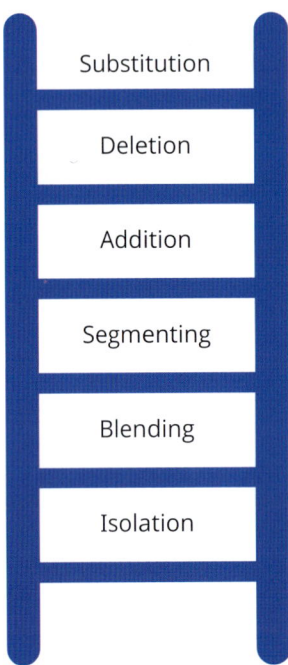

Figure 2.3 The six levels of phonemic awareness

An illustration of each step in phonemic awareness would be for an adult to say the word 'top' to a child:

Isolation: Can they tell you the first sound is /t/? Can they identify the final phoneme as /p/?

Blending: Say the individual sounds /t/o/p/. Can they blend the sounds and say 'top'?

Segmenting: Say the whole word 'top'. Can they tell you the three phonemes in the word?

Addition: What word do we make if we add /s/ to the start?

Deletion: What word do we make if we take away /t/?

Substitution: What word do we get if we change /t/ for /m/? What word if we change the /o/ to /i/?

ACTIVITY 2.4

Further Ways to Support Children's Developing Phonemic Awareness

Isolating Phonemes

What's the first sound in 'fish'?

What is the middle sound in 'pan'?

What is the final sound in 'pig'?

Can we find all the objects that begin with a /s/?

Which object is the odd one out?

Blending Phonemes

I spy a /d/o/g/

Put on your /h/a/t/

Put your hands on your /h/ea/d/

Touch your /f/oo/t/

Point to the /d/oor/

Run to the /ch/air/

It is /h/o/t/ today because the /s/u/n/ is out

Segmenting Phonemes

What are the sounds in the word 'bag'?

Use a robot voice and tell me the sounds in 'tin'

Can you clap your hands for each sound in the word 'red'?

Let's press a blob of playdough for each sound in 'set'

Adding Phonemes

What word do we make if we add /g/ to the start of 'rip'?

What word is made if we put a /h/ at the beginning of 'and'?

Let's add a /s/ in front of 'lip'

(Continued)

Deleting Phonemes

What word do we make if we take away /s/ from 'sat'?

What word can you hear if we take away the /p/ from 'play'?

What word is made if we take away /p/ from 'pit'?

Substituting Phonemes

Can we make 'tip' say 'tap'?

Let's change 'tap' to 'map'

Change 'map' to 'man'

How can we change 'man' to 'pan'?

Make 'pan' into 'pin'

As phonemic awareness is all about a child's ability to manipulate the sounds in words and honing their skills of oral blending and oral segmentation a useful tool to help this skill is to use sound buttons. The buttons could be made from a blob of playdough, dots on a page or simply moving counters (you could use actual clothes buttons as counters). Children press or move the object for each phoneme within the word. Check out Chapter 6 where I showcase my top ten manipulatives for segmenting.

TUNING INTO RHYME

We looked at the skill of listening for the onset and rime in words as part of developing children's phonological awareness earlier in this chapter, and you may have thought that I had messed up on the editing and repeatedly misspelt 'rhyme'! However, rime and rhyme are two separate terms. As we saw before, rime refers to the chunk of the word following the initial sound. It looks at the spelling of this chunk to help sort words into word families (log, dog, bog, cog), whereas rhyme is all about the *sound* that chunk makes. The rimes of words always rhyme, but the rhyme of a word is not always a rime (See Tip 2.2).

Tip 2.2 'care', 'pair' and 'their' rhyme but don't have the same rime! The rhyme is spelt differently in each of the words, so they are not part of the same word family.

As part of developing their foundational pre-reading skills, children need to practise recognising and producing rhyme – to have opportunities to join in with nursery rhymes and songs as well as listen to rhyming stories. The repetitive nature, simplicity and pre-dictability of rhymes make them fun for children to tune into the language and they readily engage with them by joining in and repeating them. Listening for rhyme and continuing a rhyming string is another way for children to practise listening for the pat-terns in words alongside isolating and manipulating larger units of sounds within words, which is a step to isolating single phonemes.

Children's knowledge of rhyme has been shown to be a predictor of later success in literacy (Dunst et al., 2011). Bryant et al. (1989) found strong links between children's early knowledge of rhyme at 3 and their reading ability at 6 years old due to rhyme enhancing children's phonological sensitivity. Mem Fox in her book *Reading Magic* (2008) also suggests that if children know 8 nursery rhymes by the time they are 4 they are more likely to be better readers by the time they are 8.

How do nursery rhymes have such an effect on children's reading?

- They expose children to rhythm, rhyme and alliteration
- They develop vocabulary
- They are repetitive so children are more likely to join in and repeat by heart
- They prompt correct enunciation
- They develop memory
- They encourage listening and concentration skills

Below is a list of 20 traditional and popular rhymes to sing with preschoolers:

1. Old Macdonald
2. Incy Wincy spider
3. Row, row, your boat
4. Baa baa black sheep
5. Miss Polly had a dolly
6. 1, 2, 3, 4, 5, once I caught a fish alive
7. Five little ducks
8. Twinkle, twinkle little star
9. Humpty Dumpty
10. Hey diddle diddle
11. Wheels on the bus
12. Jack and Jill
13. The Grand Old Duke of York
14. Rain, rain, go away
15. It's raining, it's pouring
16. This little piggy went to market
17. I'm a little teapot
18. Ten currant buns
19. Three blind mice
20. Hickory dickory dock

PRINT KNOWLEDGE

It's important for children in the early years, before they learn to match any letters to sounds, to gain exposure to print so that they begin to recognise that it carries meaning. Children notice common symbols within the environment from a very early age. How many 3-year-olds point out the sign for the local supermarket or familiar logos on the high street? The golden arches perhaps?

We can point out print in the environment and model the need to read by reading shopping lists, signs, menus, instruction manuals or demonstrating using books to find out information. This will show that words have a practical purpose. Digital print plays a big part too. You can show how you use Google to answer questions or research your favourite topics. This will develop children's interest in reading and highlight the importance of reading in everyday life.

Children will also need to develop their understanding that text is made up of words and that there are spaces between them; that words can be long and short depending on the number of letters and that, in English, we read from left to right and top to bottom. When reading story books with young children, place your finger under each of the individual words to demonstrate this. Ask them to show you where you are meant to start reading. Point to text within a speech bubble and ask children what they think it says. Ultimately, strong print knowledge lays the foundation for successful reading acquisition and literacy development.

Ensure that with young children you model writing in lowercase rather than capitals (except for the start of their names). Some literacy games and resources are culprits of this too. For a child starting out on their reading journey the sole use of uppercase is a hindrance. The very large majority of story books, decodable texts and classroom print will be written in lowercase. Simple words and captions that beginner readers practise with will be in lowercase too.

VISUAL PERCEPTION AND DISCRIMINATION

> **Tip 2.3** Visual discrimination is the ability to match exact characteristics of two shapes and notice similarities and differences between shapes, objects and symbols.

Visual perception refers to a person's ability to make sense of what they can see. Beginner readers perceive words letter by letter, which is why they can discriminate between words, for example, noticing the difference between 'bit' and 'bet' or 'chip' and 'chop'. Early readers will need practice and time to develop their eye muscles and the many visual skills that are required for reading, including the ability to pay attention to what they see, discriminate between objects and notice the similarities and differences, as well as learn and recall the visual traits of objects.

> **Tip 2.4** The eye muscles required for reading are not fully developed until around age 6–7.

We are not born with the brain connections between vision and speech (the connections that enable reading) and instead we need to build and develop these connections. Before children match letters to sounds we must first provide them with activities that strengthen these visual perception skills – this includes encouraging children to look carefully; remember what they have seen; match objects and pictures; find the differences; and look at the features of shapes. These opportunities will enhance vital visual processing skills and develop the connections between speech and vision. Here is a list of ten games and activities that can help prepare children's eyes and brains for reading success:

1 Snap card games
2 Jigsaw puzzles
3 Sequencing games – can children observe the patterns and sequences of objects and then find the next object in the sequence?
4 Visual memory game – show children a selection of up to seven objects. Cover them and take one away. Can they tell you which one is missing?
5 *Where's Wally?* books
6 Spot the difference picture puzzles
7 Pointing out features of shapes and lines – pointing out the curved, straight, wavy, horizontal and vertical lines of shapes will support children when they later learn letter shapes
8 Dominoes
9 Observational walks – go on a walk and then ask children to tell you four things that they saw on their trip
10 'Book Look' – open a small picture or story book to a given page and have the child scan it for a few seconds. Close the book and ask them to find the same page again

DEVELOP VOCABULARY

> Not knowing the meaning of words in a text is a bottleneck in reading.
> (Perfetti et al., 2005)

Studies show that children's vocabulary development plays a critical role in their literacy acquisition and that there is a 'clear association between the development of vocabulary and phonological awareness in children' (Joliffe et al., 2019). In fact, vocabulary is one of the most robust long-term predictors of good literacy development (Snow and Juel, 2005). Pupils' expressive vocabulary (the words that they can use) and receptive vocabulary (the words that they understand) are important components of their wider language skills. There is a positive correlation between a pupil's vocabulary size and their academic success (Milton and Treffers-Daller, 2013). The number of words a child has heard and can speak by the age of 3 is a predictor of later language development, so these early vocabulary gains are critically important (Hart and Risley, 2003).

A rich vocabulary enhances reading fluency, comprehension, facilitates writing proficiency, and fosters academic achievement across all disciplines. Moreover, it equips children with the linguistic tools necessary for life-long learning. Therefore, educators and caregivers must prioritise strategies to support and nurture children's vocabulary growth, recognising its pivotal role in shaping their literacy development and future success.

Talking to and holding conversations with children is the simplest, yet one of the most effective resources to develop, refine and expand their vocabulary. Try not to 'dumb down' the words you use, and use as extensive a vocabulary as you can. The types of words we learn can be sorted into three tiers (Figure 2.4), and it is good practice to use vocabulary categorised as tier 2 as often as possible with children.

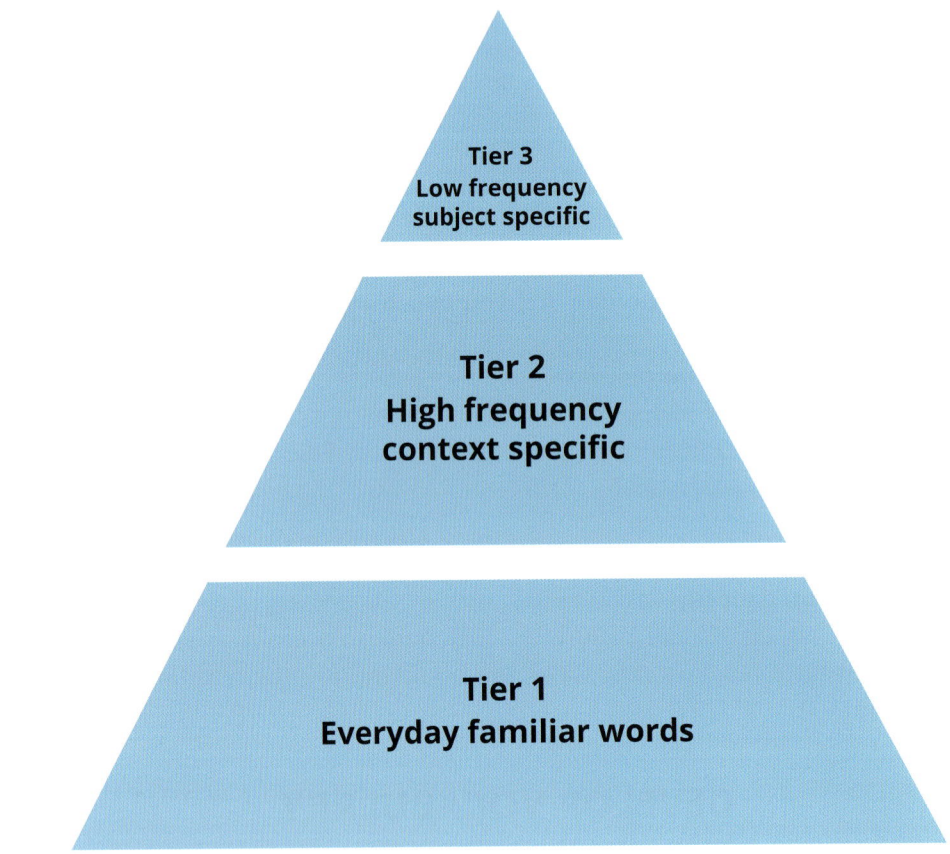

Figure 2.4   The vocabulary pyramid

Ten further techniques to expose children to new words and help expand their vocabulary are as follows:

1   At first focus on words they will want to use based on their interests, or need to use in their everyday life.
2   Create a running dialogue of everyday activities like washing the dishes, tidying up or driving.
3   Extend children's sentences: 'A bus' → 'A huge bus' → 'A huge, crowded bus'.
4   Repeatedly practice in a variety of contexts. Typically, a word needs to be heard on average ten times before becoming part of a child's vocabulary.
5   Use gesture to accompany a new word; for example, when introducing the word 'huge' spread your arms really wide.
6   Pick out key vocabulary before reading a text and discuss the meaning of these words.

7 Model using dictionaries, thesauruses and information texts.

8 Read aloud to children so they can access texts that include more challenging vocabulary.

9 Introduce children to words that have the same meaning: big – massive, huge, great, enormous, large.

10 Play vocabulary games like 'I Spy' or 'Simon Says': 'Simon says touch your palm'.

SHARING STORIES

There are few things as powerful as regularly reading to a young child.
(David, 2020)

Shared reading is the number one tool to expose children to a richer vocabulary and build their knowledge of new words. There needs to be a high priority to sharing stories both at home and in school as vocabulary is such a huge predictor of later academic success and ultimately life chances. Vocabulary equips children with the key to unlock their life-long potential. (Oxford Language Report, 2022 2024)

BOX 2.1

Researchers in the United States who had looked at the impact of parents reading with their children quoted the following figures in a news release about their findings:

Here's how many words kids would have heard by the time they were 5 years old: Never read to, 4,662 words; 1–2 times per week, 63,570 words; 3–5 times per week, 169,520 words; daily, 296,660 words; and five books a day, 1,483,300 words.

(Science Daily, 2019, quoted in DfE, 2023a, p. 11)

Despite the known benefits of sharing stories, the Oxford Language Report (2024) highlights some of the key challenges. The main reasons why sharing stories is not prioritised is the lack of time within the school day; lack of budget to invest in good-quality books; insufficient staff knowledge and training, meaning that some staff do not see the importance of sharing stories and prioritise other areas; and the varying support that children get at home. In fact, the latest National Literacy Trust report (Clark et al., 2023) found that one in five children between the ages of 5 and 8 do not own a book.

So, what are the easiest and cheapest ways for teachers and schools to overcome these barriers?

1 Prioritise book talk and story time within the daily timetable.

2 Create a book swap library.

3 Parent workshops focusing on sharing information about building vocabulary and sharing stories.

4 Create reading dens and quiet spaces to share books.

5 Visit the school or local library.

THE BENEFITS OF REPETITIVE READING

Young children will often select and ask you to read and reread and reread and reread their favourite stories and this can sometimes become a bit monotonous, but there are huge benefits to repetitive reading. It is not just the number of different stories children listen to that matters. 'On each rereading, their familiarity with a story deepens and, with that, comes a greater emotional engagement' (DfE, 2023a, p. 33). 'We know that emotional engagement is the tipping point between leaping into the reading life [and] remaining in a childhood bog when reading is endured only as a means to other ends' (Wolf, 2007). Essentially, the more you read the same book, the more emotionally engaged children become with the story, the more likely they are to develop a love of reading and want to read more books, which then has a knock-on effect of developing a life-long love of reading. Repetitive reading also means that children are given the opportunity to embed their knowledge of new words within the book. Children will also develop their oral fluency as they try to retell the story by heart, which has a positive impact on memory and imagination. If children are confident to verbally retell a story, this will help develop their reading fluency and expression at a later stage. They know what good storytelling sounds like, they join in with the pattern of the language and repeated refrains, they know when to pause, when to add expression, when to use sound effects, and they can later utilise these skills when reading books and stories aloud once they become fluent readers. Children really do thrive off repetition!

PARENTS AS THE FIRST TEACHER

> Becoming a fluent, skilled and attentive reader starts at the earliest stages, before children encounter a book for the first time, partly driven by the quality of their parents' talk with them that expands their vocabulary and comprehension. (DfE, 2023a, p. 10)

Parents have the power to influence and transform a child's literacy skills and attitude to reading by being a positive reading role model. '*Many* kids hear what you say. *Some* kids do what you say. *All* kids do what you do' (National Children's Book and Literacy Alliance, 2015; emphasis in original). Before children start to match letters with their sounds, parents and carers can model what good speaking and listening looks like with preschoolers, which will have a big impact on children's later literacy ability. Children's engagement with literacy practices at home and in the community shapes their early learning and leads into later literacy learning (Neaum, 2017). Take turns in conversation, sing nursery rhymes and songs, ask open-ended questions and show how to be a good listener. Also, it's crucial that young children see adults reading for a variety of purposes. It is thought that there are three purposes to reading – utility, pleasure and self-fulfilment – and adults can model doing them all (Stebbins, 2013; Open University, 2024). The more a child sees adults reading for a variety of purposes, the more likely they are to want to emulate this and view reading as an important life skill.

- Utility – this is the practical reason to read such as reading instructions, shopping lists, road signs and menus
- Pleasure – this is reading for relaxation and enjoyment using story books, poetry and non-fiction
- Self-fulfilment – reading to learn something new or for self-exploration

THE MATTHEW EFFECT

The Matthew effect describes what happens over time when some children enter into a positive feedback loop. Children who grow up in a language-rich environment, where reading is modelled, talk is prioritised, and vocabulary is expanded, are more likely to engage with print, read more and therefore become better readers, while poor readers will shy away from reading, which has a negative impact on their reading ability. This suggests that children's early experiences are crucial and have such an influence later in life.

Stainthorp and Hughes (1999) looked at children who read at an early age. A longitudinal study over three years found that early readers came from varied socio-economic backgrounds and were in no way exclusively economically privileged. What seemed to make the greatest difference was the home environment and parental attitudes towards reading. Print was a strong feature in homes, children were read to from an early age, regularly and from a variety of texts. Children had an extensive acquaintance with story form – introduction, development, and resolution. Parents held positive attitudes towards reading and modelled these attitudes both consciously and subconsciously. Crucially, these children had developed excellent alphabetic knowledge and high levels of phonological sensitivity – often through repetition of verse. What is perhaps most revealing is that these early readers were never forced to read by their parents, but their developing skills and interest in literacy activities ensured that they engaged in more of them.

IN SUMMARY

- Phonological awareness is the ability to listen for chunks of sounds within our language, including the ability to identify syllables and rhyme. There are four levels to phonological awareness: word level, syllable level, onset and rime, and phonemic awareness.
- Phonemic awareness is the most advanced skill of phonological awareness and is the ability for children to listen for, isolate and manipulate phonemes within words.
- Both phonological awareness and phonemic awareness are vital speaking and listening skills for early readers.
- Phonological awareness activities, developing vocabulary and sharing stories will create a solid foundation for later learning to match letters to sounds and act as a predictor for later academic success.

YOUR TURN!

Practise orally segmenting these words into phonemes. How many phonemes are there in each word?

Example 2.3   Count the phonemes practice grid

cow	pig	sheep	goat
horse	duck	farm	chicken

Worksheet 2.1   Empty answer grid

What items could you add to a silly soup for the initial sound /s/?

LEARNING IDEA 2.1
I SPY ALLITERATION BOTTLES

Develop children's ability to listen for and spot objects that begin with the same initial sound.

PRACTISE

- **Listening for alliteration**
- **Articulating sounds**

PICK UP

- **Clear bottles or jars**
- **White or dyed rice**
- **Small objects that begin with the same initial sound**

PREP

1. Place a selection of the small objects inside the container and then fill it with rice (Figure 2.5).
2. Replace the lid. You can use hot glue or strong tape around the lid to ensure that it remains closed and can't be opened.

PLAY

Children shake and manoeuvre the container to spot the objects inside. Encourage children to identify the initial sounds of each. Can they spot the same sound that all the objects start with?

Figure 2.5 Practising alliteration using objects in a bottle

LEARNING IDEA 2.2
SYLLABLE SHOPPING

Encourage children to identify and count the number of syllables within words by going syllable shopping. You can add to the role-play as much as you like too!

PRACTISE

- **Identify and count syllables**

PICK UP

- **Three paper gift bags**
- **A selection of objects and toys (Figure 2.6)**
- **Shop role-play equipment (if desired)**

PREP

1. Write the numbers 1–3 on each of the gift bags.
2. Place out the selection of toys like you are creating a toy shop.

PLAY

Children pick an object that they would like to buy. They say the word and count the number of syllables. They then 'purchase' the toy and place it into the correct bag corresponding to the amount of syllables the word contains; for example, they pick up a tractor, say the word 'tractor' and then put it in the bag with the number 2 on the front.

Figure 2.6 Practising counting syllables in words by using different toys and objects

LEARNING IDEA 2.3
SYLLABLE BINGO

Develop children's ability to identify and count the number of syllables within a word in a bingo style game.

PRACTISE

- **Identify and count syllables**

PICK UP

- **Cardboard**
- **Marker pen**
- **Bingo dabbers**

PREP

1. Create your own bingo cards by drawing a selection of objects on cardboard (Figure 2.7). Make sure that the pictures you draw vary in how many syllables they contain; for example, bike (1), pizza (2), piano (3), crocodile (4).
2. Place out the bingo dabbers next to each of the boards.

PLAY

An adult says a word and children spot the matching object on their bingo board. They then count the number of syllables in the word and dot the object with the dabber according to the number of syllables; for example, an adult says 'spider' and the child counts two syllables and then uses the bingo dabber to dot the spider picture twice. Continue until all pictures on the board have been dotted.

Figure 2.7 Bingo game using drawings on cardboard to practise syllables

LEARNING IDEA 2.4
PEG A SOUND

This activity is a fantastic way for children to really listen and isolate individual sounds within words.

PRACTISE

- **Identify phonemes**
- **Isolate phonemes**

PICK UP

- **Cardboard**
- **Clothes pegs**
- **Marker pen**

PREP

1 Cut out small rectangles of card and draw pictures of consonant–vowel–consonant (CVC) objects (pig, cat, log, bed, cot, etc.) on them (Figure 2.8).
2 Under each object draw three dots. The dots act like sound buttons and correspond to the number of phonemes in the word.
3 Place out a clothes peg next to each of the picture cards.

PLAY

Children pick up a card and say aloud the word for the picture; encourage them to identify and count all the sounds. Now, the adult says, 'clip the peg where you hear the __ sound'; for example, children pick up the sun card, the adult says, 'clip the peg where you hear the /n/ sound' and children place the peg on the final button. Repeat for the initial and middle phonemes and for all the other picture cards too.

Figure 2.8 Activity using pegs and drawings on cardboard to practise identifying phonemes

LEARNING IDEA 2.5
HUMAN BUCKEROO

An absolute joy of an oral blending activity. Children find this one hysterical, especially if it's the adult who gets to 'wear' all the objects.

PRACTISE

- **Listening for phonemes**
- **Oral blending**

PICK UP

- **A selection of objects that contain up to three phonemes that can easily be placed onto a person or large soft toy (e.g., hat, pet, pot, pen, soft toy dog)**
- **A large soft toy as an alternative to an adult**

PREP

1   Place out the objects in front of the children so they can clearly see them.

PLAY

An adult orally segments a word for one of the objects. Children orally blend the sounds together and find the corresponding object. They then attempt to place the object on the adult without it falling off (Figure 2.9). As an example, the adult says /h/a/t/, the child blends the sounds, picks up the hat and puts it on the adult's head. Repeat with all the other objects. Can the children balance all the objects on the adult without any falling off? You can play a similar game with a large soft toy, sibling or peer.

Figure 2.9   Practising phonemes by playing a human buckeroo game

LANGUAGE-RICH ENVIRONMENT AUDIT

Take some time to observe your teaching practice and classroom resources and use this audit as a tool to help develop a physical and emotional environment that actively promotes and encourages communication, language and literacy.

Worksheet 2.2   Your environment audit

Setting: **Date:**

Practice	Evidence	Development points
Relationships and interactions		
Children are confident to talk with adults and peers		
Children are taught routines for back-and-forth talk		
Opportunities to join in with classroom discussion		
Opportunities to collaborate with others		
Evidence of adults asking open-ended questions		
Adults develop children's vocabulary and challenge comprehension		
Story time		
High-quality stories to read aloud to children, including traditional and modern stories, are organised, listed and shared		
In stories and other books, children encounter others whose experiences and perspectives are both similar to and different from their own		
Teachers reread stories and talk with children about them to build familiarity and understanding		
Reading aloud occurs right across the curriculum		
Role-play		
Story props and role-play equipment are available		
Opportunities to role-play everyday experiences, e.g. shop or home corner		

Practice	Evidence	Development points
Rhymes, poetry and song		
Daily poetry, singing, rhymes and sharing stories are a priority		
Poems, rhymes and songs for each year group are listed		
Reading for pleasure		
Time allocated for classes to engage with stories and non-fiction text		
Established class or school libraries		
Parents are kept informed about how children learn to read and how they can support reading for pleasure		
Books are made available for parents to share with their children at home		
Classroom environment		
Activities are used effectively to develop children's language		
Classrooms have a designated, comfortable and uncluttered space for children to sit down with books		
Books are displayed in an appealing way and are easily accessible		
Books are rotated frequently		
Classroom resources are labelled in order to encourage independence		
Phonics displays include resources that show fidelity to the school's chosen phonics scheme		

FIFTY RECOMMENDED READS FOR PRESCHOOL AND NURSERY (3–4-YEAR-OLDS)

1 *A Thing Called Snow*, Yuval Zomer
2 *Aaaarrgghh! Spider*, Lydia Monks
3 *Aliens Love Underpants*, Claire Freedman and Ben Cort
4 *All Are Welcome*, Alexandra Penfold and Suzanne Kaufman
5 *All Kinds of Families*, Sophy Henn
6 *Axel Scheffler's Treasury of Fairy Tales*, Axel Scheffler
7 *Blow a Kiss, Catch a Kiss*, Joseph Coelho and Nicola Killen

8 *Building a Home*, Polly Faber and Klas Fahlén

9 *Colours, Colours Everywhere*, Julia Donaldson and Sharon King-Chai

10 *Daisy Eat Your Peas*, Kes Gray and Nick Sharratt

11 *Doris*, Lo Cole

12 *Everybody Has Feelings*, Jon Burgerman

13 *How Do You Make a Rainbow?*, Caroline Crowe and Cally Johnson-Isaacs

14 *I Love Chinese New Year*, Eva Wong Nava and Li Xin

15 *I Love You, Blue Kangaroo!*, Emma Chichester Clark

16 *I Try*, Susie Brooks and Cally Johnson-Isaacs

17 *Kindness Makes Us Strong*, Sophie Beer

18 *Knock Knock Superhero*, Caryl Hart and Nick East

19 *Little Robin Red Vest*, Jan Fearnley

20 *Lost and Found*, Oliver Jeffers

21 *Love Is in the Little Things*, Stella J. Jones and Jane Massey

22 *Lulu's First Day*, Anna McQuinn and Rosalind Beardshaw

23 *Mae Jemison*, Maria Isabel Sanchez Vegara and Janna Morton

24 *Mama's Sleeping Scarf*, Chimamanda Ngozi Adichie and Joelle Avelino

25 *Mavis the Bravest*, Lu Fraser and Sarah Warburton

26 *Measuring Me!*, Nicola Kent

27 *Meet the Dinosaurs*, Caryl Hart and Bethan Woollvin

28 *Mog's Birthday*, Judith Kerr

29 *My Encyclopedia of Very Important Dinosaurs*, DK

30 *Not Now, Bernard*, David McKee

31 *Owl Babies*, Martin Waddell and Patrick Benson

32 *Peace at Last*, Jill Murphy

33 *Poo in the Zoo*, Steve Smallman and Ada Grey

34 *Pop!*, Matt Carr

35 *Ready for Spaghetti*, Michael Rosen and Polly Dunbar

36 *Rosa Explores Life Cycles*, Jessica Spanyol

37 *Sam Plants a Sunflower*, Kate Petty and Axel Scheffler

38 *Shark in the Park!*, Nick Sharratt

39 *Squishy McFluff's Camping Adventure*, Pip Jones and Ella Okstad

40 *The Most Exciting Eid*, Zeba Talkhani and Abeeha Tariq

41 *The Ocean Gardener*, Clara Anganuzzi

42 *The Rabbit, the Dark and the Biscuit Tin*, Nicola O'Byrne

43 *The Runaway Train*, Benedict Blathwayt

44 *The Tiger Who Came to Tea*, Judith Kerr

45 *Tilda Tries Again*, Tom Percival

46 *Victor, the Wolf with Worries*, Catherine Rayner

47 *Watch Me Bloom*, Krina Patel-Sage

48 *What the Ladybird Heard*, Julia Donaldson and Lydia Monks

49 *When You're Fast Asleep*, Peter Arrhenius and Ingela P. Arrhenius

50 *Where the Wild Things Are*, Maurice Sendak

3
STARTING SCHOOL

If you are a parent with a preschooler starting school either this year or next, it can be a pretty anxious and stressful time thinking about how you can get your child 'school ready', especially if it's your first child starting, and you are going through the transition to school for the first time. Scrolling through social media and seeing posts and videos of 2-year-olds reading words or accounts preaching about getting toddlers to read can certainly add to these worries. I'm here to put a few myths to bed! Children do not need to start school knowing all the letter sounds of the alphabet and putting these together to read words! They do not need to be able to write their entire first and second name, know all the letter names or hold a pencil and form and write letters correctly. The best way to prepare children for starting school and formal phonics instruction is to set a solid foundation in phonological awareness and to practise all the crucial speaking and listening skills discussed in the previous chapter. Most of these areas are probably things that parents of preschoolers are doing naturally already and they don't require elaborate set-ups or expensive resources; one of the best resources to develop phonological awareness is your voice!

So, aside from the foundational pre-reading skills mentioned in Chapter 2, how else can parents prepare their child for the transition to school? What do they need to know? What things do they need to be able to do? What don't they need to know? There are some key social, emotional and independent skills that children can practise and develop before they start, and it's these skills that early years teachers would like parents to focus on: being able to ask to use the toilet and go independently; putting their shoes and coats on by themselves; following instructions; putting their belongings away; being confident to join in with small group activities; and playing with and sharing toys with other children. Here I will focus on the key communication and language skills as it's these areas of learning that will prepare your child for more formal phonics teaching once they are at school. This is not to say that the other areas of learning aren't as important. They all really have equal weight – it's just that these areas (communication, language and literacy) are more of a prerequisite for phonics.

A SCHOOL-READY POEM

Singing lots of nursery rhymes, retelling familiar tales and joining in with a tune,

Cutting, scooping and picking up my food with a knife, fork and spoon.

Hopping, throwing, catching, climbing and balancing, running and baking,

Opening lids, squeezing and brushing will make my body and hands ready for mark-making.

Organising my toys, putting them away and independently finding things I need,

Listening for sounds in words and blending them together will help me to later read.

Recognising my name will help me find my peg and drawer and put my belongings away,

Eagerness to explore, join in with games, take turns and share will help me in my play.

Asking for help from an adult if I hurt myself or need the loo,

Dressing myself by putting on my coat and shoes is something to practise too.

You will be ready, of that I am sure! Ready to start your exciting school adventure.

EARLY YEARS FOUNDATION STAGE

This is a statutory framework that outlines the standards that providers must meet for the learning, development and care of children between the ages of 0 and 5 years which will cover all preschool, nursery settings and the Reception year of school. Alongside parents, providers must target key areas of development. There are seven areas of learning and development that set out what children must be taught if they are attending an early years' setting. There are three prime areas:

Communication and language

Physical development

Personal, social and emotional development

There are four specific areas:

Literacy

Mathematics

Understanding the world

Expressive arts and design

On communication and language, the EYFS (DfE, 2024, p. 9) states:

> The development of children's spoken language underpins all seven areas of learning and development. Children's back-and-forth interactions from an early age form the foundations for language and cognitive development. The number and quality of the conversations they have with adults and peers throughout the day in a language-rich environment is crucial. By commenting on what children are interested in or doing, and echoing back what they say with new vocabulary added, practitioners will build children's language effectively. Reading frequently to children, and engaging them actively in stories, non-fiction, rhymes and poems, and then providing them with extensive opportunities to use and embed new words in a range of contexts, will give children the opportunity to thrive. Through conversation, storytelling and role play, where children share their ideas with support and modelling from their teacher, and sensitive questioning that invites them to elaborate, children become comfortable using a rich range of vocabulary and language structures.

Turning to literacy, the EYFS (DfE, 2024, p. 10) goes on to say:

> It is crucial for children to develop a life-long love of reading. Reading consists of two dimensions: language comprehension and word reading. Language comprehension (necessary for both reading and writing) starts from birth. It only develops when adults talk with children about the world around them and the books (stories and non-fiction) they read with them, and enjoy rhymes, poems and songs together. Skilled word reading, taught later, involves both the speedy working out of the pronunciation of unfamiliar printed words (decoding) and the speedy recognition of familiar printed words. Writing involves transcription (spelling and handwriting) and composition (articulating ideas and structuring them in speech, before writing).

Development Matters

Development Matters is a non-statutory curriculum guidance, published by the DfE (2023b), to assist those working with young children in the Early Years Foundation Stage, offering a top-level view of how children develop and learn. Providers can use the guidance to design an effective curriculum, alongside the requirements within the EYFS framework, to support children in their care. It consists of everything we want children to experience, and outlines everything they should learn and be able to do during the early years. Box 3.1 shows how each developmental stage within communication and language, starting from birth, builds up and provides a foundation for phonics and learning to read. Box 3.2 shows the same for each stage within literacy. Babies turning towards familiar sounds and watching someone's face as they talk is a crucial step towards later being able to identify and say the sounds that letters make; a baby babbling back and forth is a prerequisite for taking turns in conversation, and copying adult's speech and lip movements is a step towards later articulating phonemes correctly.

BOX 3.1 The *Development Matters* Statements for Communication and Language

Age Range

Birth to 3 Years Old

Children will be learning to:

- Turn towards familiar sounds
- Gaze at faces and watch someone's face as they talk
- Copy what adults do and take 'turns' in conversation (babbling)
- Try to copy adult's speech and lip movements
- Enjoy singing, music and toys that make noise
- Listen and respond to simple instruction
- Make sounds to get attention in different ways
- Babbling, using sounds like 'baba' and 'mama'
- Use gestures to communicate
- Copy gestures and words
- Use single words during play
- Use intonation, pitch and volume when talking
- Understand single words in context
- Understand frequently used words
- Understand simple instructions
- Recognise and point to objects if asked about them
- Generally, focus on an activity of their own choice and find it difficult to be directed by an adult
- Listen to other people's talk with interest but can get easily distracted
- Make themselves understood
- Start to say how they are feeling, using words and actions
- Start to develop conversation
- Develop pretend play
- Use the speech sounds /p/, /b/, /m/, /w/

- Pronounce /l/, /r/, /w/, /y/ /f/, /th/, /s/, /sh/, /ch/, /j/ and say multisyllabic words
- Listen to simple stories and understand what is happening
- Identify familiar objects and properties
- Understand and act on longer sentences
- Understand simple questions

3–4 Years Old

Children will be learning to:

- Enjoy listening to longer stories and remember what has happened
- Pay attention to more than one thing at a time
- Use a wider range of vocabulary
- Understand a question and instruction that has two parts
- Understand 'why' questions
- Sing a large repertoire of song
- Know many rhymes, be able to talk about familiar books and be able to tell a story
- Develop pronunciation but still may have problems with some sounds, e.g. /r/, /j/, /th/, /ch/ and /sh/
- Use longer sentences of four or six words
- Be able to express a point of view and to debate when they disagree
- Start a conversation with an adult or friend
- Use talk to organise themselves
- Understand how to listen carefully and why listening is important

BOX 3.2 The *Development Matters* Statements for Literacy

Age Range

0–3 Years Old

Children will be learning to:

- Enjoy songs and rhymes, tuning in and paying attention
- Join in with songs and rhymes
- Say some words in songs and rhymes
- Sing songs and rhymes independently
- Enjoy sharing books with an adult
- Pay attention and respond to the pictures or the words
- Have a favourite book and seek it out
- Repeat words and phrases from a familiar story
- Ask questions about the book
- Develop play around favourite stories using props

(Continued)

- Notice some print, such as the first letter of their name, a bus or door number or familiar logo
- Enjoy drawing freely
- Add some marks to their drawings
- Make marks on their picture to stand for their name

3–4 Years Old

- Understand the five key concepts about print:

  - Print has meaning
  - Print can have different purposes
  - We read English from left to right and top to bottom
  - The names of different parts of a book
  - Page sequencing

- Develop their phonological awareness so that they can:

  - Spot and suggest rhymes
  - Count or clap syllables in a word
  - Recognise words with the same initial sound

- Engage in extended conversations about stories using new vocabulary
- Use some of their print and letter knowledge in their early writing
- Write some or all of their name
- Write some letters accurately

GAMES WITH NAMES

Children's ability to recognise their name is an incredibly useful skill for them to acquire before they start school. In my experience, one of the first printed letters that children will recognise will be a letter that is within their name. How many times have you heard children say 'look, that's in my name!' while pointing to a label in a shop or the title of a book? Both-de Vries and Bus (2008) recognise the importance of names as an intro- duction to literacy: 'We hypothesise that children's understanding of writing as an alphabetic system starts with letters from their own name.'

Young children are egocentric and absolutely love identifying and playing games with their names, and name recognition provides a powerful route into reading and writing. It's also a fantastic tool to develop independence; if a child can identify their name they can spot it above their coat peg and know where to hang their coat, they can put artwork in their own drawer or find their missing school jumper by reading the name label.

As you can see from the *Development Matters* statements above, as children start school they should be able to both read and begin to write their names. Just like we would do for any high-frequency tricky word when we start teaching them at school, we can build up children's ability to read, spell and write their names through lots of playful practice. Try using these methods:

1   Play games where children are recognising their name as a whole, perhaps spotting their name among a list of others or finding items of clothing that have their name written on.

2   Provide children with the letters of their name for them to put back together in the correct order. You can use clothes pegs, letter cards or just bits of paper.

3   Show children their name but with some missing letters. Can they identify which letters are missing?

4   Provide them with the resources to write their name. This could be using chunky chalk or writing it with their finger in shaving foam. It doesn't have to involve holding a pencil.

> **Tip 3.1**   Ensure that children only use the capital letter for the beginning of their name. There are some children who start school writing their name entirely in capitals, and this can be tricky to rectify.

The previous chapter provided some activities that focused on pre-reading skills, so at the end of this chapter there are five fun and practical name recognition activities.

EARLY LEARNING GOALS AND THE EARLY YEARS FOUNDATION STAGE PROFILE

The early learning goals are the culmination of all the statements and requirements set out within the EYFS and *Development Matters* and are what children will be assessed against at the end of the early years, which falls at the end of the Reception year of school, as part of a child's EYFS Profile (EYFSP). The profile provides practitioners, parents and carers with a well-rounded view of a child's knowledge, understanding and abilities. Practitioners will judge children to be at the expected level and meeting the early learning goal or 'emerging' (whereby a child hasn't quite reached the goal). There are 17 early learning goals (ELGs) which span the seven areas of learning within the EYFS.

Below are the CLL goals that children will be assessed against at the end of the early years. This is not what they will be expected to be able to do when starting school, but I think it's important to highlight and reference the goals so that parents and carers can see what is expected of children, in terms of literacy, after their Reception year (DfE, 2024).

Communication and Language

ELG: Listening, attention and understanding

- Listen attentively and respond to what they hear with relevant questions, comments and actions when being read to and during whole class discussions and small group interactions.

- Make comments about what they have heard and ask questions to clarify their understanding.
- Hold conversation when engaged in back-and-forth exchanges with their teacher and peers.

ELG: Speaking

- Participate in small group, class and one-to-one discussions, offering their own ideas, using recently introduced vocabulary.
- Offer explanations for why things might happen, making use of recently introduced vocabulary from stories, non-fiction, rhymes and poems when appropriate.
- Express their ideas and feelings about their experiences using full sentences, including use of past, present and future tenses and making use of conjunctions, with modelling and support from their teacher.

Literacy

ELG: Comprehension

- Demonstrate understanding of what has been read to them by retelling stories and narratives using their own words and recently introduced vocabulary.
- Anticipate – where appropriate – key events in stories.
- Use and understand recently introduced vocabulary during discussions about stories, non-fiction, rhymes and poems and during role-play.

ELG: Word reading

- Say a sound for each letter in the alphabet and at least ten digraphs.
- Read words consistent with their phonic knowledge by sound-blending.
- Read aloud simple sentences and books that are consistent with their phonic knowledge, including some common exception words.

ELG: Writing

- Write recognisable letters, most of which are correctly formed.
- Spell words by identifying sounds in them and representing the sounds with a letter or letters.
- Write simple phrases and sentences that can be read by others.

I'M INTERESTED!

If preschool children do show an interest in letters and matching them to the sounds, then that's great, but just know that this is not something that is expected of children before they start school. There is no rush, and once children are in their first year they will be formally taught phonics using a very systematic programme. The programme might teach children certain actions for each letter and sound or introduce letter formation rhymes. If children have been taught something different at home this could potentially hinder their progress as they will have to 'unlearn' it once they are at school and follow a different scheme and progression.

If they are really showing an interest then the most important things to remember are to use the letter sounds not the letter names, avoid the schwa (see Chapter 4), and start with lowercase letters rather than capitals.

WORDLESS BOOKS

Alongside retelling stories and sharing the wonderful variety of picture books that are listed at the end of Chapter 2, you might also wish to start sharing wordless books with preschoolers. When children start school, the teacher will ensure that the books children take home are very closely matched to their phonic ability (see Chapter 13 for more information on this), and until they are confident in recognising the first few letters and sounds and using them to blend and segment CVC words, they will receive wordless books to 'read'. As a parent, these types of books can be a little daunting. They don't have any words to actually read! What's the point of them? You'll be surprised at how much learning can come from a book with no words!

Routine – receiving a wordless book at home provides parents with the opportunity to establish a routine with their child without the pressure of actually 'reading' the book. They can figure out the best time of day and space to share the book at home with few distractions.

Book care – adults can model how to hold a book correctly and turn the pages carefully. Children can take responsibility for looking after the books and deciding the best place to keep them when they are not being read. Adults can also discuss the different parts of a book such as the front cover, blurb, title and spine. Developing a good book stock can cost schools a considerable amount of money, so they will appreciate parents having these types of conversations with children.

Oracy – wordless books are an incredible opportunity to develop oracy skills in children and support literacy-rich conversations. Sharing a wordless book means that you can really focus on discussing the illustrations and story away from the demands of decoding. Encourage children to ask questions, give their point of view and talk about what is happening. 'Oral narrative skills are crucial to early literacy development, as they assist children in making the transition between oral narrative and written text' (Collins and Glover, 2015).

Vocabulary – wordless books are a great way to expand children's vocabulary by naming the objects and adding description and synonyms. As we discussed in

Chapter 2, vocabulary is a key predictor of later academic success. Studies show that children's vocabulary development plays a critical role in their literacy acquisition. In fact, vocabulary is one of the most robust long-term predictors of good literacy development (Snow and Juel, 2005).

Phonological awareness – even in a wordless book adults can prepare children with the underlying skills for later phonics learning. They could think of things that rhyme with an object, play initial sound 'I Spy', or orally segment the sounds in an object on the page for children to blend them back together.

Story structure – the story is told through the illustrations within a wordless book rather than the text, but it will still have a beginning, middle and, quite likely, a problem and resolution. Discussing the structure and events within a story can have a positive impact on children's comprehension.

Comprehension – look at the characters and their facial expressions and encourage children to make inferences about what they might be feeling and why. Adults can also talk about how the story is similar to other stories that the child might be familiar with.

Retelling and imagination – can children retell the story in their own words or use props? Can they sequence the main events? Acting out and retelling a story can further develop familiarity with story structure, expand vocabulary and develop comprehension.

Can you see the point in wordless books now?

IN SUMMARY

- Parents of preschool-aged children should not worry that they cannot identify letters of the alphabet and their matching sounds before starting school.
- Activities that develop phonological awareness skills are important to prepare children for their next step in learning, and it's these speaking and listening skills that provide a solid foundation for future phonics instruction.
- Play lots of games with children's names so that they can gain independence when at school.
- Wordless books may be used at the beginning of school, which can offer a wealth of opportunities to develop early literacy skills in preparation for books with words.

YOUR TURN!

In the following worksheet, choose three CLL *Development Matters* statements for children aged 0–3 years and think about how they are prerequisite skills for reading and how they can impact children's ability to learn phonics if they are not achieved – write your reasons in the boxes provided.

Worksheet 3.1 Development Matters reasoning

Development Matters statement 1:
Reason:
Development Matters statement 2:
Reason:
Development Matters statement 3:
Reason:

Identify two benefits to using wordless books with children in the early years.

LEARNING IDEA 3.1
SENSORY NAME BOARD

Providing children with the opportunity to practise recognising and writing their name in a multitude of practical and sensory ways will engage children with different learning styles and really embed knowledge.

PRACTISE

- **Recognise and spell names**

PICK UP

- **Large piece of cardboard**
- **Scissors**
- **Marker pen**
- **Loose parts (buttons, pom-poms, etc.)**
- **Playdough**
- **Small letter cards**
- **Parcel tape**
- **Whiteboard pens**
- **DIY dice**

PREP

1. Divide the large piece of cardboard into several sections.
2. On the top section draw the outline of your child's name and then pull off the top layer to reveal the corrugated layer underneath.
3. On the middle two sections write your child's name with a marker pen.
4. Use the space at the bottom of the board as a place for children to rearrange letter cards to spell their name (Figure 3.1). You can also cover the bottom section with parcel tape so that it becomes a wipeable board and a place for children to practise writing their name with a whiteboard pen.

Figure 3.1 Practising writing and speaking a child's name by writing it in multi-textured and multi-sensory ways

PLAY

Leave your child to explore the board and use the manipulatives to form their name. You can later extend this by adding in a dice. On each face of the dice write a way for children to read and spell their name (tactile letters, loose parts, playdough, letter cards, whiteboard pen, and roll again). Children roll the dice and form a letter of their name as instructed on the dice – for example, they roll playdough and form the first letter with playdough, they roll loose parts and form a letter with loose parts. Which section of the board will be filled first?

TIP

You can make a blank dice using a toilet or kitchen roll tube. Cut two smaller cylinders from the tube and flatten these both ways to form a square shape. Slot one of these inside the other to create the dice.

LINK

Check out activity...
Check out the DIY tactile letter cards in Chapter 4.

LEARNING IDEA 3.2
THE JUMBLED JELLYFISH

This is a really fun way for children to begin to think about spelling their names and putting the letters into the correct order.

PRACTISE

- **Ordering and spelling names**

PICK UP

- **Cardboard**
- **String**
- **Marker pen**
- **Tape/glue**

PREP

1. Draw and cut out the jellyfish head and then attach a piece of string to the head for each letter in your child's name.
2. At the bottom of each of the pieces of string stick a small disc containing one letter (Figure 3.2).

PLAY

Show the jellyfish with all the tentacles jumbled up and the letters in the child's name muddled. They work to move the strings around to place the letters in the correct order to spell their name.

Figure 3.2 Practising spelling names using a jellyfish-shaped spelling tool

LEARNING IDEA 3.3
THE NAME GAME

Help children practise both letter recognition and name recognition while developing familiarity with different fonts and expanding their maths skills too.

PRACTISE

- Letter recognition
- Name recognition
- Counting
- Subitising

PICK UP

- Large piece of paper
- Magazines and leaflets
- Scissors
- Glue
- Dice

TIP

Subitising is the ability to look at a small number of dots/objects and instantly say how many there are without needing to count them out one by one.

PREP

1   Flick through the magazines and cut out large letters that are within your child's name. Make sure you only cut the capital letters for the first letter of the name.
2   Now, write out your child's name in bubble writing.
3   Place the cut-out letters around the name outline along with dice and glue (Figure 3.3).

Starting with the first letter, roll the dice and stick that number of smaller letters inside the large letter outline. Children then move onto the next letter; once again sticking the correct number of letters inside the outline. They continue for all the letters and repeat until each large letter outline is full. Use any leftover letters for children to independently spell their name without looking at the outline.

CBeebies and Lego magazines are great for finding large lowercase letters. You can subscribe to a free Lego magazine that is delivered directly to your door four times a year.

Figure 3.3 Practising letter and name recognition using letter cut-outs of different colours and shapes

LEARNING IDEA 3.4
SUNRISE TO SUNSET

This resource offers children the opportunity to practise spelling their names twice in a day. A great one to set up over the summer before starting school. It is also a fantastic pre-writing activity to help develop fine motor skills.

PRACTISE

- **Spelling names**
- **Fine motor and pincer grip**

PICK UP

- **Paper plate**
- **Scissors**
- **Green building blocks or other base board**
- **Clothes pegs**
- **Yellow pen or paint**
- **Maker pen**

PREP

1. Cut the paper plate in half and colour or paint it yellow (your child can help with this too!).
2. Place the plate onto a base board so that it stands vertically (Duplo works well for this).
3. Grab enough clothes pegs for each letter in your child's name. Colour these yellow too and then write a letter of your child's name on each (Figure 3.4).

PLAY

Leave out for your child to access on a daily basis. In the morning they clip each peg onto the plate in the correct order to spell their name so that they look like sun rays, then before bed take off the pegs in the correct order to practise spelling their name once more.

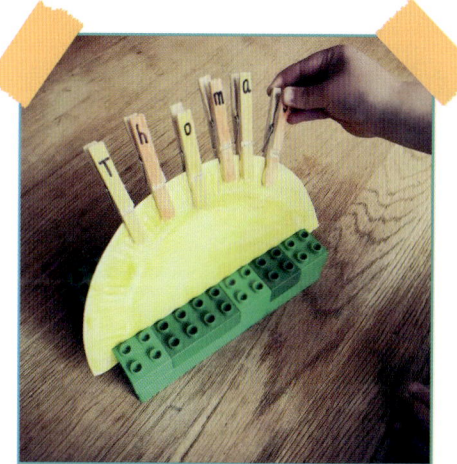

Figure 3.4 Practising name spelling using pegs and a sun-shaped craft

LEARNING IDEA 3.5
CRAYON BOX SORTING

This activity is a visually appealing way for children to practise recognising and spelling their names.

PRACTISE

- Name recognition
- Ordering letters and spelling names

PICK UP

- Large coloured craft sticks
- Scissors
- Marker pen
- White envelope
- Colouring pencils

PREP

1. Collect enough craft sticks for each letter of your child's name.
2. Carefully cut the end of each stick to create a point to form the crayon tip.
3. Use the marker pen to draw the features of a crayon on each and a letter of your child's name.
4. Cut the top off the envelope, colour in and decorate to create a crayon box (Figure 3.5).

PLAY

Place out the 'crayons' around the box in a muddled order. Children place the crayons into the box in the correct order to spell their names. You can extend this by offering children real crayons to practise writing their names and use the crayon box resource as a visual aid. Encouraging children to use small stubby crayons and chalk to make marks is a great way to encourage the tripod grip for writing.

Figure 3.5 Practising name spelling by sorting coloured crayons with letters on

4
INTRODUCING LETTERS AND SOUNDS

the common grapheme that represents that sound rather than using the symbols within the phonetic alphabet. This is so I can make the information more accessible. I might write /c/a/t/ in reference to the phonemes in the word 'cat', but using the International Phonetic Alphabet this should be written as /kæt/

And so it begins! Children have developed their phonological awareness and phonemic awareness skills and they have a wealth of experience playing with the sounds within our language, orally blending and segmenting words, and listening for and joining in with rhyme and enjoying sharing stories. They demonstrate they have a solid foundation for phonics instruction and are now ready to be introduced to letters and their matching sounds. Chapter 4 looks in depth at the phonological and phonemic awareness skills required as the foundation to phonics.

ENSURE IT'S PURE!

It's crucial when you introduce the phoneme to children that you use the pure sound and encourage them to do the same. Make sure you do not add an /uh/ sound to the end, so /ssss/ not /suh/ and /mmm/ not /muh/. This /uh/ sound is called a *schwa*. We will discuss this further in Chapter 11, but at this point you need to avoid it. Using the pure sounds will aid children's blending skills once they start to put the sounds together to read words. When showing children a letter, and getting them to say the corresponding sound, ask them to think about what shape their mouths are making. What is their tongue doing? What is the position of their teeth? Where is the sound coming from – from the back of their throat or mainly just using their lips? This will really help them focus on making the correct sound.

Tip 4.1 Make sure you model the pure sounds even outside of a phonics lesson. You never know when little ears are listening! To help avoid adding a schwa sound to the letter sounds, try whispering the sound and avoid making big movements with your mouth.

Pronunciation is not just about the sound but the movement and shape of your mouth, teeth, lips and tongue. Sounds can be either voiced or unvoiced, depending on whether they use your vocal cords. Think about and feel where the sound is coming from. Say /g/ and touch your throat to feel that your vocal cords are vibrating to produce the sound. Do the same but say /s/ and you won't be able to feel any movement in your throat.

Encourage children to say the phoneme while looking in a mirror. They can really see the shape of their mouths and position of their tongue and teeth. This will encourage them to say as pure a sound as possible.

If you are struggling to think about how to produce the pure sound, try saying a word that starts with it. It's not 'suh'trawberry but 'sss'trawberry. Also, think of a word that ends with that sound. When we say the word 'mat' we don't say 'mmmm-a-tuh'.

Table 4.1 provides a helpful guide to prompt you to produce the pure sound.

Table 4.1 Pronunciation guide for initial sounds

Letter	Example word	Mouth movement	Voiced or unvoiced
s	sun	Show your teeth and let the sss sound pass through them	unvoiced
a	sat	Open your mouth, tongue flat and say the /a/ sound from the back of your mouth	voiced
t	tap	Open your mouth slightly with teeth almost together and put the tip of your tongue behind your top teeth	unvoiced
p	pat	Bring your lips together and then use them to create a stop and release of air flow	unvoiced
i	pin	Pull your lips back, the front part of your tongue almost to the top of your mouth and say the sound at the back of your mouth	voiced
n	not	Place the tip of your tongue on the ridge of the roof of your mouth behind your front teeth. Open your lips and keep your teeth together and produce the sound through your nose	voiced
m	mat	Press your lips together. The sound is forced to be produced through your nose	voiced
d	dig	Put the tip of your tongue to the back of your teeth and the side of your tongue to the upper side teeth. Force the sound out. Every time the sound is pronounced the tip of your tongue should touch the roof of your mouth	voiced
g	got	Push the back of your tongue onto the back top teeth. Release the air flow from your vocal tract. The sound will come from your throat.	voiced
o	pot	Make your mouth form the shape of the letter and keep your tongue low and flat	voiced
c	cup	Put the back of your tongue on the back top teeth and then release the air to produce the sound	unvoiced
k	kit	Put the back of your tongue on the back top teeth and then release the air to produce the sound (the same sound as c)	unvoiced
e	peg	Open your mouth and keep your lips and jaw relaxed. Place the tip of your tongue behind the bottom from teeth	voiced

(Continued)

Table 4.1 (Continued)

Letter	Example word	Mouth movement	Voiced or unvoiced
u	mug	Open your mouth and keep your tongue flat and low	voiced
r	rat	Create a small circle with your mouth and press the side of your tongue to the back of your mouth and top teeth creating a small hump. The air flows over and around to create the sound	voiced
h	hot	Open your mouth and keep your tongue flat and low and push the air out sharply	unvoiced
b	bag	Put your lips together tightly and produce the sound as you slightly open them and release the air flow	voiced
f	fan	Open your mouth slightly and lightly touch the top front teeth onto your bottom lip and push the sound out	unvoiced
l	log	Open your mouth a little and push the tip of your tongue to the back of your front top teeth. Your tongue will almost curl back	voiced
j	jam	Air is briefly prevented from leaving your vocal tract when the side tip of your tongue presses to your side top teeth	voiced
v	van	Hold your jaw nearly closed and place your top teeth very lightly on your bottom lip	voiced
w	wet	Form a tight circle with your lips puckered. Produce a sound with your vocal cords and the back of your tongue to the roof of your mouth	voiced
x	box	Typically pronounced like /ks/ when heard at the end of words. Pronounce the /k/ sound as above and add a /s/	unvoiced
y	yet	Pronouncing the consonant sound can be tricky. Think about saying the word 'yellow'. What sound does the 'y' make? Lift the middle portion of your tongue almost to the roof of your mouth and say the sound as you lower it	voiced
z	zip	Place the tip of your tongue behind your top teeth and to the roof of your mouth. Push the air out between the teeth and tongue	voiced

Tip 4.2 Your mouth and tongue are in the exact same position to produce both /k/ and /g/ but one uses your vocal cords and one is unvoiced and uses air to create the sound. Can you work out which is unvoiced, and which is voiced?

The consonant phonemes (Example 4.1) can be categorised according to how we create each of the sounds; we don't need to go into this much detail with children, but it's worth knowing how all of the phonemes are produced so that we can encourage children to articulate them correctly. The type of sound can also affect children's ability to blend the sounds together to form words; nasal and fricative sounds are much easier to blend together than stop sounds.

Example 4.1 Phonemes according to how they are pronounced

Stop	Nasal	Fricatives	Affricatives	Glides	Liquids
p b t g c k	m n	f v s z h	j	y w	l r

Stop phonemes – consonant sounds that are made when we completely stop the airflow with our lips, teeth or tongue.

Nasal phonemes – produced by blocking the sound with your mouth and expelling air through the nose.

Fricatives – consonant sounds produced when you use the mouth to block the airstream but it is not completely closed.

Affricatives – made up of a stop sound immediately followed by a fricative sound.

Glides – these are phonetically similar to a vowel sound, often called a 'semivowel', but require more restriction in the vocal tract than vowel sounds.

Liquids – produced when the tongue makes a partial closure of the mouth.

COMMON PHONOLOGICAL ERRORS IN SPEECH PRODUCTION

As children learn to produce sounds they may often substitute easier sounds for harder ones as their speech production is not fully matured, so some common errors are developmentally appropriate; this is a natural process in young children and nothing to worry about. As children grow older, some sounds become easy, like /p/ and /m/, whereas others are more difficult, such as /z/, /sh/, and /th/. By age 5, most children should be able to pronounce almost all types of speech sounds. If children continue to produce some sounds incorrectly as they move through the first couple of years of school, then they will need to be assessed and supported by a speech and language therapist. Common phonological errors can be categorised as follows:

Velar fronting – this occurs when children attempt to produce the /k/ and /g/ phonemes. These sounds are produced at the back of the mouth but children who present with velar fronting put their tongue at the front of their mouths to create a /t/ or /d/, for example 'car' becomes 'tar' and 'goat' becomes 'doat'.

Liquid gliding – this is where children substitute a glide sound with a liquid sound, so may say 'lellow' for 'yellow'.

Stopping of fricatives – fricative sounds are replaced by sounds that do not have a stream of air, so children may say 'bish' for 'fish'.

Assimilation – children use the first sounds as the last sound or vice versa, 'bus' becomes 'bub' or 'hat' becomes 'tat'.

Final consonant deletion – children will remove the final consonant from a word, for example 'dog' becomes 'do' or 'cat' becomes 'ca'.

Cluster reduction – removing a consonant from a cluster of consonants at the beginning of a word, 'poon' instead of 'spoon' and 'wing' instead of 'swing'.

Syllable deletion – removing a syllable from a multisyllabic word so 'banana' becomes 'nana'.

Reduplication – children will duplicate the initial syllable of a word, saying 'wawa' instead of 'water'.

DISCRIMINATING BETWEEN THE VOWEL SOUNDS

A common mistake is for young children to confuse the vowels and find hearing the vowel sounds quite tricky. This is because all the short vowels are voiced and there is little difference between them in the way you move your mouth and tongue. This is particularly true for a/u and i/e. If you notice a child having trouble, try some of these ideas:

1   Have the child say the vowel sound in the mirror and use a chalk pen to draw around the shape of their mouths when saying the phoneme.
2   Sort objects that begin with the five short vowel sounds. It's easier to hear the sound at the beginning.
3   Sort objects according to their middle sounds.
4   Prepare word cards for five simple words that have the five vowel sounds in the middle (tap, ten, tin, top, tub). Say one of the words and ask the child to point to the vowel within the word that they hear – for example, say 'top' and the child points to the 'o' on the 'top' word car.
5   Show children an initial word, for example the word 'bag', and then ask how we can change it to 'big' then 'beg', 'bog' and finally 'bug'. This will really force children to focus on the middle vowel sound and discriminate between them.
6   Say the sentence 'an elephant in orange underpants'; each of the words starts with one of the short vowel sounds. This is a fun way to listen for and discriminate between them. You could display a matching image as a prompt too.

> **Tip 4.3**   Research shows that encouraging children to think about the shape and formation that the mouth makes when saying a sound has a positive impact on memorisation.

INTRODUCING GPCS

When you introduce a letter, you can show children that each letter has a name, a phoneme and a grapheme (both uppercase and lowercase). Initially when teaching young children the GPC you will need to concentrate on the phoneme rather than letter name and the lowercase grapheme rather than the uppercase. As children progress through their reading journey they will be introduced to capitals and letter names. That being said, many children start school knowing the alphabet song, so a good starting point is to show that each letter has a name and makes a sound, just as other objects have a name and make a sound. A cow is called a cow and makes the sound 'moo', a train is called a train and goes 'choo choo', and a letter has a name and makes a sound too! I feel like that would be a great song to start off with!

A cow is called a cow and makes the sound 'moo',

a train is called a train and goes 'choo choo',

and a letter has a name and makes a sound too!

'It is sensible to teach both names and sounds of letters. Names may be easier to learn because, being syllables rather than phonemes, they are perceptible, and also children expect things to have names' (Rose, 2006, para. 81).

Don't let children only associate the letter name with the capital and the sound with the lowercase letter. The capital still has a sound and the lowercase has a name. Letter names can help children understand the long vowel sounds learnt later in their phonics journey too. You'll learn more about this in Chapter 11.

Below is a simple method of introducing a letter and its corresponding sound to children. Many of the validated phonics schemes will introduce letters and sounds in a very similar way.

1   Adult models saying the phoneme (ensure it's pure!) before introducing the grapheme.
2   All children repeat the phoneme.
3   Discuss the shape of your mouth when saying the phoneme, the position of your tongue and where the sound is coming from. Children repeat, taking notice of their mouth movements.
4   Show the children the flashcard and trace around the letter while saying the phoneme again.
5   Children repeat and say the phoneme several more times.
6   Show the children a picture or object starting with the sound. Say the word, emphasising the initial sound.
7   Show children several more pictures of objects that start with the same sound.
8   Encourage children to say the word, and adults emphasise the initial phoneme.
9   Following on from this, children can sort objects according to their initial sound and have repetitive exposure to the grapheme within their classroom provision.

Example 4.2   An example list of practical activities to embed letter–sound knowledge

s	Children can trace along **s**nake images in the shape of an 's' with their fingers and hi**ss** as they do
a	Write the letter on **a**pples. Place them in a water tray and children go apple bobbing with scoops and nets
t	Form the letter using a wooden **t**rain track and move a train along the track saying the phoneme
p	Stick **p**opcorn to a p outline
i	Use sugar cubes to build an **i**gloo in the letter shape
n	Go on a **n**ature hunt, collect sticks to create a **n**est in the shape of an 'n'
m	Move a small **m**ouse toy to trace around the letter shape
d	Use **d**inosaurs to create footprints in playdough to form the letter
g	Place out lots of 'g' magnetic/wooden letters or flashcards and children **g**rab a 'g' when you say '**g**o'
o	Use small pieces of **o**range peel to collage a letter 'o' shape
c	Create a road in the letter shape and drive a **c**ar along it while saying the phoneme
k	Draw a target in chalk on a wall or fence with a letter 'k' in the middle. Children **k**ick a ball to hit the target saying the phoneme each time they kick
e	Collect half **e**gg shells, write a letter 'e' on them and children smash the shell with a spoon or hammer when you say the phoneme
u	Give children a 'u' letter card. They hold it up when you say '**u**p' or sit on it when you say '**u**nder'. Emphasise the initial phoneme as you do
r	Draw out lots of letter 'r' shapes on the pavement or playground with chalk. When you say the phoneme children **r**un and **r**ace to a letter
h	Trace around your **h**and with your finger. Say the phoneme as you go around each finger
b	Blow **b**ubbles onto the letter shape written on paper or card while saying the phoneme
f	Attach a fish picture or sticker to the children's fingers. Children trace around the letter shape with their **f**ish **f**inger as they say the phoneme
l	Make lollipops using lolly sticks and pom-poms. Children **l**ick the **l**olly and say the phoneme as they do
j	Set some 'j' magnetic letters in **j**elly. Children use a spoon to scoop out the letters and say the phoneme when they get one
v	Have a selection of **v**ehicles and draw car park spaces onto paper with the letter 'v' on them. Children park the vehicles and say the phoneme as they park
w	Write a 'w' in chalk or whiteboard pen on the window. Children use a sponge or brush to **w**ash the **w**indows and **w**ipe the letters off
x	Create a letter bo**x** from a cereal packet. Children post the 'x' magnetic letters or flashcards into the box saying the phoneme as they do
y	Draw a 'y' outline on paper and children colour it in **y**ellow
z	Children have a magic wand (could be just a pencil). They move the wand in the air to form the letter shape saying '**z**iggity **z**aggity **z**ee' as they do. Model the formation first and display the letter shape for children to copy

WHY DO WE NOT TEACH THE LETTERS IN ALPHABETICAL ORDER?

You will notice the letters in the two grids above are not in alphabetical order. This is because in phonics children will not be introduced to letters in the order of the alphabet. Although the different phonics schemes may vary the order of teaching the letters slightly, the most common letters children will be exposed to first are:

s a t p i n m d

These letters are chosen for a good reason! Once you have introduced even the first four letters and sounds children can start to put them together to form words:

at, sat, pat, tap, sap

If children learn the letters in alphabetical order then there are a limited number of simple three-letter, decodable words that can be made from a, b, c, d. 'If a child memorised ten words, the child can only read ten words, but if a child learns the sounds of ten letters, the child will be able to read 350 three-sound words, 4,320 four-sound words, and 21,650 five-sound words' (Kozloff, 2002).

FRIEZES AND SOUND MATS

Once children are secure with a group of letters and their matching sounds they can begin to practise writing them and start to spell some simple words. To help children with this it is important that the graphemes they have learnt are displayed or are easily accessible to them. Classrooms will often have a phonics display or wall frieze showing the flashcards or grapheme charts from the chosen phonics scheme. These act as a help desk so that children can refer to them when attempting to spell a word, helping to make their writing a bit more fluent and less painstaking! Imagine wanting to write the word 'cat'. You know that it starts with a /k/ sound but cannot remember what that grapheme looks like or how it is formed. Having something to refer to takes away this pressure and builds confidence.

Many of the phonics schemes will also have associated pictures alongside the letter; some will introduce specific actions or mnemonics to prompt the recognition of the GPC. All act as a hook to help children move the knowledge of the letter–sound correspondence into their long-term memory. Ensure the friezes and charts that you use contain pictures of objects that create the correct initial sound. I often see charts using, for example, an owl picture to accompany the letter 'o', a giraffe alongside 'g' or an ice-cream image with 'i'. These words start with the correct letter, but the letter is not making the phoneme that children will be initially taught. Just be mindful of this when selecting resources.

Tip 4.4 The letter 'x' will often be associated with a picture of a box or fox as we want to encourage children to remember the phoneme not the letter name. Words starting with 'x' do not have the 'x' making the /ks/ sound. Think x-ray or xylophone.

COMMON LETTER CONFUSION

When children confuse letters, wrongly identify or muddle them, parents often worry that this is an indication of dyslexia. The letters 'b' and 'd' are ones that children may frequently struggle to discriminate – for example, reading the word 'big' as 'dig' or writing the word 'dug' as 'bug'. It is very common for young children to muddle letters that look very similar. In fact, it's normal for children up to around the age of 7 to continue to do this.

MIRROR INVARIANCE

Mirror invariance is a mechanism of the visual system that we develop at a very early age which helps us to identify and recognise things such as faces, objects and places quickly even if what we are seeing is a mirror image. Children develop an innate ability to recognise that an object stays the same no matter the perspective and position. If they look at a chair it remains a chair from whichever angle – above, left side, right side, front. While this mechanism is useful in the natural world, it can be an explanation of the difficulty with and source of letter confusion. Children want to apply this natural property of the visual system to letters of the alphabet too! The letters shown in Figure 4.1 are all created using the same shape, so it is reasonable for children to assume that this shape retains the same letter (and sound) whichever way it sits on the page.

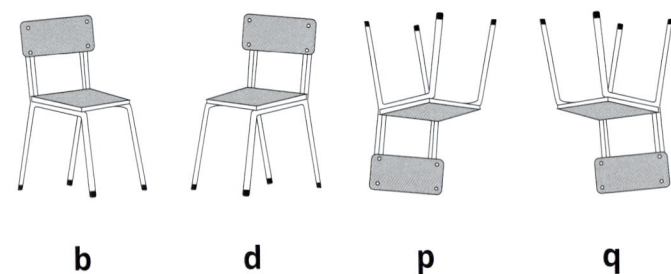

b   d   p   q

Figure 4.1   An illustration of mirror invariance

We need to explicitly teach children to learn that the direction and position of the shape *alters* the letter name and phoneme. They need to recognise these letters automatically and accurately to reduce their cognitive load. We can provide children with plenty of multi-sensory opportunities to practise recognising and distinguishing between the letter shapes, including listening for the phoneme, recognising the grapheme, rehearsing speech production of the phoneme and practising tactile letter formation to really embed recognition (Figure 4.2).

Acknowledging this multi-system interplay during language acquisition can have potential implications for educational methods. Interestingly, experiments have suggested that multi-sensory reinforcements can present an advantage for literacy acquisition (Pegado et al., 2014).

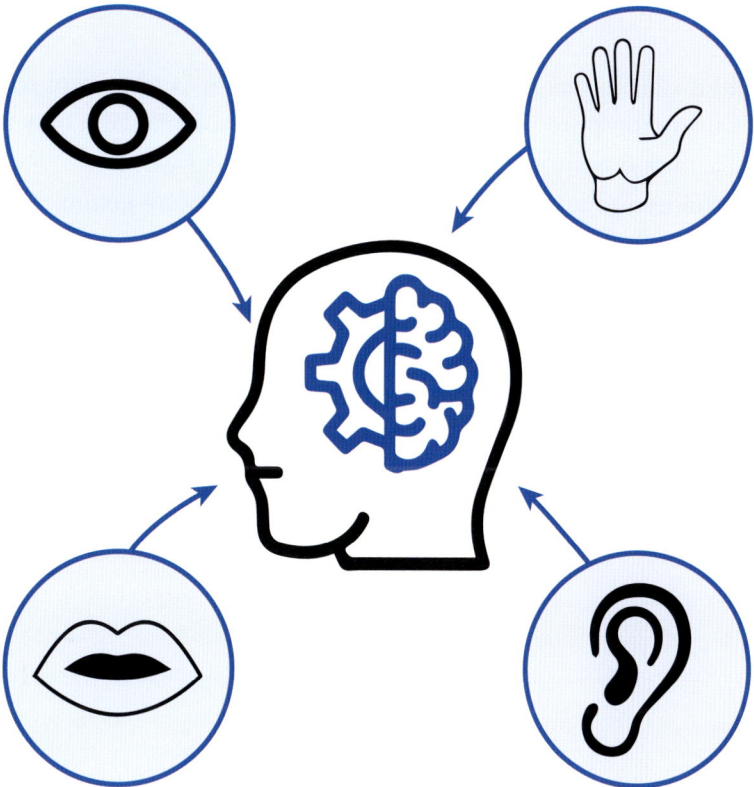

Figure 4.2 The multi-sensory factors that can influence successful language acquisition

When you teach children letters, in particular 'b' and 'd', encourage them to really look at the shape of their mouths when saying them. This will give them a clue to which letter they need to write and how to form it when it comes to spelling words:

b – your mouth starts in a closed position which reminds children that forming the letter 'b' starts by drawing the line

d – your mouth is open when saying the phoneme which can remind children to start the letter in the middle, like forming a 'c'

You might reinforce this by showing an image like that in Figure 4.3.

Figure 4.3 A useful visual tool to help children form the letters 'b' and 'd' correctly

IN SUMMARY

- Once children start to match letters and their sounds it is important to ensure that you model using the pure sound. Avoiding the schwa makes it easier for children to merge the phonemes together when learning to read words.
- Encourage children to articulate the phonemes correctly by getting them to say the sound in a mirror and look at the placement of their lips, teeth and tongue.
- Speech production errors can often occur in young children, and many will be developmentally appropriate for the age of the child. Practitioners should consult speech and language therapists if they have any concerns.
- When introducing a new grapheme, it is important to model the correct pronunciation and provide children with lots of opportunities to identify and revisit the GPC in multi-sensory activities to further embed knowledge.
- Letters are not introduced in alphabetical order, so that once children have learnt a very small selection of GPCs they can start to blend the sounds together to read simple words.

YOUR TURN!

Try saying the phonemes for the following letters in a mirror. Ensure they are pure! What do you notice about the shape of your mouth? Position of your tongue? Where is the sound coming from? Is it voiced or unvoiced?

s t p m g h r b d

LEARNING IDEA 4.1
DIY TACTILE LETTER CARDS

Children will have the opportunity to recognise letters and embed knowledge by feeling them too!

PRACTISE

- **Letter recognition**
- **Letter formation**

PICK UP

- **Cardboard**
- **Marker pen**
- **Small craft knife**

PREP

1. On a piece of card draw out a large lowercase letter using the marker pen.
2. Carefully score along the lines and through the top layer of cardboard using the craft knife.
3. Peel off the top layer of cardboard to reveal the corrugated card underneath.

PLAY

Children use their fingers to trace along the letter. This will add a sensory element to learning the letters and really embed knowledge. Encourage children to trace the letter in the direction of how the letter is formed and say the phoneme as they do.

TIP

Use a pair of tweezers to peel off the smaller bits of card. Once all the corrugated card is revealed, draw around the letter outline again to really make the letter stand out (Figure 4.4).

Figure 4.4 Practising letter recognition by using tactile letter cards

LEARNING IDEA 4.2
POSTING LETTERS

Quite literally, children can post letters! A great way for them to practise recognising the grapheme and have a go at writing the letter too.

PRACTISE

- **Letter recognition**
- **Letter formation**

PICK UP

- **Magnetic or wooden letters**
- **Postbox (an empty cereal box works just as well)**
- **Small envelopes**
- **Pencils and pens**

PREP

Place the selection of magnetic letters, envelopes and writing tools (Figure 4.5) on a table for the children to access.

PLAY

You could leave the resources out so that children can access them independently or an adult could say a phoneme and children find the corresponding letter to place in the envelope and post.

Figure 4.5 Using a postbox and 'letter envelopes' to practise recognising graphemes

LEARNING IDEA 4.3
PHONICS VIEWFINDER

Children will love taking 'photos' of objects within the environment that start with the same initial sound.

PRACTISE

- Listening for initial sounds
- Letter recognition

PICK UP

- Cardboard
- Pens

PREP

1 Draw and cut out a camera outline from cardboard.
2 In the bottom corner you can create a space to place small flashcards so that you can change the focus letter.
3 Alternatively, you could laminate the camera and use a whiteboard pen so that the letter can be rubbed away.

PLAY

Children identify the focus letter and its sound and then explore the environment, taking photos of objects that start with the corresponding initial sound that is written on the camera (Figure 4.6).

Figure 4.6 Using a home-made camera frame to practise spotting objects beginning with the same sound

LEARNING IDEA 4.4
LETTER AND SOUND PALETTE

This is a really lovely way of taking phonics outside.

PRACTISE

- Letter recognition
- Listening for initial sounds

PICK UP

- Cardboard
- Sticky-backed plastic or parcel tape
- Marker pen

PREP

1. Draw and cut a palette shape from cardboard and cut out several circles.
2. Turn the palette over and cover the holes with sticky-backed plastic or parcel tape so that small objects can now stick onto the circle.
3. On the front of the palette write a letter underneath each circle (Figure 4.7).

PLAY

Children take their palette outside and search for small objects that start with the corresponding initial sound – for example, find a small leaf and stick it in the circle above the 'l' or find a small stick and put it in the circle above 's'.

Ask children to find small natural objects that are already fallen on the ground (petals, small stones, twigs, leaves) rather than picking planted flowers or plants that are currently growing.

Figure 4.7 Outdoor phonics activity using an art palette made with objects and pens

LEARNING IDEA 4.5
FINGER HOPSCOTCH

Here is a fun and practical way to practise recognising letters and giving little fingers a workout to develop those fine motor muscles.

PRACTISE

- **Letter recognition**
- **Fine motor skills**

PICK UP

- **Paper**
- **Pens**
- **Small coin or counter**

PREP

1   Draw a hopscotch box outline.
2   Inside each box write a letter (Figure 4.8).

PLAY

Children throw a counter onto the hopscotch outline and then use their fingers to hop up the outline in a one-finger, two-finger, one-finger pattern just like you would do with your feet for playground hopscotch. They pick up the counter when they get to it and say the sound of the letter underneath. Repeat for as long as desired.

Figure 4.8   Playing hopscotch with your hands to practise recognising letters

Example 4.3 provides a list of objects that you might easily find around the home or classroom to support you when introducing the letters and their corresponding phonemes. All of the objects create the correct phoneme for the single letter.

Example 4.3   A list of objects to support the introduction of initial sounds

s	a	t	p
sock	apple	train	pig toy
scissors	avocado	tin	paper
spoon	alligator toy	teddy	pencil
soup tin	arrow picture	toast	penny
stick		tomato	paintbrush
i	**n**	**m**	**d**
insect toy	net	map	dinosaur
ink	nail	mirror	dog toy
injury – band aid	necklace	monkey toy	drink
	newspaper	money	duck toy
			dice
g	**o**	**c**	**k**
goat toy	orange	car toy	key
gloves	olives	coat	kite
game	octopus image or toy	coin	kettle
gold coin		can	ketchup
glue stick		cup	
e	**u**	**r**	**h**
egg	umbrella	rock	hat
elephant toy	underwear	ring	hands
envelope	unlock – key	rabbit soft toy	hairbrush
		ribbon	hammer toy
		rice	horse toy
b	**f**	**l**	**j**
book	football	lollipop	jam
bottle	fork	letter	jelly
bag	fruit	lightbulb	jug
boot	frog toy	leaf	jigsaw puzzle
button	flour	lock	
v	**w**	**x**	**y**
vehicle	wand	box	yoghurt
vest	wheel	six	yellow
vegetables	welly	fox	yo-yo
vase	water bottle	fix – spanner	
z			
zip			
zigzag pattern			
zebra toy			

5
BLENDING TO READ

KEY TERMS

Automaticity: the ability to do something without conscious effort. This will free up space in the working memory for other tasks

Blending: merging phonemes together to form and read a word

CVC: in phonics this abbreviation refers to a word that is made up of consonant, vowel, and consonant phoneme

Decode: the ability to accurately translate the written word into speech by employing knowledge of grapheme–phoneme correspondence

Segmenting: breaking up a word into its component phonemes for spelling

VC: in phonics this abbreviation refers to a word that is made up of a vowel and a consonant phoneme

Working memory: the small amount of information that can be temporarily stored and drawn upon to complete cognitive tasks

Blending and segmenting really go hand in hand (Figure 5.1). They are interconnected, and both skills rely on each other for children to be able to read and spell words. To read a word children need to segment the word into its individual GPCs, say the corresponding phonemes and blend them together to form the word. For children to spell, they need to have heard the whole word and then break up the word into its phonemes and recall the corresponding graphemes.

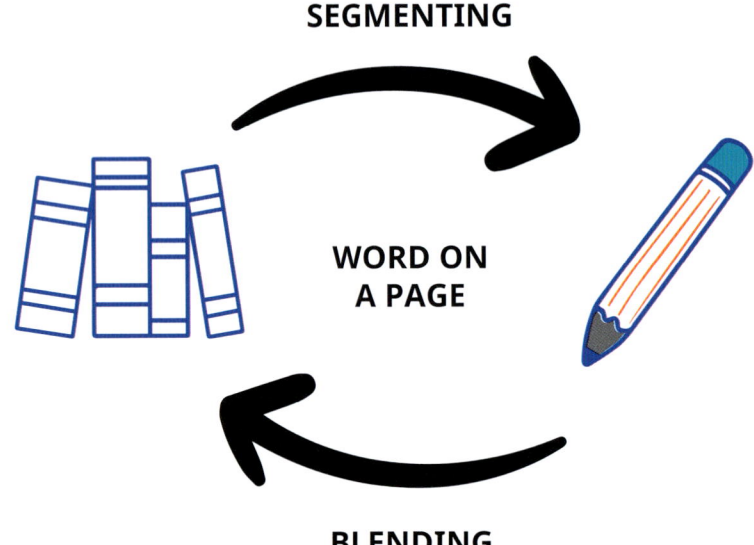

Figure 5.1　The interconnected nature of segmenting and blending

WHEN TO START BLENDING?

Once children have mastered recognising a small selection of graphemes in quick succession and can demonstrate the ability to orally blend phonemes together to form words, they can start to practise reading simple words on the page. After securing even the first four GPCs they should be given the opportunity to practise and apply their blending skills as soon as possible. At first, blending will need to be practised aloud and often rehearsed many, many times before it sticks. Some children will pick it up quickly, while for others it may take a little longer and they may need a bit more support or intervention. In this chapter we will look more closely at the different ways we can assist children with blending. The more practice children have the more likely they are to secure this vital skill for reading, the more confident and fluent they will become and, with time, the more likely to become motivated and enthusiastic readers.

THE PROCESS OF BLENDING

So, what does it actually take for us to read a word on a page? What knowledge and skills do we need to utilise?

ACTIVITY 5.1

The Mental Process of Reading

Try reading the word below and take note of the steps you need to follow in order to read it.

tip

1　At first, you need to be confident in recognising the letters (graphemes) on the page and have knowledge of the corresponding phonemes

2   Next, you need to quickly say the phonemes within the word aloud and hold them in your short-term memory
3   Then, you need to merge these sounds together aloud so that you begin to form and hear the word as a whole
4   Finally, you say the word as a whole and check it for meaning

THE READING BRAIN

While learning to speak is innate, reading needs to be taught. If a child is regularly exposed to language, then they will learn to speak. In contrast, no matter how many words and books a child is exposed to, they must be taught the appropriate knowledge and skills to decode them. They are not going to learn to read just through exposure to words. I cannot read Chinese. If I surround myself with books written in Chinese, I'm not going to be able to read Chinese. I need to be explicitly taught to match the symbols to meaning.

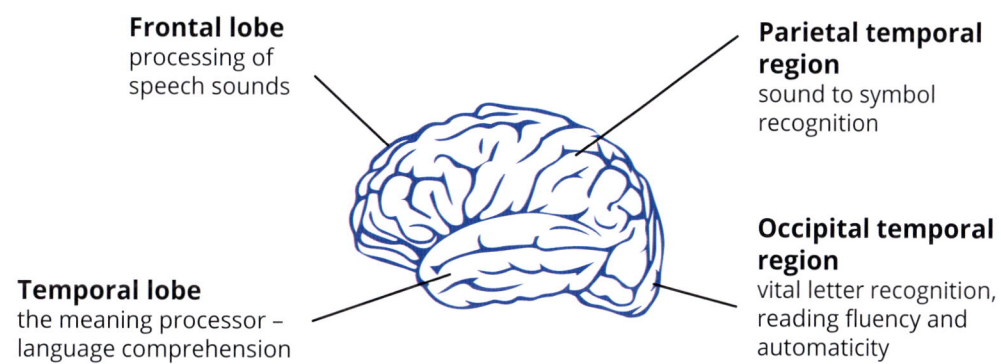

Frontal lobe
processing of
speech sounds

Parietal temporal region
sound to symbol recognition

Occipital temporal region
vital letter recognition,
reading fluency and
automaticity

Temporal lobe
the meaning processor –
language comprehension

Figure 5.2   The reading brain illustrating the key areas of the brain that are activated whilst reading

Research has found that reading repurposes several areas of the brain that are usually used for speech production. No one area is dedicated to reading but all the areas work together and play an important role (Figure 5.2):

- **Parietal temporal region** – this connects the areas that understand speech sounds and symbols.
- **Inferior frontal cortex/frontal lobe** – this area controls our speech production.
- **Occipito-temporal cortex** – when learning to read, this area recognises letters and eventually words by sight.
- **Temporal lobe** – this is where we process the meaning of words and understand context.

Learning to read requires the development of white-matter pathways which connect each of these regions of the brain. The more practice you have with blending and reading, the stronger these pathways will become (Ben-Shachar et al., 2007; Yeatman et al., 2012).

As you discovered in Activity 5.1, when you break down what it actually takes to read a word there are several steps that a reader needs to go through and several regions of the brain involved (Dehaene, 2009). It is automatic to us and I imagine, as you are a fluent reader, it is difficult for you to really think about and break down the processes involved with blending. For those just starting out on their reading journey it can be very complicated; each step can be problematic, and children may struggle and need more practice or assistance in securing the skills and knowledge required.

WHAT IS A CVC WORD?

At this stage of their reading journey children will be reading very simple, short words. For a useful word bank refer to Example 5.2 at the end of this chapter. Most of these words will be classed as CVC words. This means that they are made up of a consonant, vowel and consonant. It is important to note that, in phonics, the consonants and vowel refer to the *sound*, not the letter. So, words that contain more than three letters can be CVC words as they actually only contain three phonemes. Starting with CVC words makes it easier for children to practise blending as they only have to remember and recall three sounds to merge together and this is less taxing on their working memory.

If you are unsure whether a word is a CVC word then say it aloud and count the sounds. Say the word 'sheep' out loud and put a finger up for each sound you say. You can also think about the number of mouth movements you make; one mouth movement will equal one sound.

sheep

/sh/   /ee/   /p/

C   V   C

Example 5.1 shows further examples of CVC words that contain different numbers of letters.

Example 5.1   CVC words sorted according to the number of letters they contain

3-letter CVC words	4-letter CVC words	5-letter CVC words
cat	hill	quick
pen	mess	shell
got	buzz	shirt
hop	shop	queen
big	chip	booth
sat	thin	check
rug	sack	short

Some words may look like CVC words as they contain three letters, as the examples below show, but if you break the word down and count the sounds they only contain two sounds. We will look further at what constitutes a vowel and consonant sound within Chapter 7, but for now, in brief, know that any sound that is represented by at least one vowel letter is classed as a vowel sound.

boy		cow		say		car	
/b/	/oy/	/c/	/ow/	/s/	/ay/	/c/	/ar/
C	V	C	V	C	V	C	V

HOW CAN I HELP CHILDREN WHO ARE STRUGGLING TO BLEND?

As I discussed in Chapter 4, you really need to model saying the pure sounds with children and encouraging them to articulate the phonemes correctly too.

Ensure It's Pure!

Using pure sounds will make blending much easier as the phonemes flow and merge into each other more fluidly rather than being stopped by the /uh/. Say the word 'sun' as outlined below. Which way makes it easier for you to hear and blend the sounds?

suh/u/nuh → ssss/u/nnnn

Start Small

Practise blending initially with simple two-letter/two-phoneme words (VC words). This means that children will only need to hold and blend two sounds in their heads. As discussed in Chapter 2, an essential pre-reading skill is to practise blending two larger units of sounds. Prior experience of orally merging the onset and rime of words of two syllables provides a solid foundation for later learning to blend phonemes. It's a lot easier to blend two sounds, and children will therefore become more confident and capable at blending.

Example VC words to practise blending:

at in it on am up

> **Tip 5.1** Avoid 'is' and 'as' at this stage as within these words the 's' is making a /z/ sound. These words are likely to be taught as high-frequency tricky words a little later in children's reading journey.

Be aware that not all simple CV words are suitable at this stage. The vowels in words such as 'he', 'we', 'no' and 'go' make a long vowel sound, not the short sound that children will first learn. Again, these words will most likely be taught as high-frequency tricky words and then later discussed in more depth when learning alternative phonemes for graphemes.

Assisted Blending

Before children can independently read a simple word from a page you can demonstrate blending the sounds together to read it. This will involve using a word flashcard or three letter flashcards side by side to create a simple CVC word. You then really emphasise and elongate each individual phoneme and then model merging the phonemes together to read and say the word as a whole. Children will then copy and repeat this process. They can see and hear what blending to read sounds and looks like, and this can be key to building confidence. You can slowly take away how much you model and assist until the child is blending without support.

Successive Blending

Some children struggle to remember more than two phonemes within a CVC word and may say 'ta' or 'ap' for 'tap' or read it backwards as 'pat'. These mistakes show that children are unable to either retain all the sounds in their heads or remember and recall them in the correct order. Successive blending is a technique that helps children to combat these mistakes. It requires children to initially blend the first two sounds together to create one chunk of sound and then blend this chunk with the final sound. This process means that children only ever have to remember and recall two sounds and it is less demanding on their working memory.

ACTIVITY 5.2

Successive Blending Technique

The following would be the steps for reading the word 'mat' using a successive blending technique:

1 The reader looks at the first letter and says /m/
2 The reader looks at the second letter and says /a/
3 The reader blends the two sounds together to say /ma/
4 The reader looks at the final letter and says /t/
5 The reader blends the /ma/ with the /t/ to make 'mat'

/ma/

→

/ma/t/

→

mat

Continuant Consonants

To help children blend more competently, be more selective with the simple CVC words that you give them. Continuant consonants are sounds that can be stretched out for as long as you have the breath – for example /s/, /l/ and /f/. Words that start with these types of sounds will give children a better chance of merging the first sound into the next than words that start with stop sounds that are quick and short, like /b/, /d/ and /p/. This will help beginner or struggling readers to listen for the sounds and blend them more successfully.

Look out for, and ask children to practise with, words that start with the following GPCs. These sounds can be elongated, stretched and merged into the following phoneme more easily:

s	m	l	f	n	r
sat	mop	lip	fin	net	rug

Speed It Up!

Often, when children begin blending it can be very labour intensive. You may notice that children just starting to blend will take quite a while to read simple words and short decodable sentences as they must draw upon their phonic knowledge and recall *every* GPC within *every* word. This can take its toll on working memory. By the time they have reached the final GPC within a word the initial sound is lost from their working memory and they have forgotten it, meaning they have to start the whole process again! To speed things up, give children the opportunity to practise identifying graphemes and their phonemes in quick succession. Place out a small selection of flashcards in a line. It's good practice to include some GPCs that the child is confident with and a couple that need more practice. By placing the cards in a line, you are replicating how children read a word from left to right. Now ask children to move along the line of cards spotting the grapheme and saying the phoneme as quickly as they can. This technique will improve recognition speed and automatic recall. If children do not have to put so much effort into recalling the phonemes, they free up space in their working memory to focus on blending the sounds.

Auditory Memory Games

As I've mentioned above one of the key skills in blending is to quickly hold on to, remember and recall sounds within our heads. Working memory can be overloaded because its capacity is limited to only a very small number of items (Gathercole et al., 2006). If children's ability to store at least three pieces of information within their working memory becomes a hurdle, try playing auditory memory games. These types of games will improve children's capacity to remember and recall a larger number of sounds, which will ultimately impact blending.

Try a few of the games below to help develop auditory memory:

1   Create a sound pattern using parts of your body – for example, clap, stamp, shout, whisper or click your fingers. Can the child remember and copy the pattern back to you?
2   Stand behind the child and clap several times. Can they count and tell you how many claps you did? Repeat with different numbers of claps.
3   Place a selection of objects on a table. List two objects for the child to pick up and pass to you. You can slowly increase the number of objects on the list before they pass you the items in order.
4   Play the shopping list game. Take it in turns to add an item that you bought from the shop: 'I went to the shop and I bought …'. How many items can they remember?

5   Play 'Simon Says', but list two actions instead of one – for example, touch your head and then touch your feet. Can they remember the instructions and complete the actions in order? Slowly add more instructions for the child to remember and complete.

Check for Gaps

The cause of some children's blending issues could be down to the inability to recognise certain GPCs. Look out for any patterns in words that they struggle blending. Perhaps they haven't secured their recognition of a certain grapheme and therefore struggle to blend any word that contains it – for example, they can't recognise and say the phoneme for 'p' so can't blend and read 'pat', 'pin', 'tap', 'top' or 'pot'. It's important to complete regular diagnostic assessments to check for gaps in phonic knowledge. If you plug these gaps, then you could potentially see an improvement in blending.

Take Away the Word

If you have modelled blending, tried a variety of different blending techniques, played lots of auditory memory games, practised with words that contain only two sounds, checked for gaps in phonic knowledge and the child is still struggling to blend sounds, then return to activities that develop phonological awareness. In particular, focus on the child's ability to listen to an adult say the sounds and to blend the sounds together to form the word. Children really need a solid foundation in oral blending before attempting to blend and read any written word on the page. A great place to start with this is for children to practise orally blending the syllables within compound words. Each syllable within the longer word is a word in its own right, so children should find blending these units of sound easier as each chunk makes sense and they will already be familiar with it as a word. Think about the word 'bedroom'. Children will be familiar with both syllables /bed/ and /room/ so should be confident to then push these two sounds together to say 'bedroom'. The skill of blending and merging sounds together is still being practised here despite working with larger chunks of sounds rather than phonemes. You can also use the same visual cues to prompt blending like moving your hands closer together or tapping and sliding down your arm.

ACTIVITY 5.3

Oral Blending of Compound Words

Try these compound words that contain two chunks of sound (syllables):

fish/tank	ice/cream
pan/cake	foot/ball
car/park	lip/stick
bed/room	hand/bag
snow/man	

Practice, Practice, Practice

Ultimately, we want children to become so good at blending that it becomes effortless and automatic. This will make space in their working memory to read longer, more complex words. They will become more fluent, and this will have a positive impact on comprehension. Children must be given plenty of opportunities, both within the phonics lesson and across all areas of the curriculum, to embed the skill of blending in a fun, engaging yet systematic way. Practice really can make perfect. Practice is what leads to fluency, automatisation, overcoming the limits to working memory, information quickly moving to long-term memory, and blending happening without conscious effort.

FURTHER STRATEGIES TO SUPPORT BLENDING

There are several other practical strategies and techniques that you can utilise to help children grasp the concept of identifying GPCs and blending the sounds to read words.

Sound Buttons

This is when a small dot is drawn under single letters. The dots act as sound buttons and there will be the same number of sound buttons as there are phonemes. Every time an adult or child presses the button they say the phoneme of the grapheme above it. Once all dots have been pressed they merge all the sounds together to form the word. Some cards may also have a longer line that swipes across the whole word to indicate that blending needs to occur.

ACTIVITY 5.4

Using Sound Buttons to Read CVC Words

pin　peg　cup　ran
•••　•••　•••　•••

Sound buttons are especially useful when children move onto learning when two or three letters work together to make one sound. A line is used instead of a dot in this case and the sound button clearly shows that one sound needs to be vocalised for this group of letters. I'll go into more detail about this in Chapter 7.

Blending Slide

Here is a useful tool to visually demonstrate GPCs merging together to form the word. Children will need a playground slide outline. The initial GPC is written, or a magnetic letter is placed at the top of the slide, the middle GPC in the middle and the final GPC at the bottom (Figure 5.3). Children then either physically move the letters down the slide to build the word or touch each of the written graphemes as they move their finger down the slide saying each phoneme as they reach it and the whole word as they get to the bottom.

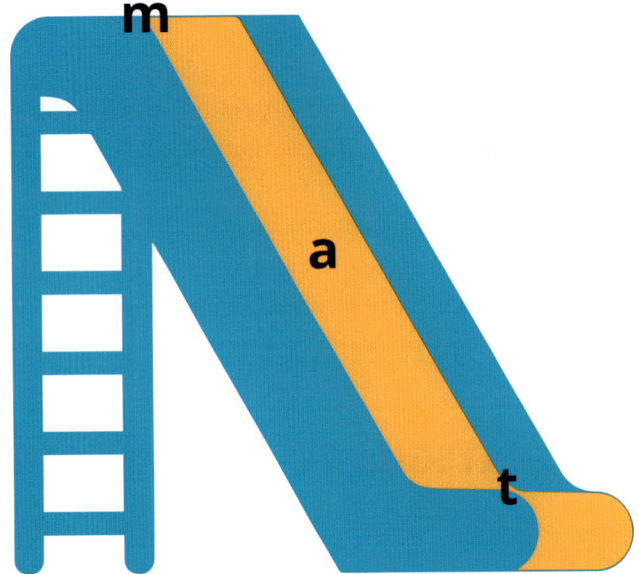

Figure 5.3 A blending slide

Blending Arms

Alternatively, instead of using a slide picture children can use their hands and arms. Holding out one arm in front of them they tap it with their other hand, starting at their shoulder and finishing at their wrist, for each phoneme in the word and then stroke their arm from top to bottom as they blend the sounds and say the word. This is a fantastic tactile way to reinforce blending as children feel each tap (sound) and the movement of their hand will illustrate the concept of blending. It's also a useful technique as it can be done at any time or anywhere and no resources are needed.

Moving Flashcards

Blending can be demonstrated by clipping cards with clothes pegs on a washing line, flashcards on an easel or simply putting cards on a table (Figure 5.4). Clip or place the cards some distance apart from each other and say the phoneme for each grapheme. Now, move them slightly closer together and repeat the process. Again, move them closer and say the phonemes until the cards are adjacent to one another and you are almost saying the word as a whole already. This is a visual way to demonstrate that phoneme recall needs to happen in quick succession to blend to read, and children can clearly see the cards coming together and 'merging'.

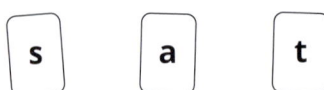

Figure 5.4 Flashcards to help model and support blending

DEVELOPING FLUENCY WITH BLENDING

The goal when teaching blending is for it to happen with little effort, in our heads rather than 'sound talking' each phoneme, and with automaticity. This will free up space in working memory to concentrate on reading sentences with fluency and give us a chance to understand what we are actually reading. But, how do we encourage children to stop segmenting words aloud and build fluency with blending? Below is a useful step-by-step guide to build up to blending occurring in children's heads rather than 'sounding out' loud. Children will get to this point at different stages on their reading journey as some may still need to hear the sounds in order to blend for some time.

ACTIVITY 5.5

Techniques to stop overt segmenting and blending

Magic Lips

When children say the phonemes within the word, instead of vocalising them encourage them to move their lips and pretend they are saying the phonemes but not actually say them aloud. They then vocalise the whole word.

Nodding

As above, but instead of moving their mouth they very slightly nod for each phoneme. Again, this is a small step towards fluent word reading without having to 'sound out' the words.

Blend in Your Head

This time ask children to segment the word entirely in their heads. They can say it to themselves internally but not vocalise the phonemes. They then say the word aloud, often when indicated by an adult – for example, an adult holds up a word card, points to the graphemes or sound buttons (children do not verbalise these) and then the adult swipes their fingers, from left to right, under the word to indicate the whole word needs to be read aloud.

IN SUMMARY

- Blending involves the ability to identify the graphemes within a word, the corresponding sounds and then merge these sounds together to read the word.
- It's important to model this process to children so that they can clearly see what is expected of them when they move to independently blending to read a word.
- There are a variety of strategies that you can use with children who are struggling to blend, including starting with smaller words, successive blending and the use of continuant consonants.

- Always revert back to developing children's phonological awareness and oral blending skills if children continue to struggle.
- Children need to build up automaticity with blending so that they can free up space in their working memory to develop their reading fluency and comprehension.

YOUR TURN!

Which of these words are CVC words?

sock   toy   saw   bug   pot   shed

Draw the sound buttons under each of these words. Practise pressing them, saying the phonemes (ensure they're pure!) and blending these words aloud.

pet   jam   leg   sun   win   dog

LEARNING IDEA 5.1
BULLDOZER BLENDING

This is a fantastic visual and physical way to demonstrate blending and for children to practise pushing phonemes together to read.

PRACTISE

- Letter recognition
- Reading left to right
- Blending sounds to read

PICK UP

- Building or Jenga blocks
- Parcel tape
- Whiteboard pen
- Small bulldozer toy

PREP

1. Cover the surface of the blocks with parcel tape so that each becomes a mini wipeable board.
2. Write letters on the blocks and then place out two or three blocks in a line with a small gap between each.

PLAY

Children use the bulldozer toy to push and move the blocks together to form a word (Figure 5.5). They say each of the phonemes as they push the bulldozer along until they say the word as a whole once the blocks are side by side.

Figure 5.5 Using a bulldozer toy and building blocks to practise phonemic blending

LEARNING IDEA 5.2
TRAIN TRACK BLENDING

Here is another really practical and engaging way to help children blend phonemes.

PRACTISE

- **Letter recognition**
- **Blending phonemes to read**

PICK UP

- **Train track**
- **Toy train**
- **Parcel tape/stickers**
- **Pen**

PLAY

Before children have a go themselves, demonstrate moving the train along the track, saying the sounds as you move along the track and then saying the whole word when you reach the end of the track. Once you have demonstrated, children can now have a go. Leave the resources out for them to independently practise blending as well as using the tracks to build their own words.

PREP

1   Just like in the previous activity, you can place a small piece of parcel tape onto the train tracks so that they become wipeable and you can change the graphemes. Alternatively, use small stickers on several tracks.
2   Place two or three of the tracks together to form a word.
3   Put the toy train at the beginning of the tracks (Figure 5.6).

Figure 5.6   Blending phonemes using wooden train tracks

LEARNING IDEA 5.3
BLENDING STICKS

This is a useful tool to demonstrate the process of blending and practise blending phonemes to read words.

PRACTISE

- Letter recognition
- Using sound buttons
- Blending phonemes to read

PICK UP

- Cardboard
- Marker pen
- Lollipop sticks

PREP

1. Create some word cards using small rectangles of cardboard.
2. Underneath each of the graphemes of the word draw a sound button.
3. Now, on a further piece of card draw a few small flying insects. Cut these out and stick them on the end of each of the lollipop sticks (Figure 5.7).

PLAY

Children select a word card to read and a blending stick. They start on the left of the word and move the insect across and underneath the word, saying the phoneme above each of the sound buttons as they reach them. They then blend all the sounds together to say the whole word at the end. They repeat with other word cards and blending sticks.

Figure 5.7 Practising blending phonemes using drawn images on wooden sticks

LEARNING IDEA 5.4
EGG BOX WORDS

Here is a hands-on way for children to practise building words and manipulating phonemes to read, as well as repurposing your recycling before it's thrown out.

PRACTISE

- **Building words**
- **Manipulating phonemes**
- **Blending phonemes to read**

PICK UP

- **Lollipop sticks**
- **Magnetic or wooden letters**
- **Egg box cartoon**
- **Scissors**
- **Hot glue**

PREP

1. Upturn the egg box and cut a small slit into the bottom of each of the egg moulds so that a lollipop stick can be slotted in.
2. On each of the sticks use hot glue to stick a magnetic or wooden letter (you can just use a small piece of card with handwritten letters if you haven't any letters available).

PLAY

Children slot the lollipop sticks into the egg carton holder to form and read words (Figure 5.8). When they have created a word, can they switch just one of the sticks to form another word? For example, once they have built and read the word 'pot' can they move just one of the sticks to create the word 'pat'? Which sound is different? Which letter do we need to swap?

Figure 5.8 Building words using recycled objects such as an egg-box

LEARNING IDEA 5.5
DUPLO WINDOWS

Repurpose a resource to create a frame to practise blending phonemes and reading words.

PRACTISE

- Letter recognition
- Blending phonemes to read

PICK UP

- Duplo windows
- Wooden or magnetic letters

PREP

1. Create a small frame using Duplo and three Duplo windows.
2. Lay the frame down onto a flat surface and place a magnetic letter inside each of the windows to spell a word (Figure 5.9).

PLAY

Children open each of the windows and say the phoneme for the grapheme they see inside. They repeat for all windows and then merge the phonemes together to read the word as a whole.

Figure 5.9 Practising blending and reading using a frame or window made using home objects

Example 5.2 Decodable CVC words organised by initial sounds

satp	i	n	m
at	it	pin	mat
sat	sit	tin	map
tap	tip	pan	man
pat	pit	nap	sam
sap	sip	nit	pam

d	g	o	c
din	gap	pot	cot
dip	dig	dog	cod
pad	pig	pod	can
sad	tag	nod	cat
	nag	mop	cog

k	e	u	r
kit	peg	cup	rug
kin	pet	mug	run
kid	net	rug	rat
	met	cut	rot
	set	sun	rip

h	b	f	l
hat	bat	fan	log
hot	bug	fit	leg
hit	bin	fog	lip
had	bag	fin	lap
hop	big	fat	lot

j	v	w	x
jam	van	wet	six
jig	vet	wag	box
jog	vat	wig	mix
jet		web	fox
jab		win	fix

y	z		
yet	zit		
yam	zip		
yak	zap		
	zigzag		

6
SEGMENTING TO SPELL

KEY TERMS

Decoding: the ability to use existing phonic knowledge to break up and blend the phonemes within a word

Dexterity: skill and ease in using the hand

Encoding: the process of translating phonemes into graphemes

Fine motor skills: the ability to make movements using the small muscles in our hands and wrists

GPC: abbreviation for grapheme–phoneme correspondence

Grapheme: the letter or group of letters that we see on the page. It's the written form of the phoneme

Phoneme: the smallest unit of sound within a word

Segmenting: breaking up a word into its smallest units of sound

Spelling: involves breaking up a word into its individual phonemes and then representing the corresponding graphemes

As we discovered in Chapter 5, segmenting and blending are tightly coupled processes that support each other:

> Blending and segmenting are, in the words of the Rose Review, 'reversible processes': that is, if you can blend the sounds together to read a word, you should be able to identify and break down (segment) the individual sounds in a word you hear to spell it. To spell the word, you need to represent each sound you hear by a letter – or more than one letter. (Ofsted, 2014, p.18)

The two processes are interconnected (Figure 6.1): 'reading is like breathing in and writing is like breathing out' (Allyn, 2015). I would adapt this slightly to say that blending is like

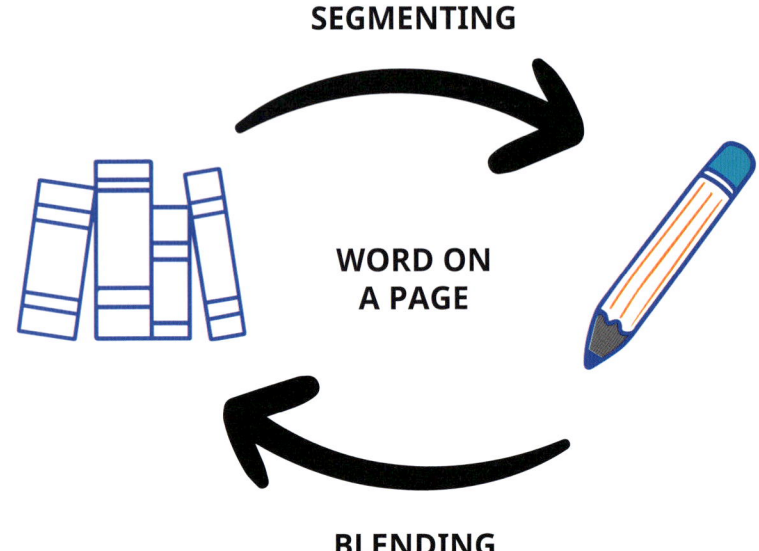

SEGMENTING

WORD ON A PAGE

BLENDING

Figure 6.1 The interconnected nature of segmenting and blending

breathing in and segmenting is like breathing out, as both blending and segmenting lie at the foundation of children's ability to read, spell and eventually write. Segmenting and encoding are the opposite to blending and decoding. Encoding is the process of breaking up a word you hear into its component sounds and then recalling the graphemes that represent these phonemes to spell and write it. In this chapter I will work through a variety of techniques that can be used to support children with segmenting and spelling words.

Segmenting → spelling → writing

Orally break up a word → recall the graphemes needed to spell it → physically write it

> **Tip 6.1** You may hear the phrases 'sound talk' or 'sounding out'. These terms may be used as a more child-friendly way of indicating that children need to use the skill of segmenting.

SPELLING DOES NOT HAVE TO BE WRITING!

If we think about the process of encoding above, it illustrates that children can demonstrate their ability to segment words before they can spell them and spell words before they physically use a writing tool to write them down on paper. This is useful to know as young children may not have the dexterity, fine motor skills or pencil control to form letters, but by using other resources and tools can clearly exhibit their ability to segment and spell. If spelling words only ever involves writing, then those children who do not have sufficient handwriting skills will have to put all of their effort into remembering how letters are formed, how to hold a pencil correctly, starting in the right place and moving the pencil in the right direction, staying on a line and worrying about making mistakes. You can see that having to focus on all of this takes up far too much space in their working memory for them to then demonstrate their ability to segment and spell! At first, taking away the demand that comes with using a writing tool to write letters and words can help children focus on spelling them.

FINE MOTOR MILESTONES

Table 6.1 Fine motor developmental milestones

Age	Activity
0–6 months	Grasping with both hands Grasping with one full hand
6–12 months	Pinching things with thumb and one other finger Transferring objects from one hand to another Picking up and dropping toys
1–2 years	Stacking three small objects Turning knobs Turning several pages of a book Painting with whole arm movement Grasping a pencil and holding it in the palm
2–3 years	Turning single pages of a book Holding a writing tool with all fingers with palm down Rolling, squeezing and pulling playdough Painting with some wrist action Copying a horizontal and vertical line
3–4 years	Copying circles Using non-dominant hand to assist and stabilise an object When using a pencil, moving the whole hand rather than the fingers Joining two dots
4–5 years	Copying crosses and squares Writing name
5–6 years	Using three-fingered grasp of a pencil
6–7 years	Writing most letters correctly Writing on a line

The milestones in Table 6.1 highlight when children are developmentally ready to hold a pencil and form letters correctly. This does not marry up with when we routinely start explicit phonics instruction at school. We must provide children with opportunities, especially in the early years, to demonstrate their knowledge using tools other than pencil and paper. The use of magnetic letters, letter flashcards and letter fans to build words can be really useful at this stage.

WHAT STRATEGIES CAN I USE TO SUPPORT SEGMENTING AND SPELLING?

Just as there are several practical strategies and techniques that children can use to help with blending, there are also many 'hands-on' resources and aids that can help children segment and spell words.

Top Ten Manipulatives

Using multi-sensory resources that children can manipulate in some way can aid children's segmenting skills. The idea is that they move, tap or press an object for each phoneme in the word; having something to physically manipulate adds a kinaesthetic element and makes the somewhat abstract concept of counting phonemes into a more concrete visual. Here is a list of my top ten manipulatives:

1 Move counters or milk bottle tops into a grid
2 Build a tower with Duplo blocks – one block for each sound
3 Clip clothes pegs onto card for each sound in the word
4 Use a Pop-It and pop a button for each phoneme
5 Draw dots onto a piece of masking tape, and children press one dot for each phoneme in the word
6 Use your arm like a blending slide and tap down from shoulder to wrist for each sound
7 Make a mark on a whiteboard or piece of paper for each phoneme
8 Count the sounds with your fingers
9 Press playdough balls
10 Hop or jump for each phoneme

Word Chains

Word chains are a really useful teaching tool for beginner readers as they help to hone children's skill of isolating and manipulating individual phonemes within a word. An adult will say, segment and spell a word. They then say a new word by substituting one of the phonemes. Subsequently, they ask the children to identify which phoneme has been changed. The adult will then change the correct GPC to create and spell the new word.

> **Tip 6.2** Try and change the beginning, middle and final sound within each word chain to practise listening for and manipulating the sounds.

There are lots of really fun and interactive ways to play this game. You could use large letter cards and give them out to the children, asking them to stand up to literally form the word at the front of a group. To create a new word a different child stands up with the correct GPC and physically swaps places with the child holding the grapheme that needs to be changed. Using magnetic letters is also a quick and easy way for children to change the GPCs. Word chains work really well for all stages of phonics instruction and are a great way to continue to focus on segmenting throughout early years and Key Stage 1. A word chain may look a little like this:

sat → pat → pit → pin → pan → can → ran → rat → sat

Notice only one GPC changes each time until you get back to the original word.

Phoneme Frames

Phoneme frames, also referred to as Elkonin boxes, are a brilliant tool to practise breaking up a word and spelling – a resource I've successfully used time and time again over the years (Figure 6.2). A child will have a grid containing a certain number of boxes in front of them. Children will often start with a frame with three boxes as they will be initially learning to read and spell simple CVC words. The child will listen to a word, segment it and place or write the corresponding GPCs into the boxes within the frame; the initial phoneme will go in the first box, middle phoneme in the middle box and final phoneme in the final box. Using this technique helps children listen for all the sounds, and it becomes visually clear how many phonemes they need to be listening for. So, using a three-box phoneme frame shows children that they will need to listen for three phonemes.

As discussed in Chapter 5, a CVC word contains three phonemes but can be made up of more than three letters. The phoneme frame will help children focus on the sounds within the word, so if a child hears a word in which they know one phoneme is spelled using two or more letters then they would place all of these letters within one box as these letters are working together to make one sound:

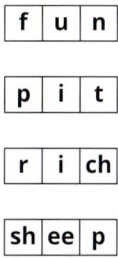

Figure 6.2　The use of phoneme frames to support segmenting and spelling CVC words

Segmenting Fingers

This involves children holding up a finger for each phoneme within a word and then counting how many fingers/sounds it contains before spelling and writing it – again, adding a multi-sensory element to phonics. This technique is especially useful when children move on to reading longer, more complex words that contain more than three phonemes, including consonants that are next to each other within a word that make separate sounds. We will look more closely at these types of words in Chapter 8.

Be a Robot!

Encouraging children to pretend to be a robot while segmenting a word can help them break it up more accurately. Children imitate a robot voice and move an arm, like a robot, for each phoneme in the word. This technique should be modelled first by an adult. They say the individual sounds really slowly, and significantly separated from each other, so that they can be clearly heard by the children. A robot toy or puppet is a great additional resource too!

Sound Mapping

This is a resource that gives children the opportunity to segment a word several times before actually writing it. Children will hear a word or look at an image (Figure 6.3), orally segment it, tap a button for each sound in the word, and then use magnetic or wooden letters to spell it and finally write it. This resource is particularly useful for children who struggle with writing words as it reduces their cognitive load because they are not attempting to both spell and write at the same time. They have already formed the word using the manipulatives and can concentrate on practising physically forming the letters and words when writing them.

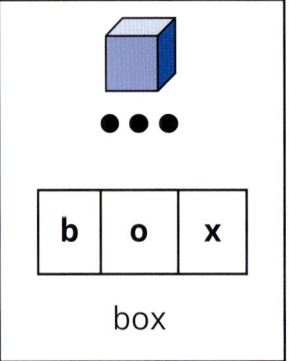

Figure 6.3   An illustration of sound mapping

Spelling Lines

One way to encourage children to move on to spelling and write words is to get them to orally segment the word while drawing a small horizontal line on a whiteboard or piece of paper for each phoneme. This clearly shows the child how many GPCs are needed. They then write the corresponding grapheme above each of the lines (a bit like a game of hangman).

d   o   g

___ ___ ___

h   a   t

___ ___ ___

Just like a phoneme frame, if children know that a phoneme is represented by more than one letter they would write the corresponding graphemes above just one of the lines.

qu   i   ck

___ ___ ___

STEPS TO SPELLING

As you can see from the techniques and tools shown above, it's important to give beginner spellers multiple chances to segment a word before actually representing and spelling the word in some form. The more practice a child has at listening for and counting phonemes within words, the more automatic this process will become. This will result in freeing up space in working memory to concentrate on making spelling choices and choosing the correct graphemes needed to represent the phonemes. We will look in much more detail at alternative graphemes and spelling in Chapter 11, but for now, with those just starting out on their reading and writing journey, try and embed the following steps when spelling any decodable word so that it starts to happen with little conscious effort.

Step 1: Say it

Step 2: Stretch it

Step 3: Count it

Step 4: Represent it

Step 5: Check it

> **Tip 6.3**   Teach children that the letter 's' never follows 'x'. They will never see words ending in 'xs' in the English language. This will avoid children making the mistake of writing plurals of words that end in a /k/ and /s/ using 'xs' rather than 'cks'. So, 'socks' doesn't become 'sox'.

PHONETICALLY PLAUSIBLE ATTEMPTS

One of my favourite things as an early years teacher was to happen upon little notes written by children during child-initiated learning and observing that they've used their phonic knowledge to make phonetically plausible attempts at spelling and writing more complex words. Sometimes these notes may have needed a lot of deciphering and to the 'untrained' eye might look like anything other than written English! But these children have utilised their current phonics based on what they have been taught and made a great attempt at putting the phonemes down on paper. The following is an example of a child's phonetically plausible attempt at spelling:

yoor d best teech yoo doo d bes wurc b cors doo d best fonix mi fens or d bes plain in d cors

(You're the best teacher

You do the best work

The class do the best phonics

My friends all the best playing in the class)

I often get asked if an adult should correct these mistakes and highlight to children their errors. We definitely don't want to discourage these attempts or dampen the child's enthusiasm for writing, so it's really about knowing that child, what they have been previously taught and what areas they are secure in. For example, a child in Reception writing 'hows' for 'house' has made an excellent attempt at using their phonics and applying their knowledge. However, if a child is at the end of Year 1 or the beginning of Year 2, and I know they are secure with the alternative spellings and have been taught 'ou' as an alternative to 'ow' and have learnt that 'se' makes the /s/ sound, I would expect them to write 'house' correctly as a common high-frequency word. I would talk to them and remind them of previous learning. Research strongly suggests that engaging children in listening for sounds in words and inventing/estimating/approximating their spelling supports their literacy development (Ouellette and Sénéchal, 2008).

IN SUMMARY

- Segmenting is the ability to hear a word and break it up into its individual phonemes.
- Segmenting is crucial for spelling. Children need to break up the word into its phonemes and then choose the correct graphemes to represent these phonemes.
- Remember that spelling does not have to involve writing. There are a variety of manipulatives that children can use to demonstrate their ability to spell.
- There are several strategies and techniques that practitioners can use to support children with segmenting, including the use of segmenting fingers and phoneme frames.
- Phonetically plausible attempts at writing are a way of children demonstrating their developing phonic knowledge, and practitioners should consider when it is best to correct their spelling errors.

YOUR TURN!

Follow the steps to spelling by saying, stretching, counting and then writing the following words in the phoneme frames.

pod

dip

rug

red

fan

box

rash

queen

sail

LEARNING IDEA 6.1
BUMPER CARS

This is such a fun and practical way to practise isolating and manipulating GPCs to build and spell words.

PRACTISE

- Letter recognition
- Isolating phonemes
- Manipulating GPCs
- Building and spelling words

PICK UP

- Toy cars
- Masking tape
- Marker pen
- Paper

PLAY

An adult says a word and children find the corresponding cars to spell that word and place them into the correct space in the car park – for example, an adult says 'park' and children find the 'p' and put it into the first box, 'ar' into the middle space and 'k' into the final space. Now, the adult says another word where just one phoneme has changed – for example, the adult now says 'dark'. Children find the 'd' car and bump the 'p' car out of the frame to create the word 'dark'. Repeat for other words.

PREP

1. On top of each of the toy cars stick a small piece of masking tape and then write a letter on each piece of tape.
2. Draw out a phoneme frame onto paper to create a 'car park'.
3. Place the selection of cars around the frame ready for children to build words (Figure 6.4).

Figure 6.4 Word building using toy cars

LEARNING IDEA 6.2
SHELL I SPELL?

This is a brilliant, engaging alternative phoneme frame.

PRACTISE

- Letter recognition
- Isolating phonemes
- Manipulating GPCs
- Building and spelling words

PICK UP

- Three shells (these can be real or cardboard outlines)
- White card

PREP

1. Cut the white card into circles to act as pearls and write a grapheme onto each.
2. Place out the shells in a line to act as a phoneme frame.
3. Set up the pearls around the shell frame (Figure 6.5).

PLAY

Begin by saying a word, and children search for the corresponding pearls to place into the shell frame to spell it. You can then say another word with only one phoneme changed, and children find the correct grapheme to change. Leave the resources out for children to explore building and reading their own words. You could have accompanying pictures to act as prompts so that children don't have to think of words to create.

Figure 6.5 Practising phonemes by framing them using sea shells

LEARNING IDEA 6.3
CRACK THE COLOUR CODE

This activity taps into children's inquisitive nature and love of code breaking!

PRACTISE

- Letter recognition
- Isolating phonemes
- Manipulating GPC
- Building and spelling words

PICK UP

- Different coloured building blocks
- Magnetic, wooden letters or flashcards
- Strip of cardboard

PREP

1. Place a variety of different coloured building blocks along the strip of card, assign and write a grapheme for each to create a key.
2. Use a compartment tray or hand-drawn frame for children to crack the code and build words.
3. Place out three of the coloured blocks such that when the code is cracked it creates a word.

PLAY

Children use the key to match the correct grapheme to the corresponding coloured block (Figure 6.6). Once they have found the three graphemes they blend to read the word. You can prepare ready-made towers of blocks for children to continue to use the key and crack the colour code.

Figure 6.6 Code breaking exercise using coloured building blocks

LEARNING IDEA 6.4
FRAME IT!

Take phonics outside and try out this alternative phoneme frame.

PRACTISE

- Letter recognition
- Segmenting words
- Spelling
- Letter formation and writing CVC words

PICK UP

- Plastic photo frames
- Paintbrushes
- Water pot
- Chunky chalk

PREP

1   Take the backing out of the photo frames so that you are just left with the plastic frame.
2   Place out the frames along with a paintbrush and pot of water. Alternatively, children could use chunky chalk.

PLAY

An adult says a word and children form the letter for each of the GPCs of the word within the frames. The first phoneme is written in the first frame, the second in the middle frame and the final phoneme in the final frame (Figure 6.7). Repeat for other words and leave the resources for children to explore writing words independently.

Figure 6.7 Phoneme framing exercise using water on tiles outside to spell 'sun'

LEARNING IDEA 6.5
MAGNA DOODLE GLOW UP

I'm sure we all have an old, cheap Magna Doodle knocking about at home. Give it a new lease of life to help further develop and support children's literacy skills!

PRACTISE

- Segmenting words
- Spelling
- Letter formation and writing CVC words

PICK UP

- Old unloved Magna Doodle
- Marker pen
- Magnetic letters
- Cardboard

PREP

1. Use the marker pen to draw a 'say it, spell it, write it' frame directly onto the Magna Doodle (Figure 6.8).
2. Create some CVC picture cards using small squares of cardboard.

PLAY

Children select one of the picture cards, say the word and segment the phonemes. They use the magnetic letters to build into the first phoneme frame and then use the Magna Doodle tool to write the word themselves into the bottom phoneme frame.

Figure 6.8 Practising literacy skills using an erasable drawing toy

7
DIGRAPHS AND TRIGRAPHS

KEY TERMS

Consonant: a basic speech sound that is produced when breath is partially obstructed

Digraph: two letters that together make one sound

Diphthong: a sound formed with the combination of two vowels within a syllable

Trigraph: three letters that work together to make one sound

Vowel: a speech sound that is produced with a comparatively open vocal tract

COMBINATIONS OF LETTERS

The next step in a child's reading journey, once they are confident in recognising the sounds for individual letters of the alphabet and blending these sounds to form words, is to learn that sometimes when you see combinations of letters written on the page they can work together to make one sound. Many phonics schemes will refer to this stage as phase 3. For a list of words that contain the digraphs and trigraphs that are commonly taught first then check out Example 7.1 at the end of this chapter. During this stage of reading children will learn that two or three letters when next to each other within a word make one phoneme. These are called:

- **Digraph**: Two letters next to each other within a word that make one phoneme. 'Di' is a prefix of Greek origin meaning 'two', 'twice' or 'double', and 'graph', also Greek, means 'written down, printed or drawn'. It might help to think of other words that start with 'di' like 'diversion' or 'dilemma' (both can have two options) to remind you that digraph means 'two'.
- **Trigraph**: Three letters next to each other within a word that make one phoneme. 'Tri', again of Greek origin, means 'three'. Perhaps think of the words 'triangle' (three sides), 'tripod' (three legs) or 'triceratops' (three horns) to help you remember that 'trigraph' means three letters written down that are working together.

Depending on the phonics scheme a school uses, the order that the digraphs and trigraphs are introduced will vary slightly, but all will introduce the GPCs in a very systematic order and learning about digraphs and trigraphs is the next step on from learning letter sounds.

WHEN SHOULD DIGRAPHS AND TRIGRAPHS BE TAUGHT?

Throughout a child's first year in school they will be introduced to multiple digraphs and trigraphs and learn the concept that letters can work together to make one sound. At the end of the Reception year children will be assessed against the early learning goals within the Early Year Foundation Stage Profile. In order for a teacher to mark a child as being at the expected level for reading they need to demonstrate that they can:

- say a sound for each letter in the alphabet and at least ten digraphs
- read words consistent with their phonic knowledge by sound-blending
- read aloud simple sentences and books that are consistent with their phonic knowledge, including some common exception words

(Early Years Foundation Stage Profile, 2021)

INITIAL DIGRAPHS AND DOUBLE LETTERS

While learning to match single letters to their sounds, children will also be taught their first few digraphs. Children will need lots of practise spotting these in words so that they segment, blend and read the word correctly. Initially the digraphs learnt will often be double letters or two letters that make the same sound anyway:

ck ll ss ff zz

Children will need practise in spotting these digraphs in words and to be encouraged to say only one sound when they see these combinations of letters:

du**ck** read as **/d/u/ck/** not /d/u/c/k/

hi**ll** read as **/h/i/ll/** not /h/i/l/l/

mi**ss** read as **/m/i/ss/** not /m/i/s/s/

hu**ff** read as **/h/u/ff/** not /h/u/f/f/

bu**zz** read as /**b/u/zz/** not /b/u/z/z/

At this stage teach children that when they hear a /ll/, /ss/, /ff/ and /zz/ at the end of a single syllable word and it follows a short vowel sound then when it comes to spelling the word they need to double the letter.

mi<u>ss</u>   b<u>uzz</u>   hu<u>ff</u>   fi<u>ll</u>   le<u>ss</u>   w<u>ill</u>

Like any spelling rule there are, of course, exceptions:

yes, is, has – are function words which we would teach up front

bus, gas – are abbreviated versions of the words omnibus and gasoline

Children also need to be taught at this stage that if they hear a /k/ sound at the end of a word and it's after a short vowel sound they should use 'ck' when spelling it.

p**i**ck   s**o**ck   l**u**ck   r**a**ck   p**a**ck   ch**e**ck

Digraphs and trigraphs can be further sorted into those that produce a consonant phoneme and those that make a vowel phoneme.

CONSONANT DIGRAPHS

A consonant digraph makes a consonant sound and is represented by two consonant letters. The initial consonant digraphs often taught are shown in Table 7.1.

Table 7.1   A pronunciation guide for consonant digraphs

Digraph	Example word	Pronunciation guide
ck	du**ck**	just as /c/ and /k/ are pronounced
th	**th**in	Place the tip of your tongue between your teeth and blow, creating an unvoiced sound
th	**th**at	The same mouth movement as above, but this sound is voiced
sh	**sh**ip	Your tongue should point towards the front teeth. Lips rounded (not fully opened but not puckered either) and blow
ch	**ch**op	Air is temporarily restricted from leaving the vocal tract by the tongue at the back of the tooth ridge and the side of the tongue is pressed to the upper sides of the teeth. The sound 'explodes' as the air is released
ng	si**ng**	Curl your tongue up at the back of your mouth and block the air. The sound is produced through your nose
nk	pi**nk**	Frequently taught as one sound unit, but it is in fact made from combining /ng/ and /k/

Both 'nk' and 'qu' are widely taught as digraphs within many of the validated schemes; however, they are actually pronounced using two separate sounds. It doesn't particularly matter, just as long as children know that when they see these letter combinations they can say the corresponding phoneme.

VOWEL DIGRAPHS AND TRIGRAPHS

A vowel digraph or trigraph will produce a vowel sound and is represented by a combination of letters, one of which will include a vowel letter.

A diphthong is the sound produced by a combination of two vowel sounds. When articulating a diphthong you will glide from one vowel sound to another (often with the tongue) and have a start and end mouth position. A diphthong is represented by a vowel digraph. The initial diphthongs/digraphs often taught are listed in Table 7.2.

> **Tip 7.1**   Children need to learn that the digraphs 'oo' and 'th' can create two different phonemes.

Table 7.2   A pronunciation guide for diphthongs

Diphthong/ digraph	Example word	Pronunciation guide
ai	rain	Place your tongue low in the back of your mouth, vibrate vocal cords and shift tongue higher and forward
ee	seek	Corner of lips wide and tongue arches up towards the roof of the mouth
oa	boat	Place your tongue in the relaxed middle position and open your mouth, continue as you move to the closer, more back position and round your lips
oo **long sound**	moon	Long, close, back and rounded. Open your mouth just a little, move your tongue to the back position and round your lips, though not as much as for whistling
oo **short sound**	book	The tongue is in the back position, the mouth is almost closed, and the lips are rounded
oi	boil	Jaw begins in an open position and the tongue is low. The jaw closes slightly, and the tongue moves up and forward

When children are writing words that end in an 'l' and contain the digraph 'oi' in the middle, they will often write 'boyl' and 'soyl'. As 'oi' is a diphthong, children are correctly tuning into the sounds they can hear when pronouncing it. Explain to children that they will never see 'yl' in common words that they need to spell and write.

Further vowel digraphs taught at this stage are listed in Table 7.3, and further vowel trigraphs are listed in Table 7.4. Note that even if the digraph or trigraph contains a consonant it is still classed as a vowel digraph because it produces a vowel sound.

> **Tip 7.2**   The 'igh' grapheme is most commonly used when it precedes a 't'.

Table 7.3   A pronunciation guide for vowel digraphs

Digraph	Example word	Pronunciation guide
ar	p**ar**k	Mouth starts in an open position and the tongue is low in the back and the tip is down. The tongue then moves up and back and pushes against the upper inside of the back teeth
or	b**or**n	The entire tongue is pushed back and kept low for this sound. The lips are made into an oval shape
ur	t**ur**n	Corner of the lips come in, pushing the lips away from the face. The middle part of the tongue lifts towards the roof of the mouth. The front of the tongue is not touching anything
ow	h**ow**	Mouth is in an open position and then becomes rounded. The tongue lifts in the back
er	lett**er**	Depending on accent, this can be articulated as 'ur' above or making an /uh/ sound (schwa)

Table 7.4   A pronunciation guide for trigraphs

Trigraph	Example word	Pronunciation guide
igh	n**igh**t	Jaw is open, tongue is in the centre and then tongue glides to the front of the mouth
ear	n**ear**	At the beginning the tongue is high and wide and then as the lips push forward the tongue pulls back and pushes against the inside of the upper back teeth
air	f**air**	The mouth starts in an open position. The tongue is forward and tip down and then the middle part of the tongue arches to the roof of the mouth. The lips flare out a little

SPOTTING DIGRAPHS AND TRIGRAPHS

As I mentioned above, the vital skill at this stage is for children to correctly spot digraphs and trigraphs within words so that they can accurately segment and blend the word to read. The more practice they have with reading words that contain them, the better they will become at spotting them. Ensure children have lots of opportunities to spot the grapheme both by itself and within a word. Before reading any word, encourage children to spot and say the digraph(s) it contains before further segmenting and blending the word. You can also model pointing out all the digraphs within a sentence before reading it or have children put the sound buttons on or circle them first.

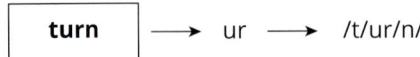

Figure 7.1   Spotting digraphs in words before reading

COMMON DIGRAPH DILEMMAS

There are digraphs that can often get muddled either because they sound very similar or they look similar; 'sh' and 'ch' have sounds that are very similar, and 'ar', 'or', 'ur' look similar as they all contain an 'r'. With digraphs that sound very similar, encourage children to look in the mirror when producing the sounds to see the slight subtleties in mouth movements, and for digraphs that look similar, play lots of sorting games with words that contain only the focus digraphs.

LETTER NAMES

As children start to learn the digraphs it is good practice to start naming the letters to spell them rather than saying the individual letter sounds. For example, when introducing the grapheme 'ai', or when a child asks you how to spell the word 'main', say the letter names for 'a' and 'i' rather than the short vowel sounds. This will get them prepared for learning alternative spellings for the same phoneme and the introduction of further spelling patterns.

Using the letter names for 'c' and 'k' will help children later spell 'ck' and understand when to use each grapheme. Try to avoid 'curly /c/' and 'kicking /k/' as children can get into the habit of 'sounding out' a word using these phrases rather than saying the phoneme. For example, they look at the work 'duck' and say '/d/ /u/ curly /c/ kicking /k/' which does not help spot the digraph and blend the phonemes.

> **Tip 7.3**
> - We usually see the letter 'k' representing /k/ before an 'e' or 'i' at the beginning of a word
> - The letter 'c' usually represents /k/ before an 'a', 'o' or 'u'
> - We use the letters 'c' and 'k' together after a short vowel and at the end of a word

SOUND BUTTONS

As we saw in Chapter 5, sound buttons are a great tool to support children's blending skills. They are also an excellent way for children to initially practise reading words that contain digraphs and trigraphs as the combination of letters is already highlighted and clearly shows that one sound is needed. Once children have lots of experience in reading words with the sound buttons you can then slowly take the support away, so they begin to spot them independently.

A long line is used under a digraph or trigraph rather than the dot which is used for a single letter that makes one sound (Figure 7.2). The line shows that this group of letters work together to create one phoneme.

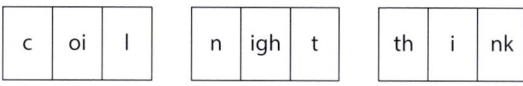

Figure 7.2   Adding sound buttons to words

PHONEME FRAMES

As we saw in Chapter 6 phoneme frames are a useful tool to help with segmenting. When children are using phoneme frames to help spell words that contain digraphs and trigraphs, the digraphs and trigraphs would go in one box as they are representing one sound (Figure 7.3).

| c | oi | l | | n | igh | t | | th | i | nk |

Figure 7.3   Placing words that contain digraphs and trigraphs into phoneme frames

IN SUMMARY

- By the end of the Reception year children will be expected to know ten digraphs to show they have achieved the early learning goal.
- It's vital that children practise identifying and spotting digraphs so that they segment and blend words correctly.
- A vowel digraph is any digraph that includes a vowel letter.
- Sound buttons and phoneme frames are incredibly useful aids for segmenting words that contain digraphs and trigraphs.

YOUR TURN!

- What's a digraph?
- What's a trigraph?

Put a sound button under all of the digraphs and trigraphs in this sentence:

In the morning, Mark and Jill might meet at the fish and chip shop in the corner of the town market.

LEARNING IDEA 7.1
DI'GRAPH'

This is a simple activity that is easily set up and adapted to focus on different graphemes.

PRACTISE

- **Spotting digraphs**
- **Reading and writing words**

PICK UP

- **Paper**
- **Pen**

PREP

- Create a blank graph template on one piece of paper with your focus digraphs along the bottom.
- On another piece of paper write a selection of words that contain the focus digraphs (Figure 7.4). Use Example 7.1 at the end of this chapter to help with this.

PLAY

Children pick one of the words on the word sheet. They spot the digraph it contains and read it. Now, they write the word above the correct digraph on the graph outline. They continue until they have crossed out and written all of the words on the word sheet.

TIP

If you want to just focus on spotting and reading words rather than writing, then you could use small word cards for children to place in the correct space on the graph.

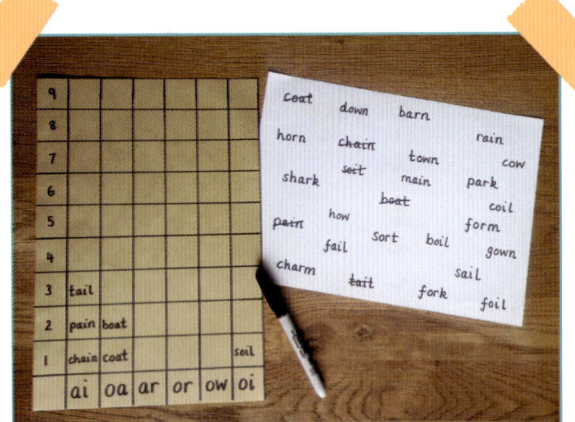

Figure 7.4 An activity using a table to learn digraphs and graphemes

LEARNING IDEA 7.2
MONSTER MUNCH

This activity works especially well if you select words that contain graphemes that often get muddled.

PRACTISE

- **Spotting digraphs**
- **Reading**

PICK UP

- **Envelopes**
- **Colouring pens**
- **Paper**

PREP

- Using the side of the envelope that contains the flap draw a monster picture. For added engagement and ownership, encourage children to draw their own monsters. The envelope flap becomes the monster's mouth.
- Write out words on small pieces of paper that contain the focus graphemes. Refer to Example 7.1 for a list of words that can be used.
- Place out the envelopes and word cards (Figure 7.5).

PLAY

Children select a word card and read it. They spot the digraph/trigraph it contains and feed it to the corresponding monster. Repeat for all other word cards.

Figure 7.5 Grapheme sorting game

LEARNING IDEA 7.3
ODD ONE OUT

This is a fantastic way to focus children on spotting the similarities and differences between words.

PRACTISE

- **Spotting digraphs**
- **Reading**

PICK UP

- **Strips of paper**
- **Pen**

PREP

Write a selection of words that contain the same digraph onto a strip of paper and include one word that contains a different digraph (Figure 7.6).

PLAY

Children read the words on the strip of paper. They spot and circle the word that contains the digraph that is different from the others. Repeat for all other collections of words.

Figure 7.6 Picking the odd word out activity

LEARNING IDEA 7.4
BUILD A DIGRAPH BINGO

This is a fun, practical way to help children recall the individual letters that make a digraph.

PRACTISE

- Spotting and identifying digraphs
- Spelling digraphs

PICK UP

- Cardboard bingo boards
- Magnetic letters

PREP

1. Draw a grid onto cardboard to create a bingo card. In each of the sections write a different digraph.
2. Find the magnetic letters needed to build each of the digraphs on the bingo cards and place them around the card or in the centre of the table if playing as a group (Figure 7.7).

PLAY

An adult says the phoneme for a digraph. If a child has the matching digraph on their bingo board, instead of crossing it off like in traditional bingo they find the magnetic letters to spell the digraph and place them over the letters on their board. The winner is the first child who has found all the letters for all of the digraphs on their card.

Figure 7.7 Digraph bingo building game on cardboard

LEARNING IDEA 7.5
ROLL A DIGRAPH

This is a great small group game to practise spotting digraphs and reading words.

PRACTISE

- **Spotting and identifying digraphs**
- **Reading words**

PICK UP

- **Word sheets per player**
- **Blank or DIY dice**
- **Coloured pens**

PREP

1. Choose six digraphs to focus on and create a word sheet for every player with a word for each of the six digraphs written in a list (six words in total for each player).
2. Each player needs a different coloured pen to mark their cards.
3. Each player will need a dice with the digraphs written on each face (Figure 7.8).

PLAY

Each player rolls their dice and identifies the digraph it lands on. They then cross out the corresponding word on their word sheet. They continue to roll the dice and cross out the words. If they have already rolled a digraph they roll the dice again. The winner is the player who has rolled every digraph and crossed out all six words first.

TIP

Laminate the word sheet so that it can be reused and the game can be played again. Swap word sheets each time to encourage children to read a different list of words.

LINK

Check out activity…
To find out how to create your own DIY dice using a toilet roll tube, check out the Sensory Name Board activity in Chapter 3.

Figure 7.8 Digraph spotting game using dice, coloured paper, and coloured pens

Example 7.1 Initial digraph and trigraph word list

ck	ng	nk	qu	sh
duck	sing	pink	quiz	shop
sock	ring	sink	quick	shed
lock	bang	tank	quiff	ship
pick	king	bunk	quack	dish
pack	long	wink	queen	wish

th	ch	ai	ee	igh
thin	chin	rain	seen	night
thick	chop	pain	meet	light
thing	chick	sail	feet	right
with	chill	mail	week	tight
this	rich	chain	seek	might

oa	oo (long and short sound)	ar	or	ur
boat	boot	farm	fork	turn
coat	moon	hard	sort	burn
toad	food	park	born	curl
load	took	harm	torn	hurt
goal	book	bark	corn	surf

ow	oi	ear	air	er
cow	soil	near	fair	bigger
owl	boil	fear	hair	better
down	join	rear	lair	boxer
town	coin	dear	chair	mixer
howl	foil	tear	pair	hotter

8
MOVING ON FROM CVC WORDS

GETTING TO GRIPS WITH ADJACENT CONSONANTS

There are no new GPCs that children learn during this stage of their reading journey. Once children are confident at blending CVC words to read and segmenting CVC words to spell and write, they will build upon these skills and start to consolidate their knowledge of reading words that contain adjacent consonants. These are words that contain different strings of separate consonant sounds, both at the beginning and end. At this stage, children will spend lots of time manipulating and playing with the phonemes within words and learning to read longer and more complex words which will also include previously taught GPCs. The stage is all about extending the knowledge and skills that children have already acquired. Many phonics schemes will refer to this stage as phase 4.

Children will need lots of practice reading words that consist of multiple consonants as they can prove problematic; one or several consonants can easily be missed when reading, spelling and writing. During this stage children really need to focus on listening for all the sounds within words in order to avoid making mistakes. A child might look at the word 'frog', segment the word correctly but then blend the sounds together and miss out the second consonant sound and say 'fog'.

frog → fog

Alternatively, they may want to spell the word 'went', segment the sounds but then miss out the penultimate consonant and write 'wet'. This mistake is particularly common in early years settings as children often want to recall and write about something they have done over a weekend or holiday. I've seen the sentence 'I wet to the park' many times!

went → wet

> **Tip 8.1** Adjacent consonants may also be referred to as consonant clusters or blends. Just note that these letter strings are not making one sound like a digraph or trigraph; each consonant letter is making its own, separate consonant sound.

VOWELS AND CONSONANTS

As a starting point, at this stage children now need to be aware of what is classed as a vowel letter and what is classified as a consonant letter. This will help them identify the part of the word that might be trickier to segment and blend and the bit they need to pay close attention to when reading and writing. I often teach children to remember what a vowel letter is by singing the vowel song while holding up a finger for each letter. Children will soon realise that the other letters of the alphabet are consonants. We then practise reading words and circling the adjacent consonants to ensure that we pay close attention to these as we blend.

a, e, i, o, u

a, e, i, o, u

a, e, i, o, u

These are the vowels we use!

> **Tip 8.2** Almost every word in the English language will contain consonants and vowels, with exception of the word 'iouea' (a type of sea sponge) which contains all five vowel letters.

Children will have lots of practice with reading CCVC and CVCC words first. Within these words it's the CC bit that is referring to the adjacent consonants.

CCVC: words that consist of a **c**onsonant sound, **c**onsonant sound, **v**owel sound and **c**onsonant sound

CVCC: words that consist of a **c**onsonant sound, **v**owel sound, **c**onsonant sound and final **c**onsonant sound we**nt**   **fr**og

CV**CC**   **CC**VC

Further examples of CVCC and CCVC words are listed in Example 8.1.

Example 8.1   A list of CVCC and CCVC words

CVCC	CCVC
mi**lk**	**fr**om
la**mp**	**st**op
ju**st**	**st**ep
wi**nd**	**gr**ip
la**nd**	**pl**ug
lu**nch**	**fl**ag
boo**st**	**tr**ain
pai**nt**	**st**ick
be**nch**	**fr**esh
toa**st**	**sp**oon

Remember that in phonics we are referring to the consonant sound and vowel sound when representing words using C and V, so CVCC and CCVC words are made up of four sounds but not necessarily four letters.

te**nth**   **sp**ark

CV**CC**   **CC**VC

> **Tip 8.3**   Tell children that when they hear a /k/ sound after an /l/ they should always spell the word using 'lk' as in 'milk', not 'milc'. We don't see 'lc' at the end of single-syllable words.

Once children are confident at reading and spelling the above type of words they can begin to practise reading words that contain more than one set of adjacent consonants and trickier consonant strings, like those in Example 8.2.

Example 8.2   A list of words that contain trickier consonant strings

CCVCC	CCCVC	CCCVCC
trust	**spr**ing	**scr**unch
twist	**str**ing	**str**and
stand	**str**ap	**spr**int
frost	**spl**it	**spl**int
stamp	**scr**ub	
crust	**str**ong	
crisp	**str**eet	
blink	**spl**ash	
ground		

SUBMORPHEMES

Submorphemes are units of language, such as certain groups of letters or consonant clusters, that linguists studying the history and morphology of words have found have similar meanings (Bottineau, 2008). For example, words that start with the two consonants 'sw' often are words that refer to something moving (swing, sway, swoop, swap). I find it fascinating to think about the connections between the meaning of words and the way we now spell them. Submorphemes can help our language make a bit more sense. Knowledge of a few could help children pick the correct letters to use within the consonant clusters; they can think about the meaning of a word and link it to other words that they already know, for example, knowing that words relating to our nose often start with 'sn'. Table 8.1 presents some of the most studied initial consonant clusters.

Table 8.1 Common submorphemes (Bottineau, 2008)

Consonant cluster	Meaning	Example words
sn	related to our nose	snooze, snore, sneeze, snub, snoot, snot, snout, snoop, sniff
sp	centrifugal rotation (operation) and/or projection (result)	spin, span, spill, speak, spit, spend, spot, spawn, spoon, spook
st	stativity or fixity in space and time	still, stop, stand, stay, step, stump, star
sk	surface (2D object and/or movement applied to it)	skin, skull, skate, skid, skittle
sw	oscillation, pendulation (back-and-forth motion)	swing, swoon, sway, swoop, switch, sweep, swap, swagger
cl	clinging	cling, clench, clasp, clutter, clutch
gl	luminosity	glint, glow, glisten, glitter, glimmer
sl	non-vertical movements	sleep, slay, slope, sleet, slot, slate, sling, slug

EXTENDING THE CVC WORD

A useful technique to help children move from CVC words on to words that contain adjacent consonants, particularly for final CC words, is to show them a simple CVC word with the final consonant hidden. They read the CVC word and then reveal the further consonant to add to the end. You can have a word card inside an envelope and children slowly pull out the card from the side to reveal the letters or write a word on a piece of paper and fold over the final consonant so that it is initially hidden from view before adding the extra consonant sound when the paper is folded out (Figure 8.1). This works best when the initial words that the children decode are already words and then by adding a consonant a new word is created.

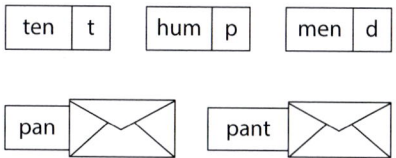

Figure 8.1   Extending a CVC word to create words that contain adjacent consonants

EXTENDING THE FRAMES

Just as a phoneme frame is a useful tool for segmenting and spelling CVC words, they can be particularly helpful for words that contain adjacent consonants too. The frame will be altered to consist of more than three boxes, depending on the number of sounds within the words you are asking children to spell. For CVCC and CCVC words children will need a phoneme frame that contains four boxes (Figure 8.2), and for words that contain more sounds more boxes can be added to the frame. The frame will clearly show children how many sounds they need to listen out for within the word.

Figure 8.2   Words that contain adjacent consonants placed into phoneme frames

There are several common mistakes that children make at this stage, particularly when they are asked to spell and write words that contain the adjacent consonants 'tr', 'dr' and 'st'. These combinations of consonants can often prove the trickiest. From experience, children will often write 'chree' for 'tree', 'dress' becomes 'jress', and 'step' is often written as 'sdep'. When you spot children making these mistakes, explain to them that English words never contain the consonant combinations of 'jr', 'sd' and 'chr' (when the 'ch' is making the /ch/ sound) and really elongate and stretch the sounds within the words so that children can hear the correct phonemes.

REVIST INTERVENTIONS FOR BLENDING AND SEGMENTING

If, after lots of practice reading and spelling words that contain adjacent consonants, children are still struggling with the longer words then refer back to the interventions that can be put in place to support children to blend and segment CVC words. Identify the hurdles and address the gaps. Is it a particular consonant blend that they struggle with? Could there be a problem with articulating certain phonemes? Words that contain more phonemes require a child to hold more sounds in their working memory; does the child need to play games that expand the capacity of their working memory?

IN SUMMARY

- Children will need lots of practice reading and spelling words that contain adjacent consonants and consonant strings as they can prove trickier for children to identify all of the sounds, segment, blend and spell.
- At this stage it is useful for children to know the difference between a vowel letter and a consonant letter.

YOUR TURN!

1   Can you spot and circle the adjacent consonants in the sentences below?

The frog can jump in the fresh pond and land on a green pad with a croak.

We can stop and camp in the tent next to this tree.

2   Which of the circled words do you think children might struggle to spell the most?
3   If a child is struggling to read a CVCC word, what interventions might you put in place?

LEARNING IDEA 8.1
BAKE A WORD

Use this commonly found household item to help children segment and spell.

PRACTISE

- **Listening for phonemes**
- **Identifying graphemes**
- **Spelling words that contain adjacent consonants**

PICK UP

- **Muffin or cupcake tin that contains four in a row**
- **Cardboard**
- **Marker pen**

PLAY

Children use the cake tin as an alternative to a paper phoneme frame. An adult will first say a word (refer to Examples 8.3–8.5 at the end of the chapter) and then children find the corresponding cookies to spell the word into the tin; four spaces means that children can build words that contain four sounds. Repeat for other words that contain four sounds. Leave out the resources for children to independently build words using the cookies into the cake tin.

PREP

1. Cut cookie or biscuit shapes out of the cardboard and draw a grapheme on each.
2. Place out the muffin tin alongside the cardboard cookies (Figure 8.3).

Figure 8.3 Segmenting and spelling words using a cupcake tin

LEARNING IDEA 8.2
ENVELOPE WORD SLIDERS

This is a useful resource to encourage children to practise adding phonemes and graphemes to words to create new words.

PRACTISE

- **Listening for phonemes**
- **Isolating and adding phonemes**
- **Reading words that contain adjacent consonants**

PICK UP

- **Paper**
- **Envelopes**
- **Pen**

PLAY

Children first read the simple CVC word. They then pull the paper to reveal the additional grapheme and read the longer word that contains the adjacent consonant.

PREP

1   Cut off one edge of the envelopes so that you create a pocket for a piece of paper to slide inside.
2   Slide a piece of paper into each envelope and, depending on whether the adjacent consonant is at the beginning or the end, have the paper pull from the left or right side.
3   You will need to write either the initial or final sound on the paper and the rest of the word on the envelope. Write an additional grapheme on the paper which is revealed when pulled from the envelope (Figure 8.4).
4   All the words you write need to be real words without and with the additional letter.

Example words could include (additional grapheme in bold) we**n**t, ne**s**t, f**r**og, b**r**ag, s**l**ick, be**n**d, b**l**ack, s**l**eep, d**r**own, s**w**ing, g**l**oat, b**l**oat, c**r**op, s**n**ail.

Figure 8.4   Creating words using overlapping sheets of paper

LEARNING IDEA 8.3
CONSONANT CASSEROLE

This is a fun and engaging way for children to practise listening for and spelling words that contain adjacent consonants.

PRACTISE

- Listening for phonemes
- Identifying graphemes
- Spelling words that contain adjacent consonants

PICK UP

- Large casserole dish or bowl
- Wooden spoons
- Sensory material such as rice or beans
- Magnetic letters
- Cardboard
- Marker pen

PREP

1 Fill the dish or bowl with the sensory materials.
2 Write out some word cards using pieces of cardboard with the adjacent consonants missing. For a list of words to use refer to Examples 8.3–8.5 at the end of this chapter. You could also draw a matching picture to act as a prompt.
3 Find the magnetic letters to complete the words – for example, the 't' and 'r' to complete the word card for 'tree'. Place all the magnetic letters into the dish and mix with the sensory material (Figure 8.5).
4 Place out some wooden spoons alongside the dish and word cards.

PLAY

Children use the wooden spoons to stir the casserole and spoon out the magnetic letters to complete all of the words on the cards.

Figure 8.5 Listening and spelling game using a casserole dish

LEARNING IDEA 8.4
PEDESTRIAN CROSSING

Build fluency in reading words that contain adjacent consonants using this word ladder technique.

PRACTISE

- Reading words that contain adjacent consonants
- Build fluency in reading

PICK UP

- Strip of cardboard
- Marker pen
- White chalk pen
- Duplo man or small world character
- Toy cars

PREP

1. Draw stripes on the cardboard strip to create a pedestrian crossing.
2. Write words on the white/blank space with marker pen.
3. Write words on the black space with white chalk pen.
4. Draw on the sound buttons if you feel this is required (Figure 8.6).

PLAY

Children walk the toy character across the pedestrian crossing reading each word as they move. You could time how long it takes for children to read all the words and then they read them again. Can they improve their time and read the words with more fluency on each read?

Figure 8.6 Game using word ladder and toys to practise fluency

LEARNING IDEA 8.5
SLIDE AND SPELL

Here's one to try to help children listen for all the phonemes within CVCC or CCVC words and practise spelling them.

PRACTISE

- Listening for phonemes
- Identifying graphemes
- Spelling words that contain adjacent consonants

PICK UP

- Masking tape
- Cardboard
- Marker pen
- Small windows

Numicon is great to act as a little window, but if you don't have access to this then use a transparent milk bottle lid or cut windows from cardboard.

PREP

1 Stick four strips of masking tape running vertically onto a table top or large tray.
2 Write graphemes on the strips to spell CVCC and CCVC words.
3 Put a window at the bottom of each of the strips.
4 Draw a selection of picture cue cards (Figure 8.7).

PLAY

Children pick a card and segment the word for the picture. They move each of the windows up the strip of tape so that the graphemes to spell the word are shown within each window.

Figure 8.7 Slide and Spell

Example 8.3 Word list of common adjacent consonants found at the beginning of words

bl	cl	fl	pl	sl
blob	clap	flag	plug	slip
black	clip	flip	plum	sling
blink	cling	floss	plot	sleep
block	clown	fling	plump	sled
bleed	clear	flash		slug

br	cr	dr	fr	gr
bring	crab	drum	frog	grab
broom	crop	drag	from	grip
bright	creep	dress	fresh	grin
brown	croak	drink	fright	greet
		drill		green
				groan

tr	sm	sn	sp	sk
trim	smell	snap	spin	skin
trap	smash	snip	spot	skip
tree	smog	sniff	spell	skill
trot	smug	snoop	spoon	skull
truck		snail	spoil	
			sport	

st	sw	tw	shr	thr
step	swig	twig	shrink	three
stop	swam	twin	shred	threat
stem	swell		shrimp	throb
sting	swing		shrug	
	sweet			
	swoop			

Example 8.4 Word list according to initial consonant string

scr	spl	spr	str
scram	splash	spring	string
screech	splat	sprang	strap
scrap	split	sprung	strong
scroll			strip

COMMON END BLENDS

Example 8.5   Word list according to final adjacent consonants

nd	nt	st
hand	went	test
sand	tent	best
bend	bent	rest
send	sent	nest
mend	hunt	lost
lend	joint	list
	burnt	twist
	paint	toast

9
READING LONGER WORDS

KEY TERMS

Compound word: when two or more individual words combine to create a new one

Diphthong: a sound formed by the combination of two vowels within a syllable

Multisyllabic word: a word that is made up of two or more syllables

Polysyllabic: another way of saying 'multisyllabic'

Syllable: a unit of speech sound within a word

Vowel: a speech sound that is produced by a comparatively open vocal tract

'This word is too long', 'I can't read this long word!', 'It's too hard'. Some of the things you might hear children saying at this stage. Moving on to read words that contain more than one syllable can often see children's progress plateau. They have become confident with reading single-syllable CVC words but may now seem stuck, struggling to make the leap to longer words. It can be daunting reading words that contain multiple syllables. The words are visibly longer, contain more GPCs to identify and require children to apply more of their phonic knowledge. As much as this step can seem intimidating, it is one that is vital in becoming a fluent reader – after all, 80% of words in the English language contain more than one syllable. It's especially important, at this stage, to develop children's confidence with longer, more difficult words. Increased confidence comes from consistent, repetitive exposure, continued instruction, plenty of practice, equipping children with some simple decoding tools and eventually the words will become a lot less overwhelming and children will take their decoding skills to the next level.

WHEN ARE CHILDREN READY FOR LONGER WORDS?

To make the step to reading multisyllabic words, children need to be confident in the important prerequisite skills discussed in Chapter 2. This will ensure that they are ready and prepared for the added level of complexity of reading longer words. Most importantly, children need to be proficient in breaking up a word into its syllables; orally segmenting and blending; and segmenting and blending CVC words. Once children have really grasped this they can begin to practise applying these skills to read longer words. Beginner readers can very early on attempt to read simple multisyllabic words once they have mastered blending simple CVC words. It's an important step to becoming a confident and fluent reader.

mag/net   **sun/set**   **nap/kin**   **pig/let**

Why are the above multisyllabic words a good starting point to reading longer words? It's all down to the syllable type. There are actually six types of syllables, which we will look at in more detail in Chapter 11, but at this stage it's important for children to be able to identify the vowel sounds within words and be aware of open and closed syllables. This will give them a better understanding of how to break up and read multisyllabic words. The above words are made up of two closed syllables, which means that they are much easier for children to decode as the single vowel letters will say their initial phonemes and the words are essentially two CVC words combined.

> **Tip 9.1**   Every syllable will contain a vowel sound. Help children recognise the vowel sound by explaining that it is a 'push of breath' within the word.

VOWELS AND SYLLABLE TYPES

When children come across an unknown multisyllabic word, having knowledge of vowels and syllable types gives them an important decoding tool. It means they can break up a word to make it more manageable to read and it becomes a lot less daunting.

Closed Syllables

A closed syllable is one where the vowel is closed in by one or more consonants, meaning the vowel letter is always followed by a consonant letter (Figure 9.1). Within a closed syllable the single vowel letter will almost always be pronounced short, as in the /o/ in 'got'.

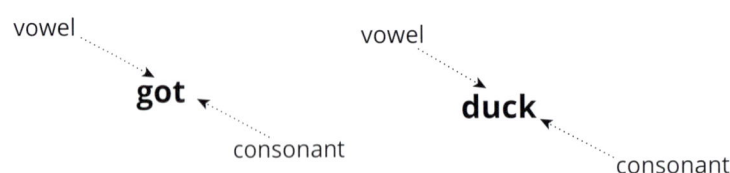

Figure 9.1   Closed-syllable words

Open Syllables

In contrast, an open syllable is one where the vowel is not followed by a consonant at the end. Several simple high-frequency words that children are taught very early on are actually words with a single open syllable: no, go, he, she, we. When the vowel letter is not followed by a consonant then it will be pronounced long (say its name) – for example, in the word 'go' the 'o' is not followed by a consonant and is pronounced /oa/.

Vowel Team Syllables

A vowel team syllable is a syllable that contains a vowel sound created by a combination of letters. At this stage children are likely to be familiar with the following vowel digraphs and trigraphs:

- Long 'a' vowel teams: ai
- Long 'e' vowel teams: ee
- Long 'i' vowel teams: igh
- Long 'o' vowel teams: oa
- Further vowel digraphs: oi, oo

raincoat   toothbrush   bedroom

R-Controlled Syllables

These might be referred to as 'the bossy r'. Anytime the letter 'r' follows a vowel, the vowel is being controlled by the 'r' and doesn't say its short or long sound. Children will be familiar with the digraphs 'ar', 'or', 'ur' and 'er', at this stage and only one 'r-controlled' vowel will be found in any one syllable.

farmyard   carpark   market   bigger

ACTIVITY 9.1

A Teaching Technique to Help Children Read Polysyllabic Words

For example, imagine that a child is attempting to read the word **rabbit** for the first time. How can we make it less overwhelming and assist them to 'break up' the word in the appropriate place so that it becomes easier to read?

1   Remind the children that each syllable must have at least one vowel. Say the word and orally emphasise the two syllables. You can encourage children to clap for each syllable too

   'rab' 'bit'

2   Work together to identify the vowels within the word. You could place a sound button under each vowel

   rabbit
    •   •

(Continued)

3   Show the children that the vowels are not next to each other, which means that there are two syllables. Look at the consonants that follow each vowel. As there are two consonants, we divide this word between the two to create two closed syllables

rab|bit

4   Now, we segment and blend each syllable. You can cover one syllable unit with your hand or paper while decoding the other

rab ☐   ☐ **bit**

5   Then put the two syllables together to form the word: 'rabbit'

'rabbit'

When dividing a word into its syllables do not split up the letters within digraphs, trigraphs or common consonant blends.

HOW CAN I HELP CHILDREN READ MULTISYLLABIC WORDS?

Here are some techniques to help you in this task.

Chunking

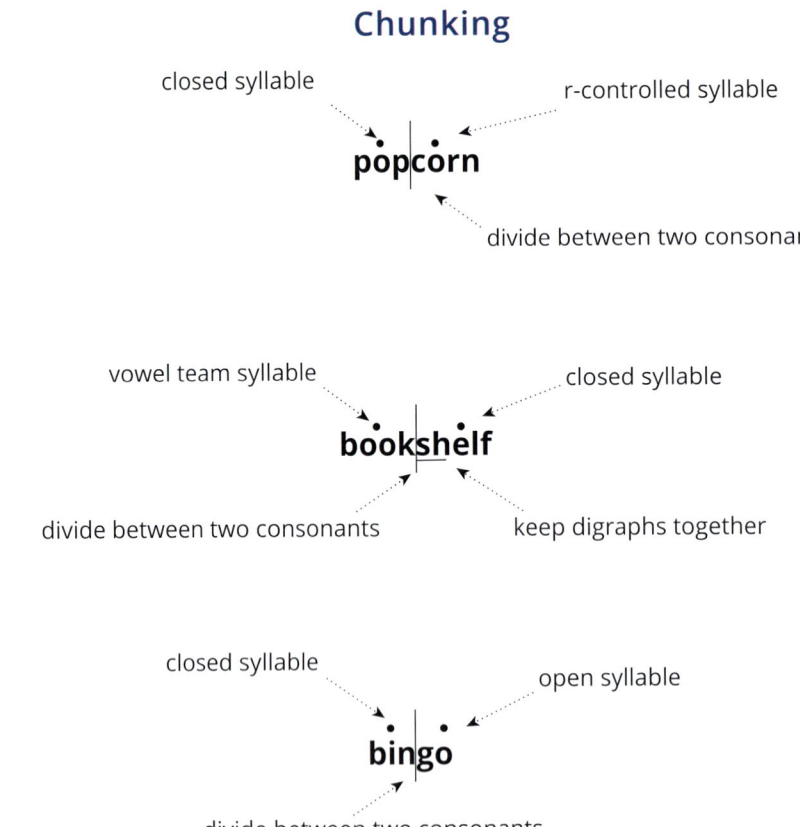

Figure 9.2   Chunking words according to the syllable type

The above steps highlight how important it is to demonstrate to children how to divide a multisyllabic word into its syllables in the appropriate place. A technique called 'chunking' is often used during phonics instruction. Children are taught to break up longer words into more manageable chunks (Figure 9.2). They will then segment and blend each chunk. Children will need to have modelled where to divide a word to create the chunks so that when they happen upon an unknown multisyllabic word in a book they can break up and tackle the word independently.

Swooping

Once children can identify and divide a longer word into its syllables they need to read them in sequence and put the syllables back together again to read the word as a whole. To help children practise this step you can display each syllable separately and then add swooping lines under each syllable (Figure 9.3). Children swoop with their finger along each line. This will develop children's fluency in blending. Another line can be drawn under the whole word to illustrate that all syllables need to be put together to read the whole word. This adds a great multi-sensory element for beginner readers too.

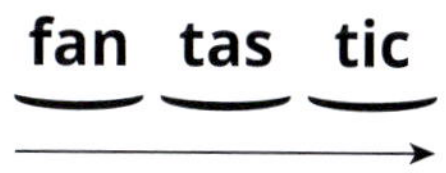

fan tas tic

Figure 9.3 Swooping lines to aid reading of polysyllabic words

Syllable Pyramids

Another method to help children read each syllable and then put them back together again is to use a syllable pyramid (Figure 9.4). This can help prevent children becoming overwhelmed when looking at longer, complex words and can build confidence. Initially, the first syllable is displayed, and children will read it. You then add the second syllable and so on until they have read the whole word.

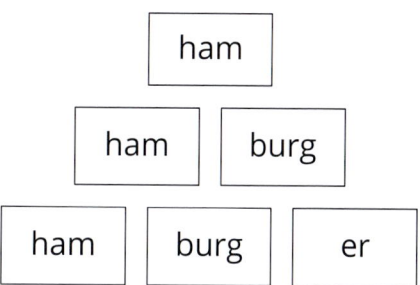

Figure 9.4 A syllable pyramid

Compound Words

A compound word is a type of multisyllabic word. It is created when two or more words, which have their own meaning, merge to create a new one. A compound word is always a multisyllabic word, but multisyllabic words are not always compound ones. Compound words are a useful starting point for beginner readers as they act as a bridge from CVC words to reading longer words. They can easily be broken into syllables that themselves make sense.

sand + pit = sandpit

wind + mill = windmill

star + light = starlight

IN SUMMARY

- Words that are made up of more than one syllable are called multisyllabic words.
- There are six different types of syllables. Knowledge of syllable types helps children break words up in the appropriate place to segment, blend and read them.
- There are several strategies that can be employed to help children identify and break a word up into its syllables so that these longer words become less overwhelming and easier to read. These strategies include chunking, swooping and syllable pyramids.

YOUR TURN!

Mark the vowel sounds within these words and divide them up according to syllable type.

robot   **treetop**   **lipstick**   **lunchbox**

children   **helper**   **turnip**   **shampoo**

caterpillar

Which of the words are compound words?

LEARNING IDEA 9.1
COMPOUND JIGSAW

Repurpose an old jigsaw puzzle to help children practise reading and spelling compound words.

PRACTISE

- **Building, reading and spelling compound words**

PICK UP

- **An old large jigsaw puzzle**
- **Marker pen**

PREP

1. Match two pieces of the jigsaw puzzle and turn them over to the blank pictureless side.
2. On the back write a compound word with one word on each of the pieces – for example, 'sun' on one piece and 'flower' on the other – so that children can put them together to read 'sunflower'.
3. Repeat for a selection of other compound words.

PLAY

Children match two of the pieces to create and read a compound word. Alternatively, draw pictures on the back of the puzzle pieces so that children match up two pieces and then write the word (Figure 9.5).

Figure 9.5 Practising reading and spelling compound words using a jigsaw

LEARNING IDEA 9.2
OPEN AND CLOSED DOORS

Use this useful tool to help demonstrate open and closed syllables and show how this affects the vowel sound.

PRACTISE

- **Reading open and closed syllables**
- **Pronouncing the long and short vowel sound**

PICK UP

- **Paper**
- **Marker pen**

PREP

1. Cut small strips of paper.
2. On each strip write an open one-syllable word on the left-hand side – for example, 'go', 'no', 'we', 'me'.
3. Now fold the right side of the strip over to create a flap/door.
4. Fold the door so that it meets the end of the word you have written.
5. On the front of the door write a consonant letter that will create a closed syllable word from the already written word – for example, put a 't' on the door to create 'not' (Figure 9.6).

Figure 9.6 Learning and practising word sounds using folded paper

PLAY

Children explore the resource by opening and closing the doors. They read the open-syllable word using the long vowel sound and then close the door to read the closed-syllable word. This will clearly demonstrate how the consonant at the end changes the vowel sound.

LEARNING IDEA 9.3
SYLLABLE TRACKS

Children practise reading and counting the syllables in words in this fun, easily adapted game.

PRACTISE

- **Count syllables**
- **Read multisyllabic words**

PICK UP

- **Masking tape**
- **Paper**
- **Marker pen**
- **Small toy or counter**

PLAY

Children can play this individually, with a partner or a small group. They pick a word and read it. They then count the number of syllables within the word and move that number of spaces along the track. How many words do they need to read to get to the finish line?

Tap into children's interest by using small car toys, Duplo figures or animal toys as the counters for the game.

Example 9.1 shows a list of decodable multisyllabic words using previously taught graphemes.

PREP

1 Use the masking tape to tape out a track on the top of a table or floor.
2 Draw lines along the track to create spaces.
3 Write up some multisyllabic and single-syllable words on small pieces of paper (Figure 9.7).

Figure 9.7 Counting the syllables game

LEARNING IDEA 9.4
THE COMPOUND WORD MACHINE

This is a fun, interactive way for children to practise creating and reading compound words.

PRACTISE

- **Creating and reading compound words**

PICK UP

- **Kitchen roll holder**
- **Toilet roll tubes**
- **Duplo**
- **Marker pen**
- **Cardboard**

PLAY

Children spin each of the tubes in turn. When they stop they read the two words that are closest to the arrow on the holder. Do they create a compound word when read together? You can extend this by encouraging children to write down the word when it creates a real compound word.

PREP

1. Build a small stand using Duplo or other resource so that you can lay the kitchen roll holder on its side.
2. Cut the toilet roll tubes in half to create smaller tubes.
3. On one tube write a selection of words that you would find as the first syllable in a compound word.
4. On the other tube write the words that create a compound word when placed alongside the words on the other tube.
5. Slide the two tubes onto the kitchen roll holder.
6. Draw and stick a small arrow on the side of the holder to act as a marker (Figure 9.8).

Figure 9.8 Using a homemade 'word machine' to practise compound words

LEARNING IDEA 9.5
THE LONG AND SHORT OF IT!

Help children read open and closed-syllable words and identify the long and short vowel sounds.

PRACTISE

- **Read open and closed-syllable words**
- **Recognise long and short vowel sounds**

PICK UP

- **Masking tape**
- **Paper**
- **Marker pen**
- **Small toy figure or counter**

PREP

1 Tape out a long strip of masking tape on a table top or floor.
2 Use the marker pen to draw spaces along the track. Ensure that there is the same number of spaces on either side of the centre space.
3 Colour in the central space and place the counter down.
4 Put a piece of tape above the right side and the same on the left side of the track. Write 'long' on one piece and 'short' on the other.
5 Write open and closed-syllable words on small pieces of paper (Figure 9.9).

PLAY

Children pick a word card and read it. They identify whether the vowel letter is making a long or short sound, depending on whether it is within an open or closed syllable. Children then move their counter accordingly along the track. They continue to read and move the counter back and forth along the track depending on whether the vowel is long or short.

Figure 9.9 Activity to help practise syllable and vowel sounds

Example 9.1 Decodable compound and polysyllabic word list

Decodable compound words	Decodable multisyllabic words
zigzag	rabbit
popcorn	cartoon
bedroom	bigger
carpark	ladder
farmyard	pocket
lipstick	jacket
desktop	garden
rooftop	hamster
driftwood	number
raincoat	fantastic
sunflower	floating
handbag	sandwich
starfish	chimpanzee
armchair	helper
earring	printer
bookshelf	twisting
airport	wooden
toothbrush	lightning
hairbrush	finishing
	caterpillar

10
HIGH-FREQUENCY WORDS

KEY TERMS

Decoding: the ability to use existing phonic knowledge to break up and blend the phonemes within a word

GPC: grapheme-phoneme correspondence

Heart words: a technique used to highlight the tricky part of the word using a heart symbol

High-frequency words: words that are common and frequently found within children's initial reading books. These are made up of both decodable and tricky words

Sight word: any word that children are now able to read by sight

Tricky word: a word that contains a part that has an irregular and uncommon grapheme–phoneme correspondence

Tricky words may also be referred to as common exception words (DfE, 2013), red words, heart words or sight words. It just means that they are not following the regular phonetic rules that children learn early on in their phonic journey.

As children move through the different stages of phonics there is a selection of high-frequency words within each stage that children will need to start to read and spell fluently because they appear frequently within matched decodable books that children will be reading to practise and embed their phonic knowledge. These high-frequency words can be decodable words, meaning that they follow the usual phonetic pattern that children have learnt – for example, 'in', 'it' and 'on'. In fact, the *Cambridge Dictionary* states that 75% of English words follow basic rules. A selection of these high-frequency words will also be classed as irregular or 'tricky' words as they contain GPCs that either do not follow the most common and regular phonetic patterns or contain a GPC that a child has yet to be introduced to. For example, the words 'go' and 'no' are useful to learn when children are first starting out on their learning journey, but this comes before they have learnt that the 'o' can produce the long vowel sound. High-frequency words (both decodable and tricky) are words that bind the English language together, and learning to read them by sight will increase children's reading fluency and ultimately engagement.

As I mentioned in Chapter 1, the current English language has several origins and influences over the course of many centuries and this has resulted in some irregularities in our spelling. All or part of each word may have held onto its original Latin, French or Germanic form. If you look at the history of some words, the spelling can become a little more logical. For example, 'said' is connected to the archaic word 'saith', pronounced /seth/, which is the third person singular of 'say'.

Example 10.1 The 100 most common words in the English language (Masterson et al., 2003)

the	are	do	about	and
up	me	got	a	had
down	their	to	my	dad
people	said	her	big	your
in	what	when	put	he
there	it's	could	I	out
see	house	of	this	looked
old	it	have	very	too
was	went	look	by	you
be	don't	day	they	like
come	made	on	some	will
time	she	so	into	I'm
is	not	back	if	for
then	from	help	at	were
children	Mrs	his	go	him
called	but	little	Mr	here
that	as	get	off	with
no	just	asked	all	mum
now	saw	we	one	came
make	can	them	oh	an

Example 10.1 lists the 100 most common words in the English language. They can further be grouped into those that are decodable at an early stage of phonic development (Example 10.2) and those that contain irregular and uncommon grapheme–phoneme correspondences (Example 10.3).

Example 10.2 High-frequency decodable words (DfES, 2007) displayed from the easily decodable to words that become decodable once children have learnt more phonemes and phonic strategies

Easily decodable			Harder to decode	
a	dad	but	look	time
an	had	put	too	house
as	back	will	went	about
at	and	that	it's	your
if	get	this	from	day
in	big	then	children	made
is	him	them	just	came
it	his	with	help	make
of	not	see	don't	here
off	got	for	old	saw
on	up	now	I'm	very
can	mum	down	by	like
			when	out

Example 10.3 Tricky words (DfES, 2007) that contain irregular and uncommon grapheme–phoneme correspondences that are not taught during the early stages of phonics. Remember, it's useful for children to build up a fluency in reading these words. I've highlighted the 'tricky' part of the word

the	me	said	little	Mrs
to	be	have	one	looked
I	was	so	out	called
no	you	do	what	asked

(Continued)

Example 10.3   (Continued)

go	they	some	**oh**	**could**
in**to**	**all**	th**eir**	she	he
ar**e**	**co**me	we	her	my
were	pe**o**ple	there	Mr	

HOW DO I TEACH HIGH-FREQUENCY TRICKY WORDS?

All phonics programmes must 'ensure that children are taught high-frequency words that do not conform completely to grapheme/phoneme correspondence rules' (DfE, 2011).

Historically, it was common practice to teach children to remember and recall these high-frequency tricky words by getting them to memorise the word as a whole, but teaching practice has moved on from teaching entire words by sight. Now, it is good practice to point out and highlight both the decodable and 'tricky' parts of the word. It is these tricky parts that children will need to learn by sight. All tricky words will contain graphemes that follow the usual phonetic pattern and a part (either a single letter or combination of letters) that does not follow the usual phonetic rules.

> **Tip 10.1**   It's important if you are using sound buttons underneath these words that you still display a button underneath the tricky part (Figure 10.1), as it does create a sound, but explain to children that this GPC is not making the sound that they already know – for example, in the high-frequency word 'said' the digraph 'ai' isn't making an /ay/ sound which children would be familiar with but is making an /e/ sound instead. This is the same for 'ey' in 'they' and the 'y' in 'my'.

said   they   my

Figure 10.1   Placing sound buttons under tricky high-frequency words

HEART WORDS

This is a method of explaining the 'tricky' part of a high-frequency tricky word. The tricky part, which children will need to learn 'by heart', is accompanied by a heart as a visual prompt for children (Figure 10.2).

you   was   have   their

Figure 10.2   Using heart symbols to highlight the tricky part of words

MNEMONICS

Mnemonics can help improve memory and can be a useful strategy to use when children move from reading to writing the high-frequency tricky words. It can be a nice individual or group activity to work with children to create their own. Children may become more engaged with their own devised mnemonics and memorise them better. Here are a few common ones for reference:

the – **t**wo **h**eavy **e**lephants

said – **s**mall **a**nts **i**n **d**anger

c**ould**/sh**ould**/w**ould** – **o**h **u** **l**ucky **d**uck!

c**ome**/s**ome** – **o**pen **m**y **e**ars

people – **p**eople **e**at **o**ranges **p**enguins **l**ay **e**ggs

w**ere**/th**ere**/h**ere** – **e**very **r**ainbow **e**nds

th**ought**/b**ought** – **o**h **u** **g**reat **h**airy **t**iger

VISUAL AIDS

The high-frequency words 'there', 'their' and 'they're' all sound the same but are spelt differently, so a good way to help children remember how to spell them and recall their meanings is to use a visual aid for these words (Figure 10.3).

the♦r

ther♦e

they^are

Figure 10.3 A visual tool to help children remember 'their', 'there' and 'they're'

There refers to a location ('there' contains the word 'here' which can be helpful to highlight to children)

Their refers to a belonging, as in 'their shoes, their socks, their bag'

They're is the abbreviated version of 'they are' where we use an apostrophe in the place of the 'a'. 'They're learning lots about phonics'

SPELLING PYRAMIDS

Another visual way to help children focus on each letter needed within a word, and help them build up to spelling it, is to use a spelling pyramid (Figure 10.4). A child starts with the initial letter at the top of the pyramid and then for each layer adds another letter until the word is written as a whole along the bottom of the pyramid. Children can write each letter or they can use other manipulatives. You could write on individual Duplo blocks with a whiteboard pen and physically build a pyramid.

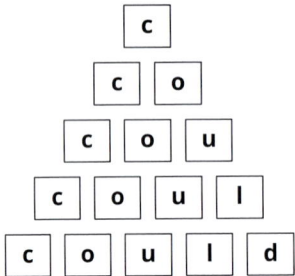

Figure 10.4   A spelling pyramid

EMPLOY A SYSTEMATIC SPELLING STRATEGY

Once children enter Key Stage 1 they will need to begin to spell these high-frequency tricky words correctly in their writing. This can be a tall order. They are tricky enough to read, let alone spell! From years of experience in the classroom, alongside helping my own children with spellings at home, I have devised a strategy which contains four steps to help practise spellings, in particular the words that are not easily decodable. This is a fun and more practical alternative to the traditional 'look, say, cover, write, check' method, which you may be more familiar with but for some children can become very tiresome, very quickly.

> **Tip 10.2   Romp** – 1. to play or frolic in a lively or boisterous manner · 2. to run or go rapidly and without effort · 3. to win easily. (*Cambridge Dictionary*)

ROMP to spelling victory!

Step 1: **R**ead and recognise – if the word is easily decodable, encourage children to segment it into its sounds and spot the familiar digraphs and trigraphs. If the word is a high-frequency tricky word, then discuss the irregular part of the word that is not following the usual spelling pattern. Provide children with the opportunity to read the word several times and play games to encourage fluency and automatic recognition. It's a good idea to put the word into a sentence to check children's understanding too.

Step 2: **O**rganise and order – next, provide children with the letters of the word written on a selection of objects that they can manipulate and put in the correct order to spell the word. You could use Duplo blocks, magnetic letters, clothes pegs, or make flashcards from cardboard. At first, children can order the letters while looking at the whole word to gain familiarity, but once they have done this several times challenge them to order the letters without looking at the whole word.

Step 3: **M**iss out letters – after children have played games where they have ordered the letters, show them the word with some letters missing. Can they identify which letter or letters are missing? This doesn't have to be actually writing the letters, children could find the correct magnetic letters or use letter flashcards.

Step 4: **P**layful practice – finally, once children are confident at reading, recognising and ordering the letters within the word, they can begin to practise spelling it by writing. There are various ways to make this more interesting and engaging. Can they write the word in as many different colours as they can? Write the word in a sensory writing tray? Write the word using chalk on the pavement? Or fill a large picture outline with the word as many times as they can? Remember, spelling doesn't have to always involve using a pen and paper!

> **Tip 10.3**   When children are initially practising spelling tricky words it can be useful for them to use a whiteboard and whiteboard pen. This takes away the pressure of getting the spellings correct every time as mistakes can easily be rubbed out. Children may be more willing to give spelling and writing a go!

IN SUMMARY

- High-frequency words are words that children will often see in their reading books.
- They can consist of words that are decodable and words that do not follow the usual spelling pattern.
- We want to encourage children to begin to read these types of words by sight, so they can develop their reading fluency.
- When introducing high-frequency words, it is important to highlight to children the parts that are decodable and the part that is irregular.
- Strategies to assist children in reading high-frequency tricky words include heart words, mnemonics and other visual aids.

YOUR TURN!

Look at these words taken from the 150 most common words (but not the 100 most common). Can you highlight the tricky part of these words?

again	**would**	**look**	**know**
want	**after**	**school**	**water**

Think about what you've learnt about phonics instruction so far: which word is actually phonetically regular? How can you help children to learn the tricky words?

LEARNING IDEA 10.1
HIGH-FREQUENCY TOWERS

Help children develop instant recall of high-frequency words to develop reading fluency.

PRACTISE

- Reading high-frequency words
- Instant recall and automaticity

PICK UP

- Sheet of paper
- Marker pen
- Duplo
- Blank or DIY dice

PREP

1. On the sheet of paper draw six bases for the towers.
2. Write a focus high-frequency word on each face of the dice.
3. Write the corresponding words next to each base on the sheet (Figure 10.5).
4. Place out a box or basket of Duplo blocks.

PLAY

Children roll the dice and read the word it lands on. They then place a Duplo block onto the correct tower base. Roll again and continue to place a block on the matching towers. Which tower will be the tallest? Which tower will be the shortest?

LINK

Check out activity...
Look at Chapter 3 to find out how to make a DIY dice out of toilet roll tubes.

Figure 10.5 Learning high-frequency words using building blocks

LEARNING IDEA 10.2
TRICKY WORD CUFFS

Is there a word that a child keeps getting stuck on? This is a fun way to develop recognition without children even realising they are reading.

PRACTISE

- Reading tricky words

PICK UP

- Toilet roll tubes
- Colouring pens
- Marker pen

PREP

1. Cut a toilet roll tube in half to create a smaller cylinder.
2. Cut down the back of the tube so that it can be flattened but also placed on a wrist.
3. Write the tricky word onto the tube with a marker pen.
4. Children can now decorate the cuffs with colouring pens (Figure 10.6).

PLAY

Place it on a wrist and children can wear them like superhero cuffs! Make sure that the word is displayed so that children can read them, and they are not upside down.

Figure 10.6 Practising reading difficult words using paper cuffs

LEARNING IDEA 10.3
SLIDE, SPELL AND REVEAL

Help children focus on the bit of the tricky words that are irregular and are not following the most common spelling rules.

Figure 10.7 Practising tricky words using a homemade cardboard sliding tool

PREP

1. Write a selection of high-frequency tricky words on strips of cardboard with marker pen. The strips need to be narrow enough to be able to slot through a flattened toilet roll tube.
2. Cut off a small piece of the toilet roll tube and flatten it.
3. Use the parcel tape to cover the top of the flattened toilet roll tube.
4. Slot the tube onto the word cards (Figure 10.7).

PLAY

An adult slides the tube along the word to cover one of the letters. Children identify the missing letter and use the whiteboard pen to fill in the missing letter and read the word. Repeat for other letters of the same word and other high-frequency word cards.

LEARNING IDEA 10.4
SEEK AND SPELL

This is a really fun, practical way to practise reading and spelling high-frequency tricky words. It's a great way to take phonics outside too!

PRACTISE

- Reading tricky words
- Spelling tricky words

PICK UP

- Clothes pegs
- Cardboard
- Marker pen

PREP

1. Create a base board by cutting a small rectangle of cardboard and writing 'Seek and Spell' at the top.
2. Write the letters to spell a tricky word onto clothes pegs and hide them around the environment (Figure 10.8).
3. Prepare other clothes pegs to spell a selection of other tricky words.

PLAY

An adult says the tricky word that children are hunting for. They then search around to find the clothes pegs. Once all the pegs have been found they organise them and clip them onto the card in the correct order to spell the word. Repeat for other words.

Figure 10.8 Game using cardboard and pegs to practise reading and spelling

LEARNING IDEA 10.5
PASSWORDS AND PIN CODES

Give this a try to help children practise reading and spelling those trickier high-frequency words that can become a stumbling block for fluency. It's ideal to stick up on the classroom door in school or even the snack cupboard at home for continued exposure.

PRACTISE

- **Reading tricky words**
- **Spelling tricky words**

PICK UP

- **Paper**
- **Pens**

PREP

1 Draw a keypad onto paper.
2 Write the tricky word in full at the top and randomly place its letters on some of the buttons underneath.
3 Write other letters on each of the remaining buttons (Figure 10.9).
4 Stick up at the side of a door or on a cupboard.

PLAY

Before entering or opening a cupboard children read the password on the keypad and press the 'buttons' in the correct order to spell it. The keypads can be up for a few days before being replaced with a different high-frequency word.

Figure 10.9 Learning tricky words using a keypad-style activity

11
LEARNING TO READ AND SPELL MORE COMPLEX WORDS

KEY TERMS

Digraph: two letters that together make one sound

Grapheme: the letter or group of letters that we see on the page. It's the written form of the phoneme

Phoneme: the smallest unit of sound within a word

Phonogram: the letter symbols that comprise a phoneme. A phonogram can be made up of one letter or a group of letters

Quadgraph: four letters that together make one sound, for example 'ough' and 'eigh'

Schwa: the laziest but most common vowel sound in the English language. It's essentially the /uh/ sound that vowels can make within words

Syllable: a unit of speech sound within a word

Trigraph: three letters that work together to make one sound

Vowel: a speech sound that is produced with a comparatively open vocal tract

There are 44 sounds in the English language, and children will have learnt the initial ways that they can be represented by previously learning the letters and sounds of the alphabet and matching the sounds to a selection of digraphs and trigraphs. At this stage of phonics things can get quite complicated (if you don't think that already!). There are 44 sounds, but these sounds can be spelled in around 250 different ways. Letters and combinations of letters can make several different sounds (for example, 'ow' can make the sound /ow/ in 'cow' or /oa/ in 'snow'), and phonemes can be represented in lots of different ways (/ai/ could be written as 'ai', 'ay', 'a-e', 'eigh', 'ey', among others). This phase is all about broadening children's knowledge of graphemes and phonemes and providing them with opportunities to learn the alternatives and apply this knowledge in both reading and spelling.

WHEN ARE CHILDREN READY TO MOVE ON TO THIS STAGE OF PHONICS?

As this stage of phonics is more complex and demanding of children's phonic knowledge it is essential that they have completely mastered all the previous stages before they attempt to learn the alternatives. Are they secure in recognising all the initial digraphs and trigraphs? Can they read and spell both CVC words and words that contain more phonemes? Are they confident in reading multisyllabic words? Do they recognise a selection of high-frequency words? In fact, the ability to identify the tricky part of a tricky word is a great introduction to alternatives. Many of the high-frequency tricky words that children have previously learnt will now become easily decodable once they start to learn the alternative ways they can represent phonemes. Words such as 'like' and 'out' are initially taught as high-frequency tricky words in order to increase reading fluency, but once children have been introduced to split digraphs and the first alternative grapheme these words will become fully decodable.

FIRST ALTERNATIVE GRAPHEMES

Leading up to this stage, aside from /c/, children would have been taught one way to represent the 44 phonemes. Now, children will learn that a phoneme can be spelled in a variety of different ways. Typically, they will be introduced to one other way to represent a phoneme first as shown in Table 11.1 (the order of introduction may vary between phonics schemes, but the premise is the same).

Table 11.1 Alternative graphemes commonly taught first

Previously taught	Alternative grapheme
ai	ay
ee	ea
igh	ie
oa	oe
or	aw
oo	ue
ur	ir

Previously taught	Alternative grapheme
ow	ou
oi	oy
f	ph
w	wh

SPLIT DIGRAPHS

A further alternative way to represent vowel phonemes is to use a split digraph. There are five split digraphs for children to learn. You may know these as 'magic "e"' or 'silent "e"'. A digraph is split up and a consonant is placed in between the two letters. The letters to create the digraph are now not adjacent but they are still working together to create one phoneme. I often explain to children that the 'e' at the end of the word or syllable is making the vowel in the middle say its name not its sound (say the long vowel sound rather than the short). A sound button for a split-digraph word looks like an arch linking the 'e' at the end with the middle vowel letter (Figure 11.1). You may see the arch go above or below the word, but both are just illustrating that the letters are linked and together create one sound.

Figure 11.1 Split-digraph words with sound buttons

Children need lots of practice spotting split-digraph words so that they segment and blend the word correctly and avoid 'sounding out' each letter – for example, if a child does not spot that the word 'bike' contains a split digraph they will likely segment the word b/i/k/e rather than b/ie/k.

You can encourage children to emulate an alarm sound (/ee/, /ee/, /ee/) whenever they spot a short word that ends in an 'e' so that they are prompted to check if it is a split digraph and consequently segment the word correctly.

> **Tip 11.1**   If children hear a /c/ sound and they know it is within a split-digraph word then use the grapheme /k/, for example, in the words 'bike', 'take' and 'poke'. A 'c' in the middle of a split-digraph word will make an /s/ phoneme, as in the words 'race', 'spice' and 'face'.

FIRST ALTERNATIVE PHONEMES

During this phase children will also be taught that familiar graphemes can also make alternative phonemes. This is particularly the case for single vowel letters, which we look at in a bit more detail below, but there are other graphemes that children will come across in words that can make a different sound than what they have been previously taught. Common alternative phonemes that children will be taught first will include those listed in Table 11.2.

Table 11.2 Alternative phonemes for graphemes already learnt

Grapheme	Previously taught phoneme Example word	Alternative phoneme Example word
a	hat	/ai/ – bacon
e	pet	/ee/ – behind
i	pin	/igh/ – find
o	pot	/oa/ – cold
u	fun	/ue/ – unit
g	goat	/j/ – giant
c	cat	/s/ – circle
ow	cow	/oa/ – snow
ie	tie	/ee/ – field
ea	seat	/e/ – bread
y	yes	/ee/ – happy
ch	chin	/sh/ – chef

FURTHER ALTERNATIVES

Once children have mastered reading words that contain the above alternative graphemes and phonemes they can slowly, but systematically, be introduced to further alternatives for reading and spelling. Table 11.3 shows the most commonly found alternative graphemes.

Table 11.3 Further alternative graphemes for phonemes

Phoneme	Graphemes	Example word
/s/	s	sit
	ss	mess
	c	city
	se	house
	ce	science
	sc	scent
	st	whistle
/n/	n	net
	gn	sign
	kn	know

Phoneme	Graphemes	Example word
/m/	m	mat
	mb	lamb
/c/	c	cot
	k	kit
	ck	sock
	ch	school
/f/	f	fit
	ff	huff
	ph	phone
/l/	l	let
	ll	fill
	le	apple
	al	total
/j/	j	jam
	g	gem
	dge	bridge
	ge	large
/v/	v	van
	ve	have
/w/	w	wet
	wh	whale
/z/	z	zip
	zz	fizz
	s	as
	se	please
	ze	maize
/ch/	ch	ch
	tch	pitch
/sh/	sh	ship
	ch	chef
	ti	station
	ssi	passion
	si	tension
	ci	special
/ai/	ai	rain
	ay	play
	a-e	cake
	a	taken

(Continued)

Table 11.3 (Continued)

Phoneme	Graphemes	Example word
	eigh	eight
	ey	hey
	ei	reindeer
	aigh	straight
	ea	break
/ee/	**ee**	seed
	ea	leaf
	e	she
	e-e	theme
	ie	field
	y	funny
	ey	key
/igh/	**igh**	night
	ie	tie
	i	tiger
	i-e	ride
	y	fly
/oa/	**oa**	boat
	o	token
	o-e	poke
	oe	toe
	ou	mould
	ow	snow
/oo/ or /yoo/	**oo**	moon
	ue	true
	ew	new
	u	uniform
	u-e	flume
	ou	group
	ui	fruit
/ar/	**ar**	farm
	a* (*accent dependent)	father
	al	half
/or/	**or**	form
	aw	straw
	au	launch
	aur	dinosaur
	oor	floor
	al	talk
	a	water

Phoneme	Graphemes	Example word
	oar	roar
	ore	more
	our	four
	ough	thought
	augh	caught
/ur/	ur	turn
	er	herb
	ir	first
	or	work
	ear	heard
/ear/	ear	dear
	ere	here
	eer	deer
/air/	air	fair
	ear	bear
	are	care
	ere	there
/zh/ (new phoneme)	su	casual
	si	vision

BEST BET DECISIONS

As children start to build up a large bank of alternative graphemes for reading, they will need to start applying this knowledge in their writing. But how do children know which grapheme to use to represent a phoneme? For example, a child wants to spell the word 'play' and has learnt several alternatives for the /ai/ phoneme; which grapheme do they use to spell the /ai/ phoneme? To assist children with their spelling and grapheme choices we can together think about where the focus phoneme is within a word. Certain graphemes are more likely to be represented at the end of a word and others are frequently found in the middle (Table 11.4). We can teach children to make 'best bet decisions'; that is, they start to learn where certain graphemes are more likely to appear within a word. In the example word 'play', children can be taught that if they hear an /ai/ phoneme at the end of a word or syllable then it is represented by the 'ay' grapheme rather than 'ai'; we don't see 'ai' at the end of words.

In fact, Hodges (1966) and Fry (2004) completed studies looking at the top spellings of graphemes within 17,000 most frequently used words which I think is really interesting research. Obviously, children don't need to know all of the percentages for all of the graphemes, but I think it's worth highlighting here as a reference for adults to further support children to make appropriate grapheme choices (see Table 11.5).

Table 11.4 Where alternative graphemes are commonly found within a word

Beginning and middle	End
ai a-e	ay
ee ea	ey e ea (one syllable words) y (two or more syllables)
i-e igh	y ie
oa	oe ow
oo	ew ue
oi	oy
ow ou	ow
or aw ough	ore oor aw
	are
	ear eer

Table 11.5 Frequency of common alternative graphemes within words (only including graphemes that account for at least 3%) and the most frequently used GPC for each phoneme in bold

Phoneme	Principal spellings in order of frequency
/a/	**a** (cat) 97%, a-e (have) 3%
/ai/	**a** (bacon) 45%, a-e (bake) 35%, ai (main) 9%, ay (play) 6%
/ar/	**ar** (car) 89%, are (are) 5%, ear (heart) 3%
/ch/	**ch** (chair) 55%, ture (feature) 31%, tch (catch) 11%
/e/	**e** (bed) 91%, ea (bread) 4%
/ee/	**y** (happy) 41%, e (behind) 40%, ee (seed) 6%, ea (seat) 6%
/ear/	**er** (experience) 32%, ear (fear) 25%, eer (deer) 18%, e-e (here) 14%, ier (tier) 7%
/ul/	**le** (table) 95%
/er/	**er** (hammer) 77%, or (author) 12%, ar (cellar) 8%
/f/	**f** (fox) 78%, ph (phone) 12%, ff (stuff) 9%
/i/	**i** (hit) 92%, i-e (give) 6%, y (gym) 2%
/igh/	**i-e** (hide) 37%, i (kind) 37%, y (fly) 14%, igh (right) 6%

Phoneme	Principal spellings in order of frequency
/j/	**ge** (large) 66%, j (jam) 22%, dge (edge) 5%, d (soldier) 3%
/k/	**c** (cat) 73%, k (kit) 13%, ck (sock) 6%, ch (school) 3%
/oa/	**o** (focus) 73%, o-e (hope) 14%, oa (boat) 5%, ow (row) 5%
/oi/	**oi** (soil) 62%, oy (toy) 32%
/oo/	**u** (push) 61%, oo (hook) 35%, o (woman) 5%
/ow/	**ou** (shout) 56%, ow (cow) 29%
/s/	**s** (sun) 73%, c (cent) 17%, ss (miss) 7%
/sh/	**ti** (action) 53%, sh (shed) 26%, ci (special) 5%, ssi (mission) 3%
/ue/	**u** (human) 59%, u-e (use) 19%, oo (moon) 11 %, ew (few) 4%
/z/	**s** (was) 64%, z (zip) 23%, es (flies) 4%, x (xylophone) 4%
/zh/	**si** (incision) 49%, s (pleasure) 33%

So, how can this help children? Once they have been exposed to all of the likely alternatives we can start teaching them about the most likely graphemes to use in their spelling and encourage them to think about where the phoneme is sitting within the word too. For example, if children want to write the word 'bike' they segment the word b/ie/k. What have they learnt about how the phonemes are represented to help them spell the word correctly? They identify that the /igh/ phoneme comes in the middle of a single syllable word so a best bet would indicate that it's either an 'i-e' or an 'igh'. They would have learnt that a /t/ follows 'igh' so it's not this GPC in this case and the split digraph 'i-e' is found to be the most common representation of /igh/ (37%) if it's not before multiple consonants (as in 'kind' and 'child'). So, they have utilised their phonic knowledge to work out that it's a split digraph. Now, what have they learnt about how the /c/ phoneme is represented within a split-digraph word? They need to use the grapheme 'k'! With the right teaching and tools children have encoded and deduced that it must be spelt 'bike'.

SILLY SENTENCES

To help children recognise the role of alternative phonemes and graphemes you can introduce them to some silly sentences. In each sentence below the same phoneme is being represented by different graphemes or the same grapheme is creating a different phoneme within each of the words. Create your own with children for added fun and engagement!

Alternative graphemes:

Her bird was hurt

The jewel in a large gem badge

Hey, eight reindeer have taken the great cake

I ride the tiger at night in the sky

Alternative phonemes:

My stretchy yoga gym

A great bread treat

SYLLABLE TYPES AND VOWEL LETTERS

Understanding syllable types is another vital tool in children's reading and spelling toolkit. In Chapter 9 we looked at how we can 'chunk' a multisyllabic word into syllables so that these longer words become more manageable to read. This knowledge can now help children work out the best way to pronounce graphemes and how the phonemes are best represented.

At this stage of their phonic journey children would have learnt that the five vowel letters can make a short or a long sound – for example, 'a' can say /a/ as in 'cat' or /ay/ as in 'acorn' – and it's the type of syllable that the vowel letter is within that will determine this. If a vowel is within a closed syllable (closed in by a consonant) then it will make the short sound (one that children are initially taught when learning to match letters and sounds) whereas if the vowel is at the end of the syllable and therefore not closed in by a consonant, then it will make the long vowel sound (say its name).

Within these words the vowel letter within the open syllable will create a long vowel sound (/igh/, /ee/, /ue/). 'i' and 'o' will make their long sound within a closed syllable when it is before two consonants, for example, 'wild', 'child', 'cold', 'gold'.

ti/ger   fre/quent   hu/man

We looked at four syllable types in Chapter 9 (open, closed, vowel team and r-controlled). There are two further types of syllables that children should be aware of and I will explain them in more detail below. To help children remember the six syllable types it might be useful to use the CLOVER acronym.

C – closed syllable

L – 'le' syllable

O – open syllable

V – vowel team

E – magic e (split digraph)

R – r-controlled

The 'le' Syllable Rule

This type of syllable always occurs at the end of a word. It is where a consonant is followed by 'le'. The vowel sound within this syllable type creates more of a schwa sound, /uh/. Think about how you say the words 'purple', 'turtle' or 'circle'. The 'le' at the end makes an /uhl/ sound. So, if children hear an /uhl/ sound at the end of a multisyllabic word their best bet when spelling it is to use 'le'.

pu͜r/p**le**   tu͜r/t**le**   ci͜r/c**le**

Split-Digraph Syllable Rule

This is when one of the syllables within a multisyllabic word is made up of a split digraph (it has a silent 'e' on the end). There will only be one consonant between the vowel and the final 'e'.

for/t͡un͡e   po/l͡it͡e   mi͜s/t͡ak͡e

MAGNIFYING GLASS

Now that we have looked at the six syllable types (CLOVER) let's put this knowledge into practice to see if it helps us decode multisyllabic words correctly. Figure 11.2 below shows how to apply the syllable rules to the multisyllabic words 'photograph', 'caterpillar' and 'dandelion'.

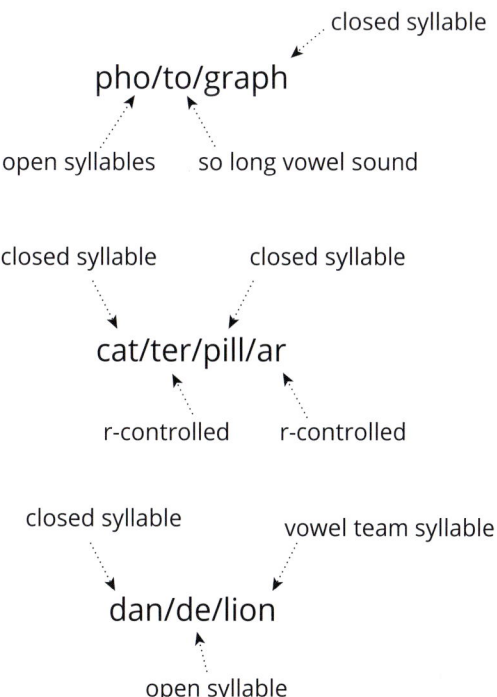

Figure 11.2   Syllable segmentation of polysyllabic words

How do we know where to chunk (break up) a multisyllabic word, aside from knowing the syllable types? There are some spelling pattern rules for this! It's about looking at the position of the consonants and vowels within the word. Table 11.6 indicates the different spelling patterns that can occur. To break a word into its syllables, highlight the vowels in a word and then divide in the middle.

Table 11.6   Consonant and vowel patterns to identify syllables

Pattern	Examples
VC/CV	rab/bit mon/key
V/CV	mu/sic pi/lot
VC/V	cam/el haz/ard
VC/CCV	ham/ster chil/dren
V/V	li/on di/et

WHAT'S A SCHWA?

Earlier in the book I talked about trying to avoid adding the schwa sound /uh/ to the end of letter sounds to create the pure sound and therefore make it easier to blend sounds to form words. But the schwa sound is in fact the most common vowel sound in the English language, and once children have moved on from initial letter sounds and beginning to read multisyllabic and more complex words then they will come across the /uh/ sound very frequently.

The schwa is often described as the laziest speech sound as you hardly open your mouth and your jaw is relaxed when you say it. It can be represented by any of the vowel letters or it can be unwritten but heard. The schwa sound plays an important role in making our speech more fluent and natural. One of the first high-frequency tricky words that children learn, 'the', contains the schwa sound; within this word the schwa is represented by an 'e'.

Example words that contain a schwa represented by each vowel are listed in Example 11.1.

Example 11.1   Words where the vowel creates a schwa sound (accent dependent)

a	e	i	o	u
balloon	children	animal	ribbon	bonus
banana	telephone	pencil	dinosaur	supply
salad	camel	accident	police	virus

In multisyllabic words we tend to pronounce and stress one syllable more than the other. Within the stressed syllable the vowel tends to make its regular long or short sound. It's within the unstressed syllable that the schwa sound can be found lurking! The stressed syllables in the words below are in bold, and the schwa indicated.

seven ᵊ   **ba**con ᵊ   **tun**nel ᵊ   **rib**bon ᵊ

The schwa can cause particular problems for spelling as the word will not be written like it sounds and can be represented by all the vowels. There are some spelling tips and rules that you can teach children to help them recognise the vowel sound and choose the appropriate graphemes in their writing.

R-controlled vowel digraphs can often become a schwa, especially when they are found at the end of a word. Again, this can vary according to accent.

lett**er** ᵊ   doct**or** ᵊ   sug**ar** ᵊ

When you find an 'a' at the beginning or end of a multisyllabic word it can create a schwa sound.

yog**a** ᵊ   past**a** ᵊ   **a**way ᵊ

A vowel before an 'l' at the end of the word can become a schwa.

met**a**l ᵊ   foss**i**l ᵊ   bag**e**l ᵊ

Below are some useful ways to help children identify and practise reading words that contain a schwa:

1   Identify the stressed and unstressed syllables within words.
2   Encourage children to segment and blend words and check if they sound correct. If they don't, get them to replace one of the vowels with a schwa and check again.
3   Hunt for schwas in words.
4   Model breaking up a word into its syllables and highlighting the regular vowel and the one that makes a schwa.
5   Sort words according to the vowel letter that is making a schwa.

SING A SCHWA SONG!

(To the tune of 'Wheels on the bus')

The schwa sound goes like uh, uh, uh,

uh, uh, uh, uh, uh, uh.

The schwa sound goes like uh, uh, uh,

in a word that has two vowels.

The schwa sound is in about and around,

about and around, about and around.

The schwa sound is in about and around,

do you hear the schwa?

The schwa sound is in pizza and sofa,

pizza and sofa, pizza and sofa.

The schwa sound is in pizza and sofa,

do you hear the schwa?

GHOST LETTERS

Often referred to as silent letters, these are letters that are unpronounced but are used in the spelling of particular phonemes. Often, we will find these silent letters next to the same letters when we spell them (kn, mb, gn, gu, sc, mn, st, wh). In all of these digraphs the phoneme is only saying the sound of one of the letters. Many of the current day spellings are the result of the word hanging on to its original form from hundreds of years ago.

mb – /m/

kn – /n/

gn – /n/

su – /s/

sc – /s/

mn – /m/

st – /s/

wr – /r/

wh - /w/

Just like any other digraph, children need to learn that when they see these two letters next to each other they only create one sound and they will need to practise them accordingly. It can be a fun idea when spotting these digraphs that have silent letters to place or draw a ghost outline over the letter that is unpronounced (Figure 11.3).

Figure 11.3 Ghost letters

> **Tip 11.2**   In Old English the 'k' in 'kn' would have been articulated, but over time we have dropped the sound but not the letter (Philps, 2012).

As we saw in Chapter 8, knowledge of submorphemes can help us make more sense of our language. Words that have a common cluster of letters will often have the same meaning and have their roots in Anglo-Saxon. This is particularly true for words that have silent letters. We can encourage children to think about the word's meaning which might give us a clue on how we should spell it. Words that start with 'kn' are often related to the bending of joints, words that start with 'wh' are linked to creating a sound, and 'wr' can convey turning or bending (Example 11.2).

Example 11.2   Submorphemes

kn	wh	wr
bending of joints	**create a sound**	**turn or bend**
knee	whistle	wrap
knuckle	whisper	wreck
knead	whimper	wrestle
knot	wheeze	wrench
knit	whine	wrist
knock	whack	wreath

FURTHER SPELLING RULES

Studies have shown that introducing children to spelling rules as you introduce the phonogram can help children work out 80–90% of the words within the English language (Adams, 1990; Crystal, 2005). That said, it is important to remember the approximately 10% of words that have an irregular spelling pattern and there will be exceptions to these rules. However, knowing the spelling rules for alternative graphemes (English programmes of study: Key Stages 1 and 2) in Table 11.7 (DfE, 2013) and having an understanding about where certain graphemes sit within a word provides children with an excellent tool to both read and spell almost every word they come across.

Table 11.7   Spelling rules for alternative graphemes

Rules and guidance	Example words
The /ch/ phoneme is usually spelt 'tch' if before a single vowel letter	pitch, match, witch, catch, fetch Exceptions: which, rich, much, such
English words do not end with a 'v' so if a /v/ is heard at the end of a word spell it as 've'	have, live, give

(Continued)

Table 11.7   (Continued)

Rules and guidance	Example words
If the ending sounds like /s/ or /z/, it is spelt as 's'. If the ending sounds like /iz/ and forms an extra syllable in the word, it is spelt as 'es'	cats, dogs, spends, rocks, thanks, catches, matches
The past tense of some verbs may sound as if they end in /id/, /d/ or /t/, but all these endings are spelt 'ed'	hunted, buzzed, jumped, pulled, filled, watched, skipped
The only common English word that ends in 'ou' is 'you'	you, about, sound, found, mouth, around
English words do not end in 'i' unless an abbreviation or a word borrowed from another language	hi, sushi, safari, tai chi
The /f/ phoneme is not usually spelt as 'ph' at the beginning of short everyday words	fat, fit, fix, fun
The letter 'j' is never used for the /j/ sound at the end of words. Use 'dge' at the end straight after short vowel sounds. After everything else use 'ge'	edge, bridge, fudge, badge, dodge age, large, charge, huge, change
Use 'g' to represent the /j/ phoneme at the beginning of words before 'e', 'i' and 'y'	gem, gym, gentle, giant, giraffe, energy Exceptions: give, get
Spell the /s/ phoneme using 'c' before 'e', 'i', and 'y'. This is often referred to a 'soft c'	race, space, rice, cell, city, circle
The /r/ sound can be spelt as 'wr' at the beginning of words	wrist, write, written, wrap, wrong
Th /l/ and /uh/ sound is most commonly spelt 'le' at the end of words	table, apple, bottle, middle, little
The 'el' spelling at the end of words is often used after m, n, s, v, and w	model, tinsel, camel, tunnel, travel
The most common spelling of /igh/ at the end of a word is 'y'	cry, fly, spy, try, sky, reply, July
The /or/ sound is usually spelt as an 'a' before 'l' and 'll'	ball, call, fall, walk, talk, always
After a 'w' the 'a' says /o/	want, watch, wander
A 'w' can make 'ar' say /or/ and 'or' say /er/	war, warm, swarm, award, towards world, work, word, worm

Rules and guidance	Example words
Vowel teams that end in an 'i' or 'u' are not found at the end of a word	
Use 'wh' to represent /w/ at the beginning of question words	what, when, why, which
The /z/ sound is represented by 's' almost 70% of the time – when it is after a vowel or a voiced consonant such as 'g', 'd' and 'b'	logs, beds, tubes, moves, clothes

IN SUMMARY

- Once children are confident with reading words that contain the initial digraphs and trigraphs they can begin to learn the alternatives.
- They will learn that the same grapheme can make different phonemes and the same phoneme can be represented by different graphemes.
- Children will also be introduced to split digraphs at this stage.
- Knowledge of open and closed syllables will help children know the correct phoneme for single vowel letters.
- Children can learn to use 'best bet decisions' to help them with spelling and writing words.

YOUR TURN!

How many phonetically decodable ways can you write the words 'germ', 'race' and 'circle'? In Example 11.3 an example is given for each word.

Example 11.3 Rewriting the words 'germ', 'race' and 'circle' in phonetically decodable ways

germ	race	circle
jirm	rais	surkll

GIVE ME FIVE!

1   What phoneme can be represented by the most graphemes?
2   Why does the word 'swan' have the 'a' making an /o/ sound?
3   Can you spot the schwa in the word 'dinosaur'?
4   What is the only common English word that ends in 'ou'?
5   When do we see 'c' making a soft sound?

LEARNING IDEA 11.1
COIN FLIP BINGO

Use this game when children first start to learn alternative ways to spell the same phoneme. It is also a good way to focus children on two graphemes that look similar, for example 'ay' and 'oy'.

PRACTISE

- Spotting digraphs and trigraphs
- Recognising alternative graphemes

PICK UP

- Cardboard
- Marker pen
- Counter
- Bingo dabber or felt tip pen

PREP

1. Write two focus graphemes on either side of the counter with marker pen (use a small sticker if you would prefer not to directly write on the counter).
2. Create a bingo board and write on it a selection of words that contain the two focus graphemes; one will be a grapheme previously learnt and the other will be the alternative spelling – for example, 'oi' and 'oy' (Figure 11.4). Use Example 11.4 at the end of the chapter to help with this.
3. Place the resources out alongside a bingo dabber or pen.

PLAY

Children flip the counter and read the grapheme displayed. They then spot the same grapheme in a word on their bingo card and mark it off with the bingo dabber. They keep flipping the counter and marking off the words until all the words have been marked.

Later on, children can flip the counter and write a word with the matching grapheme on a whiteboard or piece of paper.

Figure 11.4 Game to help with graphemes and phonemes

LEARNING IDEA 11.2
BEST BET BOARDS

Create some 'best bet boards' to help children think about how to represent phonemes and the best graphemes to choose.

PRACTISE

- **Recognising alternative graphemes**
- **Making best bet spelling decisions**

PICK UP

- **Cardboard**
- **Marker pen**
- **Clothes pegs**

PLAY

Children use their knowledge of alternative graphemes and understanding of where they would most likely see the graphemes within a word to choose the correct spelling. They clip the clothes peg on the correct spelling of the word. Repeat for all other best bet boards.

PREP

1 Cut rectangles of cardboard and draw lines to section off the card to make space for a picture and three words.
2 In the top section of the card draw a picture.
3 In the bottom three spaces write the word for the picture three times, but only once using the correct graphemes – for example, the whale picture with 'whail', 'whale' and whayll' (Figure 11.5).

Figure 11.5 Representing phonemes and graphemes with text and drawings on cardboard

LEARNING IDEA 11.3
ROLL AND READ

This classic activity can be adapted to suit any stage of phonics by changing the graphemes and words you want to focus on, but it does work particularly well for the five split digraphs that children need to learn.

PRACTISE

- **Identifying graphemes**
- **Reading words**

PICK UP

- **Paper**
- **Pen**
- **Ruler**
- **Dice**
- **Bingo dabber or felt tip pen**

PREP

1   Divide the paper into five or six columns depending on your focus.
2   Draw a horizontal line around 2 cm from the bottom and across all columns.
3   In each of the bottom spaces draw dots, or write numbers, to represent each number on the dice.
4   Within each column above write words that contain the same alternative grapheme – for example, a-e, i-e, o-e, u-e and e-e words, with the number 6 being 'roll again' (Figure 11.6). Use Example 11.4 at the end of the chapter to help with this.

PLAY

Children roll the dice and read a word above the corresponding number on the sheet. They then cross it out and roll again. Continue until all words have been crossed off the sheet. They could also draw the sound buttons on each of the words before marking them off the sheet.

Figure 11.6   Game to identify graphemes using dice and marker pen

LINKS

Check out activity...
Look at Chapter 3 to find out how to make a DIY dice out of toilet roll tubes.

LEARNING IDEA 11.4
THE MAGIC OF THE LETTER 'e' LADDER

Create a practical word ladder to help children practise reading alternative graphemes and realise the power of the letter 'e'!

PRACTISE

- Spotting alternative graphemes
- Reading words

PICK UP

- Cardboard
- Marker pen
- Star stickers
- Magnetic letter 'e'

PLAY

Children move the magnetic letter up the ladder and place it over each star sticker. They recognise and recall the digraph or trigraph that has been made by adding the 'e' and read the word accordingly. Continue with the words all the way to the top of the ladder.

Later on, children can time themselves to see how quickly they can move the letter and read all of the words. Can they beat their time on the following attempts?

PREP

1. Cut a long strip of cardboard and divide it up into smaller sections with the marker pen as if you are drawing a ladder.
2. Write a word in each of the sections which contains a digraph/trigraph or split digraph and the letter 'e' (ea, ee, ie, oe, er, ear, ue, ew, i-e, a-e, e-e, o-e, u-e) but replace the letter 'e' with a star sticker. Use Example 11.4 at the end of the chapter to help with this.
3. Place a magnetic letter 'e' at the bottom of the word ladder (Figure 11.7).

Figure 11.7 Practising reading graphemes using a word ladder

LEARNING IDEA 11.5
SPELLING TRACKS

This is an engaging way to practise spellings, and once you've created the board you can use it with any words you want children to focus on.

PRACTISE

- **Reading and spelling high-frequency words**

PICK UP

- **A3 sheet of paper**
- **Marker pen**
- **Word cards**
- **Toy car**
- **Pens/pencils**
- **Timer or dice**

PREP

1. Draw a car track on the A3 sheet of paper and divide it into small spaces like a board game.
2. Within each space write down a way for children to practise spelling the focus words – write it small, big, dotty, backwards, rainbow coloured, with eyes shut etc.
3. Create or gather some high-frequency word cards (Figure 11.8).
4. Place the toy car at the start alongside a timer or dice.

PLAY

Children either move the car around the track for an agreed amount of time (10 seconds) or roll the dice and move that number of spaces. Wherever they land they choose a word card from the pile and then practise spelling the word however the space they have landed dictates.

Figure 11.8 Practising spellings using a homemade 'track' game

Example 11.4 Alternative grapheme word bank

/s/			
se	**ce**	**sc**	**st**
house	fence	science	whistle
mouse	force	scent	listen
cause	since	descent	castle
pause	brace	crescent	bustle
loose	niece	fascinate	fasten

/n/	
kn	**gn**
know	gnat
knew	gnome
knot	align
kneel	assign
knit	sign

/m/	/c/	/f/
mb	**ch**	**ph**
lamb	school	phone
limb	anchor	photo
numb	character	elephant
comb	chrome	alphabet
climb	monarch	phantom

/l/	
le	**al**
apple	total
table	medal
title	mental
angle	coral
cable	central

/j/		
g	dge	ge
gem	badge	large
gym	bridge	hinge
magic	fudge	merge
ginger	edge	change
giant	lodge	strange
gentle	dodge	challenge

/v/	/w/
ve	wh
have	whale
give	when
live	which
love	whisk
sensitive	wheel
	whirl

/z/		
s	ze	se
dogs	maize	please
bugs	snooze	cheese
moves	gauze	because
clothes	seize	choose
becomes		praise
		noise

/ch/	/ear/	
tch	ere	eer
catch	here	deer
pitch	sphere	cheer
match	severe	beer
witch	sincere	career
stitch	interfere	steer
batch		

(Continued)

Example 11.4 (Continued)

/sh/				
ch	**ti**	**si**	**ssi**	**ci**
chef	station	mansion	passion	special
machine	action	tension	session	magician
brochure	nation	extension	mission	vicious
parachute	section		admission	facial
chalet	direction		discussion	artificial
	potion			

/ai/							
ay	**a**	**a-e**	**ey**	**eigh**	**ei**	**ea**	**aigh**
day	acorn	make	they	eight	vein	break	straight
play	baby	cake	hey	weigh	reign	steak	
say	apron	take	obey	weight	reindeer	great	
relay	basic	lake	survey	neigh			
delay	lady	flake		sleigh			
stray	table	shape					

/ee/					
ea	**e-e**	**e**	**ey**	**y**	**ie**
neat	these	he	key	happy	field
seat	theme	she	donkey	lucky	shield
dream	eve	we	chimney	funny	thief
leaf	delete	behind	valley	carry	chief
each	complete	beside	alley	baby	piece
sea	concrete	vegan	turkey	suddenly	

/igh/			
ie	**i-e**	**i**	**y**
pie	like	wild	fly
lie	time	child	try
spied	fine	final	spy
cried	bike	spider	cry
tried	fire	tiny	deny

/oa/

o	o-e	oe	ou	ow
no	note	toe	soul	snow
go	poke	woe	mould	glow
cold	hope	hoe	boulder	show
gold	rope	Joe	shoulder	blow
post	broke	foe		grow
total		goes		flow

/oo/ or /yoo/

ew	ue	u	u-e	ui	ou
new	cue	unit	tube	fruit	you
few	clue	unicorn	cube	suit	soup
chew	value	uniform	huge	suitcase	group
stew	venue	music	use	juice	youth
nephew	pursue	human	rude	cruise	route
knew	rescue	stupid	June		coupon

/or/

aw	au	oor	aur	al
saw	launch	door	dinosaur	all
raw	haunt	floor		walk
paw	haul	poor		talk
claw	August	moor		always
jaw	author			wall
lawn	astronaut			ball

/or/

a	ore	oar	ough	our	augh
water	more	oar	thought	four	caught
	snore	soar	bought	your	taught
	store	roar	fought	pour	naughty
	wore	board		fourth	daughter
	score			court	
	before				

(Continued)

Example 11.4 (Continued)

/ur/			
er	ir	or	ear
her	girl	work	learn
herb	bird	word	earn
fern	shirt	world	earth
stern	third	worth	pearl
servant	first	worse	heard
	thirteen	worst	rehearsal

/air/		
ere	ear	are
there	wear	care
where	tear	dare
nowhere	bear	fare
somewhere	pear	square
everywhere	swear	share

/zh/	
si	su
television	treasure
vision	pleasure
explosion	leisure
discussion	visual
occasion	measure
	casual

12
YEAR 1 PHONICS SCREENING CHECK

Tetching chylldrun tue ried yuizing fonickce meenz yoo proevighd theam whyth the tuells tew deacowd unphamilere whirdz.

The Phonics Screening Check was first announced as part of government policy in 2011 and introduced to schools across England in 2012. It's a statutory assessment administered to Year 1 pupils during the second half of the summer term and it is designed to assess children's progress, checking whether they have achieved the expected standard of phonics by the end of the year.

WHY WAS IT INTRODUCED?

The Rose Review (2006) highlighted the importance of teaching children to read both synthetically and systematically and so the short, statutory assessment was introduced by the DfE to further ensure a focus on synthetic phonics and strengthen phonics teaching in schools.

WHAT DOES THE CHECK INVOLVE?

Children must apply their phonic knowledge and decoding skills to read a list of 40 words. The word list consists of both real words and pseudowords (also called alien, nonsense or non-words). Pseudowords are accompanied by a picture of an alien to highlight to children that these words are non-words and they won't make sense. There are two sections to the check: section 1 includes words using graphemes from the earlier phases of phonics, including the first digraphs and trigraphs; and section 2 includes words that contain consonant clusters and alternative graphemes, including split digraphs.

WHAT HAPPENS DURING THE CHECK?

The check is administered on a one-to-one basis in a quiet, relaxed environment by a familiar adult; often children don't even realise they are sitting it! There is no time limit to the check, but it will usually take no longer than ten minutes. Children can go at their own pace and are allowed rest breaks to make reading more manageable, though administrators must ensure that children do not return to the classroom. Children will attempt to use their phonic knowledge to read each word and be given a mark for each word read correctly. If a child is struggling, then the check can be stopped at any time.

WHY INCLUDE PSEUDOWORDS?

Pseudowords are words that use combinations of GPCs that children will have learnt but they do not have any meaning attached. These made-up words are used to force children to utilise and demonstrate their knowledge of phonics and apply their decoding skills. Try reading these pseudowords:

trelvait

bargawl

criseelor

quorturfet

In order to read the quote at the beginning of the chapter and the words above you probably had to revert back to your knowledge of phonics and draw on your experience of reading other similar, more familiar words. For example, you know that when you see a double 'e' then it makes the sound /ee/ or that 'bargawl' could rhyme with 'shawl' so you know how to pronounce it. Imagine now that you are a child just starting out on your reading journey with limited knowledge and experience of letters and sounds; all words are unfamiliar to you at this point. Teaching children phonics provides them with the key to crack the code of the English language, meaning it equips them with the skills to tackle *all words*, whether real or made up. The use of non-words means you can check whether children have really developed the appropriate decoding skills and are not relying on sight word memorisation or picture clues. Having this letter–sound knowledge prepares children for when they come across an unfamiliar word later – they can revert back to their phonic knowledge to decode it.

ADMINISTERING THE CHECK

Schools must submit data for all pupils, including those where the headteacher has decided that administering the check would not be appropriate. This might be for children who are yet to complete the first year of the Key Stage 1 English programme of study or have shown no understanding of grapheme–phoneme correspondences; pupils for whom English is an additional language and who have limited fluency in English; pupils who use British Sign Language or other sign-supported communication to spell out individual letters; and those pupils who are non-verbal or selectively mute. Modified versions of the check are available with coloured, black and white, and no images, and schools can also modify the check themselves by changing the font, showing fewer words on the page or using coloured overlays.

Those who administer the check need to have completed training, and while administering and scoring will have to follow tight procedures in terms of making sure that papers are locked away and stored appropriately and the same introductory script is followed for all pupils. They will need to have a good knowledge of phonics themselves and when scoring they will need to refer to the guidance as some of the graphemes used in the check can represent several different phonemes. When decoding a real word children have to select the correct phoneme for the word – for example, 'snow' would need to use the /ow/ in 'glow' not 'cow'. When decoding a pseudo word, all plausible alternative and regional pronunciations are acceptable.

According to the 2024 Phonics Screening Check administration guidance (https://tinyurl.com/yc7wacfc), administrators should also consider the following points when scoring:

- if a pupil sounds out the phonemes but does not blend the word, you must not prompt them to do so, and you must score as incorrect
- pupils may elongate phonemes but if they leave gaps between phonemes and do not blend them, you must score as incorrect
- alternative pronunciations when deciding whether a response is correct – for real words, you must mark inappropriate grapheme–phoneme correspondences as incorrect – for example, reading 'blow' to rhyme with 'cow' would be incorrect
- you can allow alternative pronunciations of graphemes in pseudo-words – the scoring guidance gives some alternative pronunciations, but the list of acceptable pronunciations is not exhaustive
- a pupil's accent when deciding whether a response is acceptable – there must be no bias for or against a pupil with a particular accent, and pupils can use any acceptable regional pronunciation even if it is not within their usual accent
- any pronunciation difficulties when deciding whether a response is acceptable – for example, a pupil unable to form the 'th' sound who instead usually says 'f' should have this scored as correct
- if a pupil shows their ability to decode by revising an attempt, you must mark this as correct – you should not, however, prompt pupils to 'have another go' and must score the final attempt even if this is incorrect and a previous attempt was correct

WHAT IS THE EXPECTED STANDARD?

Although the pass mark is subject to change each year it has remained at 32 since the check's introduction. Children who achieve 32/40 are assessed as being at the expected level of word reading. Those that do not achieve the pass mark will sit the screening check in Year 2. The percentages of pupils achieving the expected standard in recent years are shown in Table 12.1.

WHAT DO SCHOOLS DO WITH THE RESULTS?

Although schools' individual screening results are not published, and they will not be placed in any sort of league table, the data are submitted to their local authority and a national average score is published. Often schools will publish their score on the school website. Ofsted will also look at these data during any inspections, in particular during 'reading deep dives'. The main drive of the check is to encourage schools to evaluate and reflect on their practice; get a better picture of their current phonics instruction; identify gaps in both teaching and children's knowledge; offer interventions and additional support; and adapt their practice accordingly. Children's individual scores are reported to parents usually within the end-of-year report.

Table 12.1 Percentage of pupils achieving the expected standard in the Phonics Screening Check, 2012–2023

2012	2013	2014	2015	2016	2017	2018	2019	2020	2021	2022	2023	2024
58%	69%	74%	77%	81%	81%	82%	82%	–*	–*	75%	79%	80%

*There were no assessments in 2020 and 2021 due to the Covid pandemic.

WHAT IF A CHILD DOES NOT ACHIEVE THE EXPECTED STANDARD?

Those children who do not achieve the pass mark at the end of Year 1 will sit a screening check again during the summer term of Year 2. While administering the check it is good practice for the adult to take notes and jot down any mistakes that the child has made. This will be passed onto the Year 2 teachers who will then be able to adapt their planning to plug children's gaps in phonic knowledge. This might be through ability grouping, small group interventions, changing the level of decodable books the child is reading or offering more tailored one-to-one sessions – the aim being for them to pass the check when they re-sit. In my experience there are a few common errors that children make year on year:

- not identifying digraphs. instead 'sounding out' each letter
- struggling to blend words with adjacent consonants and consonant clusters
- reversing certain letters (d/b) or making adjacent letters into digraphs (strom to storm)
- struggling to read multisyllabic words
- struggling to spot and read split-digraph words
- making non-words into real words
- rushing through reading the words

Confident readers, who have secure phonic knowledge, may sometimes not achieve the pass mark as they tend to be more prone to rushing through the check or making pseudowords into real words.

TOP TEN TIPS TO HELP PREPARE

To properly prepare children for the check here are my top ten tips to focus on during the first half of the summer term before the check is administered in June:

1 Revisit all initially taught digraphs and their first alternatives (ai, ay, oi, oy, igh, ie, ow, ou, ee, ea, oo, ue, ew, ar, or, aw, au, ur, ir).

2 Revisit the trigraphs ear and air, particularly concentrating on reading 'air' as /air/ not /ai/r/.

3 Practice reading words that contain the digraphs that look similar (sh, ch, th and ar, or, ur).

4 Saying aloud the digraphs/trigraphs within the word first before going on to segment and blend the word as a whole – for example, look at 'blue' and say 'ue', '/b/l/ue'.

5 Devising a system to make spotting split-digraph words easier. Encourage children to spot short words that have an 'e' at the end and check if it is a split digraph. There are always at least five split-digraph words within the check, and this can easily make the difference between passing the check or not.

6 Reading words that contain a consonant before the vowel and ensuring they are not made into a digraph ('ro' is not read as /or/, 'ra' is not read as /ar/).

7 Practise chunking multisyllabic words.

8 Encourage all children to 'sound out' and blend all of the words even if they are a confident, fluent reader. This way mistakes can be spotted more easily and this can combat making pseudowords into real words.

9 Practise reading pseudowords and highlight the image of an alien next to the word to prompt children to read it as a non-word.

10 Encourage children to take their time and not rush their word reading.

COMMON CRITICISMS OF THE CHECK

Since its introduction the check has been subject to a varied amount of criticism and contention. Among the criticisms are the following:

1 The arbitrary nature of the pass mark. Why is achieving 32/40 judged to be meeting the expected standard? Why not 35? 25? Year 1 children have to achieve a pass percentage of 80% to be assessed as 'on track'.

2 The inclusion of pseudo words is a particularly contentious subject. Critics of the check suggest that children can easily demonstrate their phonic ability through real word reading.

3 When marking pseudowords, the scoring guidance states that administrators can accept any possible alternative phonemes – for example, accepting the long vowel sound for single vowel letters. Children's knowledge of alternatives, and experience of open and closed syllables, can vary from school to school and therefore the marking of pseudowords can also vary. As an example, if children read the word 'splet' as 'spleet' (using the long vowel sound for 'e') it is not clear if administrators should accept this as correct or not. In a real word example, it would be a short vowel sound as it's within a closed syllable, but guidance states that all acceptable alternatives can be used for pseudowords.

4 Issues around testing 5- and 6-year-old children.

IN SUMMARY

- The Phonics Screening Check was first introduced in England in 2012 to further focus on the use of synthetic phonics as the prime approach to teaching reading.
- The check is administered to children in June of Year 1.
- It involves children reading a list of 40 words made up of real words and pseudowords.
- Pseudowords are used to force children to utilise their phonic knowledge to decode words.
- Those who do not pass in Year 1 will sit the check in the summer term of Year 2.
- Teachers can use the outcomes of the check to plug any gaps in knowledge, offer interventions and adapt planning.

YOUR TURN!

Try reading the pseudowords from past screening papers in Worksheet 12.1 and write a description on how to pronounce them (refer to the scoring guidance at the end of the chapter).

Worksheet 12.1 Table of pseudowords with space to write a description on how to pronounce them

Pseudoword	Description
zeg	uses the 'z' from 'zip' and rhymes with 'peg'.
slimp	
splew	
craint	
flards	
deebs	
kig	
remp	
smung	
vair	
whike	

LEARNING IDEA 12.1
REAL AND NON-WORD BASKETBALL

PRACTISE

- Reading real and non-words

PICK UP

- Two tin cans or paper cups
- Cardboard
- Paper
- Marker pen

PREP

1 Take the labels off the tin cans (make sure the tin cans do not have sharp edges).
2 Cut two squares of card and draw on the lines to create two basketball backboards, labelling one as 'real' and the other as 'non-words'.
3 Cut into the backboards so that they can be slotted onto the cans/cups.
4 Write a selection of real and non-words on small pieces of paper (Figure 12.1).

PLAY

Children pick a word card and read it. They identify whether the word is real or pseudo and then screw it up and throw it into the correct basketball net. Repeat for all the other words in the pile.

Figure 12.1 Paper basketball game to identify real and pseudo words

LEARNING IDEA 12.2
GIVE A DOG A BONE!

PRACTISE

- **Reading real and non-words**

PICK UP

- **Small dog bones (real or cut from card)**
- **Two dog bowls**
- **Two soft toy dogs**
- **Box or bag**
- **Marker pen**

PLAY

Children pick a bone from the box or bag and read the word written on it. They then place it into the correct dog bowl according to whether it is a real word or not. Repeat by reading and sorting all the other bones.

PREP

1 Write real and non-words onto the dog bones and place them into the box or bag.
2 Place out a food bowl for each of the soft toy dogs and assign one to collect the real words and the other to collect the non-words – the dogs could have a tag for this (Figure 12.2).

Figure 12.2 Identifying real and non-real words using dog bowls and bone treats

LEARNING IDEA 12.3
CE'REAL' AND NON-WORDS

PRACTISE

- Reading and sorting real and non-words

PICK UP

- Small cereal packets
- Scissors
- Cardboard
- Marker pen
- Plastic bowl
- Spoon

PREP

1. Choose two cereal boxes that have characters on the front.
2. Cut out the mouths of the characters to create a little postbox and assign one for collecting real words and the other to collect non-words.
3. Write words on small pieces of card to act as cereal and place in a bowl. For a list of words to use refer to Table 12.3 at the end of the chapter.
4. Place out the boxes, bowl and spoon (Figure 12.3).

PLAY

Children use the spoon to pick up a piece of 'cereal' and read the word. They then 'feed' the cereal to the correct character on the cereal boxes.

Figure 12.3 Sorting real and non-real words using cereal boxes

LEARNING IDEA 12.4
ALIEN WORD PUZZLES

PRACTISE

- **Reading and writing pseudowords**

PICK UP

- **Cardboard**
- **Marker pen**
- **Whiteboard and whiteboard pen**

PLAY

Children mix and match three squares (head, body and legs) to create an alien. They then identify the graphemes on the three cards and blend the sounds to form the word. This is the alien's name. They write the name onto the whiteboard and read it again now that it is written horizontally. Repeat for other cards and alien names.

PREP

1. Cut up the cardboard into small squares and sort into piles of three squares.
2. Place the squares on top of each other and draw an alien's head on the top, body in the middle and legs on the bottom square. Repeat to create several alien figures.
3. Write graphemes on the cards: consonants on the head and legs and the vowel digraphs on the body.
4. Place out the resources next to a whiteboard and pen (Figure 12.4).

Figure 12.4 Creating and reading pseudo words using alien-word figures

LEARNING IDEA 12.5
DINO RACES

PRACTISE

- Reading and writing real and non-words

PICK UP

- Masking tape
- Marker pen
- Small dinosaur toys
- Dice
- Whiteboard and whiteboard pen

PREP

1 Place out three vertical strips of masking tape.
2 Divide each of the strips into six spaces.
3 On the left-hand strip write six consonant graphemes in each space, on the middle strip write six vowel graphemes, and on the final strip write six consonant graphemes.
4 Place a toy dinosaur at the bottom of each track.
5 Place a dice (or three) next to the tracks (Figure 12.5).

PLAY

Roll the dice three times (or three dice once) and move each of three dinosaurs up the strips accordingly. Children write down each of the three graphemes they land on to create a CVC word. They read the word and decide if it is a real word or a pseudo one. Return the dinosaurs to the start of the strips and repeat.

Figure 12.5 Practising real and non-real words using dinosaur toys and word ladders

TIP

A small jewellery organiser with three sections acts as a good dice holder and is a great way to roll the dice without them getting lost.

Example 12.1 Phonics Screening Check (Year 1 Phonics Screening Check, STA, 2024)

Section 1	Section 2
nop	bew
yim	clune
zeg	bawp
ild	cheve
jick	blenk
sheb	froast
deeg	scrup
quish	sprace
brop	bar
sleen	sneak
sint	curl
doilt	doze
shin	plank
fang	shrimp
sort	split
chill	stripe
fled	relay
speck	ending
ramp	dolphin
corns	crackers

Section 1: When decoding a pseudoword, all plausible alternative and regional pronunciations are acceptable.

Table 12.2 Scoring Guidance of Non-words Section 1 (Year 1 Phonics Screening Check, STA, 2024)

Pseudoword	Acceptable pronunciation
nop	This item uses the 'n' from 'net' and rhymes with 'mop'
yim	This item uses the 'y' from 'yell' and rhymes with 'dim'
zeg	This item uses the 'z' from 'zip' and rhymes with 'peg'

Pseudoword	Acceptable pronunciation
ild	This item combines the 'i' from 'ill' and the 'ld' from 'hold'
jick	This item uses the 'j' from 'just' and rhymes with 'pick'
sheb	This item uses the 'sh' from 'ship' and rhymes with 'web'
deeg	This item combines the 'd' from 'doom' with the 'ee' from 'weed' and the 'g' from 'big
quish	This item uses the 'qu' from 'quick' and rhymes with 'swish'
brop	This item uses the 'br' from 'brew' and rhymes with 'chop'
sleen	This item uses the 'sl' from 'slurp' and rhymes with 'green'
sint	This item uses the 's' from 'salt' and rhymes with 'mint'
doilt	This item uses the 'd' from 'dairy' and rhymes with 'spoilt'

Section 2: When decoding a pseudo word, all plausible alternative and regional pronunciations are acceptable.

Table 12.3 Scoring Guidance of Non-words Section 2 (Year 1 Phonics Screening Check, STA, 2024)

Pseudoword	Acceptable alternative
bew	This item uses the 'b' from 'bar' and rhymes with 'grew'
clune	This item uses the 'cl' from 'close' and rhymes with 'prune'
baup	This item combines the 'b' from 'bell' with the 'au' from 'audio' and the 'p' from 'hop'
cheve	This item uses the 'ch' from 'chime' and rhymes with 'Steve'
blenk	This item combines the 'bl' from 'blast' with the 'e' from 'bless' and the 'nk' from 'sink'
froast	This item uses the 'fr' from 'frost' and rhymes with 'toast'
scrup	This item uses the 'scr' from 'scrape' and rhymes with 'cup'
sprace	This item uses the 'spr' from 'sprint' and rhymes with 'pace'

13

DEVELOPING A LOVE OF READING

When you open a book and start to read, the words on the page become a seed. They sprout in your mind and grow with delight, planting you in places far out of sight. (Katie Whitehead)

Reading for pleasure is the single biggest indicator of a child's future successes, more than their family circumstances, parent's educational background or their income (OECD, 2002), and yet, worryingly, research tells us that one in five children between 5 and 8 years old do not own a book at home and over half (56%) of young people between 8 and 18 years old do not read for pleasure in their own time (Clark et al., 2023). It's crucial then that we not only equip young children with the skills to decode the written word but also establish and embed a 'love of reading' at an early age, altering children's tendency to view reading as not only for utility but promoting, enticing and inspiring reading for pleasure, for expanding knowledge, for self-fulfilment and for personal development.

Having access to resources and having books of their own really does have an impact on children's attainment. Studies show there is a positive relationship between the estimated number of books in the home and attainment and children who have books of their own enjoy reading more and read more frequently (Clark and Poulton, 2011). There is also consistent evidence that age affects attitudes to reading and reading behaviour – that children enjoy reading less as they get older (Topping, 2010).

The Teachers as Readers project identified three main practices that impacted reading for pleasure pedagogy (Figure 13.1). All three key influencing factors are encompassed by a social reading environment and hinge on the teacher's knowledge of children's literature and how well they know the children in their care.

The research found that reading for pleasure pedagogy must be explicitly planned for and must be:

- **L**earner-led
- **I**nformal
- **S**ocial and supported by
- **T**exts that tempt

Developing a reading for pleasure culture must be planned for and implemented alongside discrete phonics instruction in order for it to be most effective. Children must be taught the hows, whats and whys of reading. Learning specific skills and gaining phonic knowledge provides children with the *how*, but they must also be taught and gain experience of *what* to read and *why*.

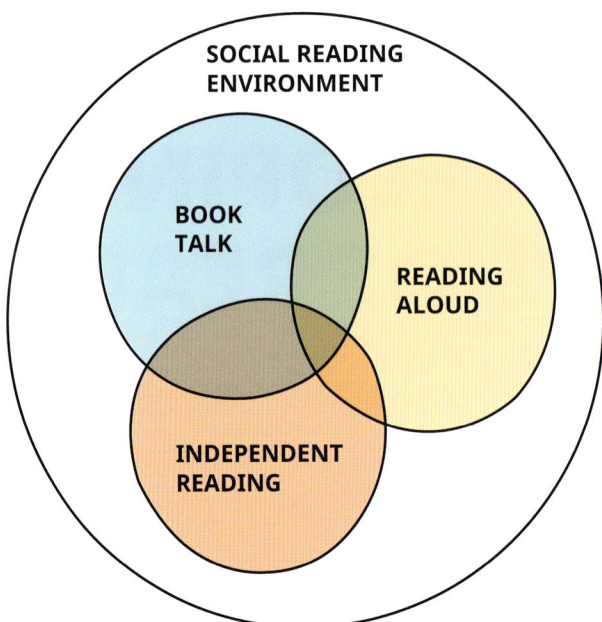

Figure 13.1 The reading for pleasure pedagogy (Open University, 2024)

DECODABLE BOOKS

Children just starting out on their reading journey first need to embed their developing phonic knowledge, develop fluency, achieve independence in reading and gain a sense of accomplishment. It is essential that we provide these children with books that are matched to their current phonic ability. In fact, one of the validation criteria for phonics schemes is to ensure that children have access to decodable books. Resources must be provided to enable teachers to deliver the programme effectively, including sufficient decodable reading material to ensure children can practise by reading texts closely matched to their level of phonic attainment and that do not require them to use alternative strategies to read unknown words (DfE, 2023d).

The very large majority of words within decodable books will be words that children can decode and read independently. Decodable books must be available for children to take home to ensure that they experience success; embed and utilise their phonic knowledge; expand their vocabulary; and develop fluency and comprehension. Some schools may refer to these books as 'show-off' books: children will be familiar with the book from reading it in class and can read the very large majority of the words fluently, so by the time it gets taken home to read to parents they will be 'showing off' their reading ability and independence. Most phonics schemes are aiming for children to be able to read nine-tenths of the words within the book fluently. Any words that children come across that they cannot read fluently they should still be able to decode using their phonic knowledge. There should not be any unfamiliar graphemes or words within these types of books as they can act as a barrier and stop the flow of reading. The National Curriculum (DfE, 2013) outlines statutory requirements that Key Stage 1 children should:

- read aloud accurately books that are consistent with their developing phonic knowledge and that do not require them to use other strategies to work out words
- re-read these books to build up their fluency and confidence in word reading

As an example, a child who is in Reception class and confident in recognising the first digraphs and trigraphs introduced and the stage-appropriate high-frequency words, takes home a book with the following text. The words crossed out are words that are not matched to their currently phonic ability. How can we expect them to develop their fluency, understanding of what they are reading and enjoy it if they cannot read most of the words?

~~What do they like to eat?~~

~~What does~~ a ~~bird like~~ to ~~eat~~?

~~A bird likes~~ to ~~eat worms~~.

~~What does~~ a ~~giraffe like~~ to ~~eat~~?

~~A giraffe likes~~ to ~~eat leaves~~.

~~What does~~ a ~~seal like~~ to ~~eat~~?

~~A seal likes~~ to ~~eat~~ fish.

~~What do you like~~ to ~~eat~~?

(DfE, 2023a)

Learning phonics and reading decodable books are the first crucial steps in developing an enthusiasm for and love of reading. If children can't read the words on the page, they will not build up their fluency, not develop comprehension and will become resistant to reading for any purpose. It's essential that children are not left to fall too far behind and that rapid catch-up programmes are put in place to identify problems and interventions implemented so that this resistance and view of reading does not get embedded and become a life-long trend.

DEVELOPING FLUENCY

Once children are confident at recognising a bank of GPCs, and can use their knowledge to easily decode, the focus needs to shift to supporting their fluency skills. 'Teachers need to ensure that all pupils can read at a speed that allows them to enjoy and understand the books they want to read themselves' (DFE, 2023a. p. 91). It's important that we recognise and appreciate the importance of fluency in the journey to become effective and enthusiastic readers. The Education Endowment Foundation defines reading fluency as: 'The ability to apply and identify the correct pronunciation of written words immediately and without conscious effort. It involves smoothly and effortlessly decoding words while also comprehending and interpreting the text.' There are three factors to fluency:

accuracy – the ability to decode words accurately at a glance and with little effort

automaticity – reading words at an appropriate pace for the text

prosody – using appropriate expression and intonation while considering punctuation

> **Tip 13.1** Fluency is not about being a fast reader! Faster reading does not lead to better reading.

Fluency is the bridge between decoding and comprehension. Building fluency means that children are not having to concentrate all their energy and effort into decoding words, and this therefore frees up cognitive space to really understand what they are reading.

STRATEGIES TO DEVELOP FLUENCY

The Gradual Release of Responsibility Model (Pearson and Gallagher, 1983), heavily based on Vygotsky's Zone of Proximal Development (Vygotsky, 1962, 1978), sets out a strategy of shifting from teacher-modelled tasks to independent practice:

Modelled ⟶ Shared ⟶ Guided ⟶ Independent

We can keep this model in mind when asking children to complete activities that develop fluency, or any learning task for that matter! Students can move back and forth between each of the components as they master skills and strategies.

(1) Modelled

Model reading with fluency – it's important to demonstrate to children what reading with fluency sounds like. Adults can model reading aloud a variety of different texts so that children can hear how they vary pace, add expression and intonation.

Model reading with disfluency – talk like a robot, stop to overtly decode words, read too fast or too slowly, miss pausing at full stops, or read a passage with a monotone voice. Can children spot the problems?

Read aloud across the curriculum – take the chance to read aloud and model fluency across all curriculum areas.

(2) Shared

Read poetry – lots of poems have predictable rhyme and repeated refrains. Poems are great to read aloud and perform too.

Choral reading – ask children to read aloud in unison as part of a whole class or group. This is a useful strategy to build self-confidence and practice reading at an appropriate pace.

(3) Guided

Echo reading – model reading a short passage of a text and ask the children to repeat it back. This is a great way to model adding expression and taking account of punctuation.

Paired reading – children are paired with a reading helper, often a child who is reading at a slightly higher level. This provides a chance to build fluency with a peer.

(4) Independent

Repeated reading – ensure that children have the chance to read the same book several times. This will build their confidence, automaticity and familiarity.

Scooping phrases – instead of pointing at each word, encourage readers to scoop their finger under a group of words and read them in phrases (Figure 13.2). Think about how you would say the sentence below. You don't say each word in a chopping fashion but group words/phrases together. The scooping lines can be pre-drawn or ask children to draw the lines as they initially read and then practise reading the sentence again.

The small wild elephant   sat down next to the watering hole   and began to drink.

Figure 13.2   Scooping phrases

Fluency pyramids – another useful technique is to create fluency pyramids with decodable sentences (Figure 13.3). Children start at the top of the pyramid and a word in the sentence is added at each level until the complete sentence is read at the base. This develops automaticity as children will reread the words a number of times within each pyramid.

A
A boat
A boat can
A boat can sail
A boat can sail in
A boat can sail in the
A boat can sail in the stormy
A boat can sail in the stormy sea.

Figure 13.3   A fluency pyramid

Reading for just 30 minutes a week:

- produces greater life satisfaction
- enhances social connectedness and sense of community spirit
- helps protect against and even prepare for life difficulties.

(Billington, 2015)

SOCIAL READING ENVIRONMENTS

Alongside phonics instruction, the use of decodable books and developing reading fluency, it is crucial to promote a culture of sharing stories and developing a community of readers. Children need to experience the enjoyment and desire to read and realise the importance of reading for pleasure. This starts with the adults around the child having a positive attitude towards reading and children witnessing these same adults reading for a variety of different purposes. Having a positive reading role model can be transformative for children (Cremin et al., 2009). *The Reading Framework* says: 'The main aim of storytelling is to breathe life into the words, capturing children's attention rather than simply entertaining them' (DfE, 2023a, p. 33).

Reading aloud – ensure that there is time planned to read aloud to children but also embrace those *ad hoc* moments to share stories. Reading aloud enables children to access a variety of rich texts that are otherwise above their reading ability. It helps develop a bond between reader and listener; expands oracy skills; prompts discussions; and builds comprehension. There are definitely books that work better than others to read aloud. Books that elicit a strong response and emotional engagement, have a strong narrative that can sustain multiple reads, reflect children's background and cultures and have more opportunities to dramatise and role-play are books that work best to read aloud.

To effectively engage children while reading aloud think **PPP**!

Prepare – read the book beforehand and decide which words, phrases or sentences to emphasise. Are you going to use different voices for the characters? Are there any sentences you are going to say quietly, loudly or with a rushed voice?

Practice – rehearsal and frequent practice will build up the storyteller's confidence and soon you might not even need the book to retell the story.

Pausing – knowing when to pause (and not pause) before a certain word to add emphasis can be really effective. As can knowing when to take time to stop and discuss word meanings.

Special books – adults share texts that they love, but books and stories are chosen that enthuse the children too. Pupil voice is really important here. A nice way of doing this is to regularly ask children to vote for which book is read aloud.

Story time – make sure story time and sharing stories are planned and prioritised. Ensure that they are valued as an essential part of the daily timetable and avoid, as much as possible, dropping story time due to other time constraints. I know this is not always easy. Use story time and independent reading actively rather than as a passive time filler or holding activity. Will children actively engage with stories and books if they only ever get to choose a book to read after they have finished their work? What is the message we are sending about how we value reading in this scenario?

Reading buddies – a lovely way to promote a social reading environment is to arrange children from older year groups to come and share books with children. Peers can act as great reading role models.

Book talk – multiple opportunities, both formal and informal, for readers to share recommendations, discuss reading preferences and explore different reading experiences are a key feature of healthy reading communities.

BOOK NOOKS, CORNERS AND CLASSROOM LIBRARIES

Rich, engaging spaces, both physically and socially, need to be created within the learning environment that send a message about the value you place on reading for pleasure and where the books themselves are made the priority; soft toys, canopies, bean bags and cushions are lovely, but a book corner without the books is just a corner! Book areas need not be made 'for show' but are inviting, cosy and comfortable spaces for children to sit, read and share stories. 'The focus of teachers' time and attention when establishing book corners should be on the quality of books rather than elaborate decorations' (DfE, 2023a). Children need to be given time to access these spaces and know that they can be used spontaneously. Outward-facing texts are displayed to tempt and spaces may also be complemented with role-play opportunities and resources, such as story sacks or boxes, which will prompt children to engage more deeply with stories and gain a greater understanding of the characters. Often the most effective and engaging reading spaces encourage pupil voice and are ones that provide children with the opportunity to take ownership of the area and are designed to be 'reader-led, reader-directed and reader-owned' (Cremin, 2019). Use Worksheet 13.1 at the end of this chapter to audit your book corner and highlight any areas in need of improvement.

CHOICE AND VARIETY

Choice is crucial to foster engagement; it can take just one book that captivates a reader to act as a hook and gateway to developing a reading for pleasure habit. Gambrell (1996, cited in Clark and Rumbold, 2006) found that when children were asked which book they had enjoyed most, 80% of them said that it was the one they had chosen themselves. Ensure that areas are supplied with a feast of books, including fiction, traditional tales, joke books, non-fiction, graphic novels, magazines, comics, newspapers and information leaflets and text they might choose to read again and again. This variety will entice both boys and girls. In all countries, boys not only are less likely than girls to say that they read for enjoyment, but also have different reading habits when they do read for pleasure; girls are more likely to read fiction or magazines, and boys are more likely to read newspapers or comics (OECD, 2010).

DIVERSITY

In order to become enthusiastic and committed readers, children need to meet characters that look like them and read stories that reflect their lives. It's essential that the books that children access feature positive role models, challenge stereotypes and reflect the diverse range of cultures and communities of the school. A lack of representation can have a tangible negative impact on engagement. Representation matters! Research shows that 34.4% of UK school children are black, Asian or minority and yet only 0.7% of pupils study a book written by an author of colour and only 7%

of pupils study a book written by a woman at GCSE (Elliott et al., 2011). The CLPE *Reflecting Realities* (2023) report shows the percentage of children's books published that feature a character of colour. In 2017 just 4% included a character of colour, rising to 20% in 2021. This is a positive step in the right direction, but there is still work to be done. It is vital that teachers develop a clear picture of the diversity of the cultures and communities of the school and gain an understanding of the particular needs of their pupils to help fully engage young learners with reading and develop a reading community; activities and books that work for one school might have very little impact in another setting.

READING BEYOND THE BOOKSHELF

Celebrating World Book Day, dressing up and marking the occasion with an assembly is a lovely way of engaging children with books and bringing the whole school community together, but we must also be persistent and positive in our endeavour to establish a reading culture, not just promoting reading during a yearly event that can quickly get forgotten about. It's vital that there is a whole school effort to celebrate the majesty of literature on a daily basis. So, besides all of the above strategies, how else can we engage children with reading outside of the classroom walls?

Reading outdoors – those children who are not actively engaged with reading in the classroom may become more enthusiastic about choosing to read if there is an opportunity to select books, sit and read in spaces outside the classroom. Book sheds in the playground, cosy book nooks in corridors or a regular 'booknic' could prove to be very popular and effective.

Library visits – if you have a school library then make sure you have allocated time to visit and for children to browse the books on offer. All local libraries encourage school visits if this is feasible, and many welcome the opportunity to come into the school and talk about the library services and seasonal reading challenges on offer. Research has found that students' engagement and interest in reading is strengthened when they visit a well equipped library (Iheakanwa et al., 2021).

Author visits – where the school budget allows, arranging author visits to share their books is a great way to engage children. You can also listen to authors read their work aloud online. In fact, the National Literacy Trust recently published a report analysing data from the National Literacy Survey, and found that more children and young people who had experienced an author visit said that they enjoyed reading in their free time compared with their peers who hadn't had a visit (58.6% versus 39.3%) and these children also rated their reading skill as high compared with their peers who didn't have an author visit (Clark and Picton, 2023).

Reading aloud across the curriculum – make sure that time is planned for reading and reading aloud to take place in curriculum subjects other than English.

Subject knowledge – all staff need to be knowledgeable about children's literature and aware of their power to influence children's views of reading.

Parents – ensure that parents have an understanding of why reading for pleasure is crucial and share ways they can support their child with reading at home.

IN SUMMARY

- Reading for pleasure is the single biggest indicator of a child's future successes, more than their family circumstances, parent's educational background or their income (OECD, 2002).
- To develop a love of reading children need to practise and consolidate their phonic knowledge by reading matched decodable books.
- Once children are confident at decoding, the focus then needs to shift to developing fluency to free up space in their working memory to comprehend and enjoy what they are reading.
- It's vital that children view reading not just for utility but for self-fulfilment and for developing knowledge.
- It's important that a school aims to establish a reading for pleasure culture where children are inspired to read.

BOOK AREA CHECKLIST

Worksheet 13.1 A checklist of your book area

Classrooms have a designated quiet, comfortable and uncluttered space for children to sit down with books. These spaces are not placed in an area that has a constant stream of traffic	
Books are displayed in an appealing way and are easily accessible	
Interesting books are displayed at eye level	
Books are rotated frequently	
Include a variety of texts, including fiction, non-fiction, comics, magazines and graphic novels	
The diversity of the school community is reflected in the books on offer	
Key vocabulary is displayed	
Chance for children to take ownership of the area, including choice of books	
Role-play or story sacks available to deepen understanding of stories	
Evidence of children reading alone, in pairs and small groups	
Time allocated for all children to visit the book area, but also children know that they can access it spontaneously	
Curriculum books used in lessons are made available for children to also access independently	
Books are regularly checked for damage and quickly replaced	
Include around 30–40 books that have already been read aloud to pupils	
Decodable books used as part of phonics programme are stored separately	
Regularly audit the book stock	
Key questions are displayed to support adult–child interactions	
Adults regularly model using the book area	
Adults regularly survey how, when and who uses the book area	

14

WHAT DOES AN EFFECTIVE PHONICS LESSON LOOK LIKE?

In 2021 the government introduced a process whereby publishers of phonics schemes could submit a self-assessment, apply to be assessed against core criteria and obtain government-validation. This process was designed to help schools choose a scheme that had been rigorously scrutinised by a panel of experts, met a list of standards and would prove to be an effective systematic, synthetic phonics programme. When the validation process closed, after three rounds of applications, the government listed 45 validated schemes.

Choosing a validated phonics scheme is not a statutory requirement and those schools that consistently achieve good outcomes, particularly in the results of the Year 1 screening check, are able to design and follow their own scheme, albeit ensuring they still meet the core criteria. The key word here is *fidelity*. Whether using their own scheme or buying into a validated one, a school must prove that they are remaining consistent and follow the programme with rigour in terms of teaching, planning, training, resourcing, assessment and interventions on offer. They need to ensure that they are not cherry-picking from a selection of different programmes and resources. As a result, many schools chose to purchase and follow one of the validated schemes to ensure fidelity across the school and, more realistically, aim to limit the amount of scrutiny from Ofsted that they might receive if they were to follow a school-devised programme.

Considering this process, schools across England are currently implementing a variety of different phonics programmes. However, it's worth noting that all these programmes must meet core criteria and standards, and all have the ultimate goal of children becoming fluent, enthusiastic and committed readers. I like to think of the choice of different schemes a bit like choosing toothpaste. There is a whole variety of different brands and flavours to purchase but they all need to contain the ingredients that help to keep our teeth clean. All the schemes, whether validated or self-made, need to contain the key elements of an effective phonics programme. It's these key elements that make for effective and successful instruction. So, what are these key elements and what does an effective phonics lesson actually look like?

KEY ELEMENTS OF A PHONICS LESSON

Here are some components that are important to teaching phonics well.

Systematic and Synthetic

An effective lesson will clearly demonstrate progression from the previous lesson. This could be following the scheme's progression map and introducing the next GPC for the children's stage or providing a chance for children to practise and embed skills, such as blending or segmenting. It also needs to be obvious that the use of synthetic phonics is your prime approach to teaching reading so, for example, you model segmenting the phonemes within words or children can utilise their phonic knowledge to segment and spell words. You are not asking them to guess words from a picture or sight-read newly introduced tricky high-frequency words without discussing the part of the word that is irregular first.

Revisit and Review

Effective lessons will always start with revisiting and reviewing previously taught knowledge and skills. This ensures the movement of knowledge and skills from short-term to long-term memory and also that lessons do not become 'bubble' lessons (i.e., once you've introduced a GPC it's never revisited). Successful reviews will include children revisiting previously taught GPCs both outside and within a word. This could be through reading both GPC and word flashcards, stand-up/sit-down type games, drawing sound buttons or sorting word cards according to the graphemes they contain. The focus will be to recap and embed knowledge from previous lessons.

Teach

The next element of a good phonics lesson will be to teach a new GPC or skill. Adults need to explicitly share the learning intention with the children; they need to know what they are learning and how they can achieve this. Within this section of the lesson it is really important that adults model to children. They need to ensure that they are articulating the phonemes correctly when introducing a new GPC and that they are encouraging children to do the same. New skills are also modelled so that children can clearly see and hear what the outcome needs to be – modelling blending sounds to read a word, breaking up a word to spell or demonstrating what a fluent reader sounds like.

Practice

Within a good phonics lesson children are given time to practise using the newly introduced GPC or practise the newly taught skill. This is quite often the part of the phonics lesson that involves a game or interactive element. Again, it's essential that lessons do not become 'bubble' lessons, so the large majority of the words children will be reading will include the new GPC but a few will revisit and review other GPCs previously taught.

Apply

Once you have taught a new GPC or skill, and children have had a chance to practise, they will also need the opportunity to apply their phonic knowledge. This will be the part of the lesson where children will be either reading or writing words and sentences that contain the new GPCs and putting new knowledge into context.

Pace

To help keep children actively engaged with a lesson it's essential that you pace the lesson appropriately. This will be about knowing the children in your lesson and realising when it's time to move on with the lesson or time to pause and revisit. You will need to keep a look-out for the obvious signs that children are becoming disengaged. Phonics lessons shouldn't need to have children sitting on the carpet for extensive periods of time. Make sure there is some movement involved to keep children on task. Think also about things that might affect the pace of the lesson, such as not having resources ready and easily accessible. If you use whiteboards and whiteboard pens, when is the best time for children to get them? If you need groups of children for a game, have them pre-planned or find a quick strategy to group them so that the pace of the lesson is not affected. If children take too long to sort out working with a partner, then they are missing vital teaching time. Make every second of the phonics session count!

Well Resourced

An effective phonics scheme should 'provide resources that support the teaching of lower-case and capital letters correctly, with clear start and finish points, and that will move children on by teaching them to write words made up of learned GPCs, followed by simple sentences composed from such words and any common-exception words learned'. It should also 'include guidance and resources to ensure children practise and apply the core phonics they've been taught' (DfE, 2023d). This means that all schemes will be accompanied by a selection of scheme-matched appropriate resources, and it's these resources that teachers need to use to show fidelity. The resources should also be available for children to access independently outside of a phonics session as an aid for reading and writing. Sound mats, grapheme charts and high-frequency word lists are also displayed and made available on 'help desks' to support children. Any further non-scheme specific resources (whiteboards, highlighters, pens, etc.) need to be easily accessible to the children, frequently checked for damage and quickly replaced.

Multi-Sensory

Again, multi-sensory resources and activities will help keep children actively engaged and provide movement to the lesson. Children are not just sitting for the entire lesson reading word cards, but opportunities are provided to consolidate learning through the use of games, writing on whiteboards, watching a skill being modelled, writing in phonics books, putting hands on their heads to respond to questions, among other things. All of these methods, however, still have a clear focus on practising and applying new knowledge. Strategies are also in place to avoid 'hands-up' responses and singling out individual children to answer questions. A good lesson will see children reading in unison and ensure all children participate and join in.

Planned Decodable Words

Effective phonics planning will have pre-planned decodable words to introduce during the lesson. This not only ensures that there is progression across lessons but also that the words contain both the newly taught GPCs and GPCs that need to be revisited. Planned words will have a positive impact on the pace of the lesson too as adults will not have to think of words to use in the moment. Imagine teaching the grapheme 'ir' without any pre-planned words. What words are you going to ask children to read and write? Are they fully decodable and do they contain graphemes that children know? This same logic applies to asking children within the lesson for words that contain a certain GPC. For example, suppose you are teaching 'ai' so you ask children to think of 'ai' words. You are going to get responses such as 'play', 'day' and 'cake', all of which do not contain the correct grapheme. Having pre-planned word cards ensures that the lesson remains focused on the learning intention rather than children randomly plucking words from their heads.

Reading and Writing Opportunities

Lessons need to ensure that children can frequently apply their phonic knowledge in both reading and writing and that there is a balance of both within a lesson and across the weekly plan. Time needs to be spent practising both blending for reading and segmenting for spelling and writing.

Assessment for Learning

There must be opportunities for adults to assess children's knowledge within the lesson. This could be through children's verbal responses, reading of word cards, spelling words on whiteboards and writing sentences on paper or in books. Adults need to assess whether the large majority of the children have achieved the learning intention and can move on with their learning or perhaps spend some time revisiting.

Adaptations

Based on assessment for learning, adults should be confident to adapt planning in order to address misconceptions or plug gaps in knowledge. The children may need more time to practise a new skill or to embed their knowledge of certain GPCs, and lesson plans should reflect this. This is a vital process. Never be afraid to adapt plans and revisit; this is a sign of excellent teaching practice.

Subject Knowledge

For phonics instruction to be effective it is essential that *all* staff working with the year groups that receive phonics instruction are appropriately trained. They need to be trained in delivering the specific school scheme but also have been allocated time to develop their own subject knowledge and get to grips with all the terminology that comes with teaching phonics (this might be the reason why you are reading this book!).

A Phonics-Rich Environment

Just as we create a language-rich environment to help develop all the key foundational skills of phonics, we need to provide children with opportunities to consolidate and embed their phonic knowledge outside of the phonics lesson, within reading matched decodable texts and across other areas of the curriculum. Children need to see a purpose and use for phonics in their reading and writing and that learning phonics is not exclusive and constrained to a phonics lesson. Previously taught graphemes, focus graphemes and high-frequency words should be on display within the environment, with children knowing how and when to refer to these displays to assist them. When children are independently able to demonstrate their phonic knowledge, this is a sure sign that this knowledge is embedded and secure. If children are never provided with opportunities to self-direct and play literacy games, access resources and read and write independently, without the support of an adult, then they aren't ever able to demonstrate their independent phonic ability. An adult's role here is to observe, assist if needed and address any misconceptions, but also allow children to consolidate and embed as independently as possible.

Data-Driven

There are also systems in place for regular assessment of children, both formatively through observations and assessment for learning opportunities and through planned summative assessments at the end of a unit of teaching. The assessment should cover grapheme recognition, decodable word reading and high-frequency word reading. Teachers then need to show evidence that they are analysing the outcomes of these assessments and adapting their planning to plug any gaps in phonic knowledge. Don't feel like you have to rush and plough through the scheme in order to fit everything in! If gaps are not addressed, which could mean reteaching to a small group or whole class, then these gaps only get wider and children will struggle to move on to more complex concepts if they are not secure in the previous step.

The ABC Rule

For effective phonics instruction I like to follow the ABC rule. It really is as simple as ABC! This rule essentially simplifies the key elements I discuss above. It is a cycle of teaching where you are data-driven; teach new knowledge and skills; and then provide chances to consolidate learning and repeat (Figure 14.1).

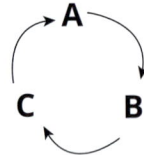

Figure 14.1   The ABC of effective phonics teaching

Assess – regular diagnostic assessments, both formative and summative, highlight if children have any gaps in knowledge or are not confident with certain skills.

Build knowledge – using assessment, aim to plug the gaps and develop skills by revisiting and reviewing prior learning and adapting planning. Teach new knowledge and skills in a systematic way, starting with the simplest sounds and building up to the most complex.

Consolidate – make sure children have the chance to practise and apply new knowledge as frequently as possible within the lesson and also provide opportunities to independently embed new learning in a fun, engaging and practical way.

INTERVIEW LESSONS

So, you have got to the end of your teacher training course and have successfully secured an interview for a teaching position. During the interview process you will most likely be asked to teach a lesson, and this lesson can often be to deliver a short phonics session to a class or group of children. It can be a little overwhelming when you receive the 'invite to interview' letter and read that you need to plan and deliver phonics to a group of unfamiliar children. If you are in this scenario, here are a few of my top tips to hopefully settle your nerves and put you in the best possible position to deliver a great lesson and receive a call that you've got the job!

1   If the school has not mentioned the scheme they follow in the invite letter, then contact them to find this out. It will show them that you are aware of how phonics needs to be taught using a systematic programme – whether it be a validated scheme or a school-based one – and that you want to show fidelity and remain aligned to how children are usually taught. Find out where the children are in their learning and ask the school to send you the weekly or daily plan that they should be working on. If you are not familiar with the scheme used, then many of the validated ones have videos and resources available to access on their website. Just do a Google search and find out a bit more about the programme they follow.

2   If the school do not offer you the current phonics plans and would like you to plan and deliver your own session based on their brief overview then ensure that you plan time to revisit and review, teach a new grapheme or skill, give a chance for children to practise word reading with the new grapheme and then apply their

knowledge by either reading or writing a short caption or sentence (age-dependent).

3   If you are unable to find out the specific graphemes the children are working on and just have to go off the outline of the lesson from the letter (e.g., 'children are working in phase 3') then plan to teach to the middle-ability children but demonstrate how you would extend and support the learning of the higher- and lower-ability children.

4   Even though you are only delivering the phonics lesson during the interview you can show in your planning how you would provide opportunities to consolidate and embed learning after the lesson, within the provision and within other curriculum areas.

5   Ask the school to give you a little more information about the make-up of the children. How many children will you be teaching? How many are included as part of their focused lower 20% of children that are currently working below the expected standard in reading? Are there specific learning needs you need to be aware of or children with special educational needs and disabilities? You can adapt your planning to target and support these children within the lesson. Do they have carpet spaces? Regularly move to tables during the session? Try to get a picture of the children and the usual teaching practice.

6   Enquire about the resources that will be available to you. Will there be an interactive whiteboard? Word cards? Can the children access wipeable whiteboards and pens easily? This will indicate to you the resources you need to prepare before the interview day. Try to keep the lesson as simple as possible and not rely too heavily on technology; typically, it will not work properly on the interview day!

7   If you are following a plan from a scheme, or have written your own lesson plan, then ensure that it includes time for movement and is as interactive as possible within the time and space constraints. Think about behaviour strategies that you are confident with and can easily implement with a group of unfamiliar children – hands on your head, copy me or speaking quietly so children really need to listen can work really well. Avoid using hands-up: firstly, you won't know the children's names; and secondly, phonics is a perfect lesson to model and have children repeat in unison.

8   Try and practise the lesson with a group of children before the interview day. You will be able to judge things that worked well or things that you may need to adapt. It will also give you an idea of timings and pace.

During the interview day you will also take part in a formal interview with members of the senior leadership team (SLT). They may ask you to reflect on how well the lesson went. Was there anything that you would do differently? What worked and how would you extend the learning? This is a real chance for you to show that you are a reflective teacher and be confident to talk about the positives as well as identify some areas of development. Remember, the SLT will not be expecting the lesson to be perfect, especially if you are new to teaching, they just want to gain a sense of your enthusiasm for the role and that you are willing to continue learning on the job. Other than more generic questions about safeguarding, teamwork or behaviour management, they may ask you some more subject-specific questions. Below I've written a few potential questions, along with example answers.

Why use a systematic, synthetic phonics programme? Children need to be taught to read, it doesn't come naturally. Synthetic phonics gives children the key to decode all words, from simple CVC words to the more complex, and if introduced systematically it gives children the best possible chance of becoming successful fluent readers and moving from learning to read to reading to learn.

How would you promote a love of reading within your classroom? I would ensure that I plan in time for children to independently read and choose from a range of materials, including fiction, graphic novels, information texts and magazines. I would make sure that I create an inviting and accessible reading area where children feel comfortable to sit, read and share stories. I would also make sure that the books available to children reflect the diversity and cultures of the children. It is crucial that children see themselves reflected in the stories they read, and this will impact their engagement. I would ensure 'pupil voice' and create a voting system so that children can choose the book that is read aloud daily and make sure that I read aloud not only in English lessons but across all areas of the curriculum. It is also vital to get parents on board to create a reading for pleasure community, so I would aim to arrange workshops and information meetings to explain to parents why reading for pleasure is so important and talk to them about how they can support their child's reading at home.

How would you support the bottom 20% of readers? I would ensure that I completed regular diagnostic assessments so that gaps in knowledge are highlighted and consequently adapt my planning to address the gaps within the phonics lessons. If I am teaching the whole class, then I would ensure these children are positioned so that I can support them if needed and they remain engaged with the lessons. It's crucial that additional support and interventions are given to the bottom 20% so they rapidly catch up and the gap does not widen. These interventions might be through small group work, one-to-one support or more tailored teaching daily. This would be dependent on what assessments tell us and where the gaps are.

What strategies would you use to help struggling readers develop their fluency and comprehension? I will ensure that the decodable books are completely matched to their phonic ability so that children can actually decode and read the words within the book and gain confidence. Repetitive reading of the books will also develop fluency and comprehension, and I would ensure that children have multiple opportunities to read the same book in class. I would also model 'thinking aloud' and talking about the story to develop comprehension. I would read aloud regularly to demonstrate what reading with fluency looks like and what the end goal is.

What would you say to a parent who says that the reading book their child brings home is too easy? I would explain that the book is completely matched to their child's current phonic ability. This means that they should be able to fluently read around nine-tenths of the words and use their phonic knowledge to decode the rest. There should not be any words within the book that they can't read. This might mean that it seems too easy because they can read all the words, but that is exactly what we are aiming for! We have been reading the book in class too, so by the time the child brings it home they should be showing off their independent reading skills and the focus needs to shift to showing they can read fluently and have a chance to talk about the story. This method of repetitive reading will build confidence, fluency and a deeper understanding of the text. Please be assured that through regular assessments the books will always reflect the child's phonic knowledge.

IN SUMMARY

- No matter the phonics scheme, there are key elements that make for an effective phonics lesson that will remain consistent across all schemes.
- These factors include time to revisit and review previously taught graphemes, modelling, the pace of the lesson and ensuring that the lesson is well resourced.
- It's essential that a school completes regular diagnostic assessments to highlight gaps in knowledge and is confident to adapt planning in order to address the gaps.

LESSON OBSERVATION TEMPLATE

Worksheet 14.1 A lesson observation template where you can write in your notes

Essential characteristics	Achieved	Comment
Clear **planning** is available identifying the parts/sections of the discrete lesson and showing progress over a series of lessons	Yes No	
All children can clearly hear/see the teaching input, or the object(s) being used to support the teaching	Yes No	
The session is **fully interactive** for most children for most of the time	Yes No	
The teacher's **articulation of phonemes** is correct	Yes No	
Children are required to **articulate phonemes** themselves, not just listen to the adult doing so	Yes No	
Children are being taught how to **blend and/or segment**	Yes No	
The session is **multi-sensory** but tightly focused on the learning goal	Yes No	
There is an effective leadership of **additional adults** to support effective learning for all pupils	Yes No	
There is evidence of **new learning (challenge)**, not just consolidation	Yes No	
Resources are pre-prepared and used effectively to support pupil learning	Yes No	
The **pace of the learning** is appropriate for the group	Yes No	
There is evidence of **differentiation** within the discrete phonic session	Yes No	
Assessment opportunities are built into the discrete phonic session	Yes No	

15
OFSTED INSPECTIONS AND READING DEEP DIVES

Above all, remember you know your children and the best way to support them to become effective and enthusiastic readers! Make sure you tell Ofsted this! (Katie Whitehead)

With early reading remaining at the forefront of education, when Ofsted visit a school for a graded inspection they will conduct a reading deep dive. This is a mandatory process for every infant, middle and primary school as Ofsted wants *all* children to experience good phonics teaching, to be able to learn to read early and read fluently as quickly as possible. The deep dive will entail a thorough subject inspection and the examination of how reading is taught across the school. If you are the reading subject lead you will most certainly be timetabled to meet with the inspectors and perhaps complete learning walks and lesson observations alongside them. If you are not the reading subject lead then it's still really important that you have knowledge of how reading is taught across the school, and what is involved in a reading deep dive, as inspectors can ask questions to any member of the school community, including parents.

Inspectors will consider the *intent* of the curriculum, how well children gain skills and knowledge to achieve the appropriate age-related expectations. They will evaluate how effectively you *implement* the curriculum through teaching and learning, and the overall *impact* it is having on pupil outcomes. Ofsted will want to drill down into teaching and learning, look for trends and identify any tendencies in practice. Its primary purpose, as outlined in the *Education Inspection Framework*, is to be 'a force for improvement through intelligent, responsible and focused inspection and regulation' (Ofsted, 2023).

Intent $\longrightarrow$ Implementation $\longrightarrow$ Impact

Perhaps during an inspection, a Year 2 child says that they 'don't like reading'. Through observations and book looks, does this statement marry up with teaching practice? Is this the current trend across the school, or is it just one child's opinion? Inspectors will pick up and follow this line of inquiry to fully assess the quality of education, identify areas of good practice and areas in need of improvement. They will consider a variety of different sources when making their judgements and triangulate evidence from teaching practice, pupil outcomes and pupil voice (Figure 15.1).

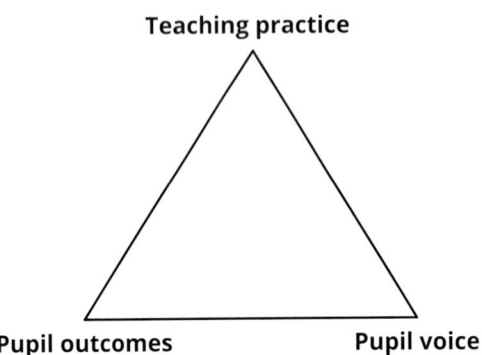

Figure 15.1   The triangulation of evidence for Ofsted

The *School Inspection Handbook* (2024) contains key expectations which inspectors will consider when making a judgement about the quality of reading provision within a school. They will consider whether:

- The school is determined that every pupil will learn to read, regardless of their background, needs or abilities. All pupils, including the weakest readers, make sufficient progress to meet or exceed age-related expectations.
- Stories, poems, rhymes and non-fiction are chosen for reading to develop pupils' vocabulary, language comprehension and love of reading. Pupils are familiar with and enjoy listening to a wide range of stories, poems, rhymes and non-fiction.
- The school's phonics programme matches or exceeds the expectations of the national curriculum and the EYFS early learning goals. The school has clear expectations of pupils' phonics progress term by term, particularly from Reception to Year 2.
- The sequence of reading books shows a cumulative progression in phonics knowledge that is matched closely to the school's phonics programme. Teachers give pupils sufficient practice in reading and re-reading books that match the grapheme–phoneme correspondences they know, both at school and at home.
- Reading, including the teaching of systematic synthetic phonics, is taught from the beginning of Reception.
- The ongoing assessment of pupils' phonics progress is sufficiently frequent and detailed to identify any pupil who is falling behind the programme's pace. If they do fall behind, targeted support is given immediately.
- The school has developed sufficient expertise in the teaching of phonics and reading.

This all sounds like an incredibly daunting process and my hope is that in the future this chapter will not be necessary. I have faith that with a change in government the focus of Ofsted will also change, and a school inspection will become a much more collaborative, supportive and reflective experience rather than it feeling like something that schools are subjected to. However, at the time of writing the Ofsted inspection and rating system is still in place. Unfortunately, you can't disregard this chapter just yet! I have not written it to worry or add to anxiety, but offer a little support. My aim here is to equip you with everything you need to know about reading deep dives, the questions that inspectors might ask and the supporting evidence you could provide to answer them.

Although I can't give you the exact questions inspectors might ask during their visit, as this will vary according to the particular focus of the school and the School Development Plan (e.g., whether you have adopted a validated scheme or are showing a downward trend in Year 1 screening results), I can offer a list of the potential questions that may arise. I have been part of this process, either during the full inspections or through arranged 'Mocksteds', many times during my teaching career and there is definitely a pattern to the types of questions that are asked.

THE FIVE WS OF OFSTED EVIDENCE

Firstly, to help prepare for the inspection and the reading deep dive it is useful to think about the five Ws.

(1) What?

This is your curriculum content for teaching phonics and reading. Do you follow a validated scheme or have you created your own to follow? What ways do you teach reading outside of phonics? What does phonics look like in Key Stage 2? What do you assess?

(2) Why?

Why have you chosen the particular scheme to follow (validated or school-derived)? Did you choose it to tighten up teaching? Did it offer a good selection of matched decodable books that you previously didn't have? Is there a rigorous assessment procedure in place that you were lacking before?

(3) When?

This is your specific teaching timetable. When is phonics taught across the school? When do intervention groups happen? Is there an allocated time during the week to read with an adult as part of a small group?

(4) Where?

Where does phonics teaching take place and does it reflect the recommendations in *The Reading Framework* to be within a quiet space with few distractions? Are there displays in the classroom that children can access to support their reading and writing? Do the resources you use across the school show fidelity to your chosen scheme?

(5) Who?

This is all about accessibility of the phonics teaching for all learners. Who are the children in need of interventions? Is there a SEND programme as part of your chosen scheme? Who are your bottom 20% of children that are currently working below the expected standard? Are assessments used to adapt planning and plug gaps in phonic knowledge? Who still needs to access phonics teaching in KS2?

HOW WILL OFSTED GAIN EVIDENCE TO EVALUATE THE TEACHING OF READING?

As I mentioned above, Ofsted will almost certainly arrange an interview with the phonics or reading subject lead. This may or may not be alongside other members of the SLT. It's useful to take along any evidence you have. Inspectors will complete observations of phonics lessons and reading sessions across the school, they will look at classroom displays, help desks and reading areas. They will likely take a sample of the books that you send home for children who are still accessing the main phonics programme to ensure that they are fully decodable and matched to children's phonic ability. Inspectors will also read with a selection of pupils, normally a few children who sit within the bottom 20% from Years 1–3. They may want to observe any intervention groups that are taking place and during learning walks speak with individual children as well as potentially having a group discussion with a small group of pupils; these children will likely be chosen by the school, so select carefully those who are confident to speak as part of a group, offer their opinion and paint the school in the best light!

POTENTIAL QUESTION AND RESPONSE BANK

Example 15.1   Reading deep dive questions and potential supporting evidence

How do you assess and track pupils' progress? **How do you identify and support the bottom 20% of pupils?**
Potential evidence: • Regular phonics assessments completed to identify gaps in phonic knowledge and used to inform planning • Assessments identify children who are 'on track', and for those who are at risk of falling behind regular and rigorous intervention groups are in place • Additional tutoring groups for children who need rapid catch-up • Targeted support offered within the whole class phonics lesson for children who are working at a lower level, i.e. consideration of seating, tailored questioning or support from additional adults

- Assessment data are inputted into a system so that children's progress can be tracked
- Additional one-to-one reading is offered outside of the reading sessions
- Staff attend regular pupil progress meetings with members of the SLT to identify and track children within the bottom 20% and have the opportunity to reflect on their practice and ask for additional support
- Parents are regularly informed of their child's progress through parent–teacher meetings and information is regularly shared on how best to support their child at home

How do you promote a love of reading, expand vocabulary and develop comprehension?

How does reading fit within the wider curriculum?

Potential evidence:

- Time is allocated for staff to model reading for pleasure
- Regular opportunities are taken for adults to read aloud to the class across all curriculum subjects
- Children participate in frequent small group reading sessions
- Story time is planned into the daily timetable
- Children have free access to a wealth of books and other reading materials
- Every class has an inviting and comfortable book area where the books are made the priority
- Time is given for children to visit the school library
- Core texts are identified for each year group
- Planning includes poetry and non-fiction texts
- A whole-school programme is in place to develop oracy skills
- Regular book audits are completed and reading areas show that they are well looked after
- There is evidence of pupil voice in the decision-making, i.e. choosing the types of text that are included in the book area
- Books reflect the diversity of the school community
- Reading is celebrated across the school, including special events such as author visits and World Book Day
- Parents are informed about the importance of reading for pleasure and there is evidence of a positive and effective home–school link

Are the books children read matched to their phonics knowledge, and when are children given time to practise?

Potential evidence:

- Children have access to a collection of fully decodable books for each phonics stage
- A system is in place to track children's progress and this information is used to match ability with book
- A home reading timetable is in place for children to take home both decodable books and quality picture books to share
- Regular book audits are in place to check for damage, and books are quickly repaired or replaced
- There are timetabled group reading sessions across a week
- One-to-one reading time with an adult
- Children have the opportunity to embed their phonic knowledge outside the phonics lesson within the classroom provision and other subject areas
- Adults complete formative assessments during the daily phonics lesson
- Adults complete regular summative assessments, and this information is used to match books

(Continued)

Example 15.1 (Continued)

How is reading taught from the very beginning?
Potential evidence: • There is a focus on phonological awareness in the early years and children are provided with experiences that develop foundational speaking and listening skills   • An aspirational long-term plan is in place that shows the progression of skills   • A collection of wordless books are available for those children who are not yet secure with a small number of GPCs to blend and read   • A collection of systematic and synthetic decodable books are available for children right from the beginning of school once they are secure with a small bank of GPCs   • Observations, monitoring visits and learning walks demonstrate a consistency in teaching all through the school   • Medium-term plans demonstrate an immediate practice of blending to read once enough GPCs have been learnt   • Parents have the opportunity to attend workshops and information meetings to find out how to support their child right from the very beginning   • Evidence of links with feeder nurseries and preschools   • Baseline assessments are carried out and these are used to inform planning and track pupil progress
How are staff trained in the delivery of phonics and reading in order to gain sufficient expertise?
Potential evidence: • Regular lesson observations, monitoring visits and learning walks are in place to support staff in delivering the programme and ensure a consistency and fidelity to the scheme   • Opportunities to team teach, observe model lessons and receive coaching   • Time is allocated in staff or team meetings to focus on phonics and reading and share good practice   • Evidence of CPD training for all staff   • Outside support via School Improvement Partners or English Hubs   • Staff are given opportunities to visit other settings   • Attendance at Local Authority or Trust network meetings   • New staff are immediately trained   • Support staff are trained and CPD routinely offered   • Planning, preparation and assessment (PPA) time is protected so that lead staff can observe others or complete learning walks

Ofsted inspectors may also ask questions to individual children during learning walks or prearranged group discussion with a selection of pupils. What questions might they ask pupils? It's useful to know these as it's not only a good way to prepare them for the Ofsted visit and walkaround but it is also really good practice to regularly ask children these questions in order to develop pupil voice within the school.

What is your favourite book?

When do you read with an adult?

What books have you taken home?

Does your teacher read stories aloud to you?

What other subjects do you read in?

Do you enjoy phonics?

Do you enjoy reading?

Ultimately, the most valuable piece of supporting evidence during a reading deep dive is to demonstrate that you know the children in your school really well and you can confidently articulate this to inspectors. You really do know your children best and what is the most effective way to support them to become fluent, confident and enthusiastic readers. Let this knowledge and enthusiasm for teaching reading shine through. You are the expert!

IN SUMMARY

When completing a reading deep dive, Ofsted inspectors will:

- consider the *intent* of the curriculum and how well children gain skills and knowledge to achieve the appropriate age-related expectations
- observe how effectively you *implement* the curriculum through teaching and learning
- evaluate the overall *impact* your curriculum is having on pupil outcomes

SELF-REVIEW FRAMEWORK

To help prepare for the potential questions and collect your supporting evidence, use the proforma below to gather your ideas and collate your notes.

Worksheet 15.1   A self-review framework with space to make reflective notes

How do you ensure early reading is prioritised?
Notes:
How do you assess and track pupils' progress?
Notes:
How do you identify and support the bottom 20% of pupils?
Notes:
How do you promote a love of reading, expand vocabulary and develop comprehension?
Notes:
How does reading fit within the wider curriculum?
Notes:

Are the books children read matched to their phonics knowledge, and when are children given time to practise?

Notes:

How is reading taught from the very beginning?

Notes:

How are staff trained in the delivery of phonics and reading in order to gain sufficient expertise?

Notes:

What do you do to ensure pupils in Key Stage 2 continue to make progress in reading?

Notes:

What plans do you have to improve next year?

Notes:

REFERENCES

Adams, M.J. (1990) *Beginning to Read: Learning and Thinking about Print*. London: MIT Press.

Allyn, P. (2015) Reading is like breathing in; writing is like breathing out. Literacy Now. *International Literacy Association*. www.literacyworldwide.org/blog/literacy-now/2015/07/16/reading-is-like-breathing-in-writing-is-like-breathing-out

Ben-Shachar, M., Dougherty, R.F. and Wandell, B.A. (2007) White matter pathways in reading. *Current Opinion in Neurobiology*, 17, 258–270.

Billington, J. (2015) *Reading Between the Lines: The Benefits of Reading for Pleasure*. Quick Reads, Centre for Research into Reading, University of Liverpool.

Both-de Vries, A.C. and Bus, A.G. (2008) Name writing: A first step to phonetic writing? *Literacy, Teaching and Learning*, 12(2), 37–55.

Bottineau, D. (2008) The submorphemic conjecture in English: Towards a distributed model of the cognitive dynamics of submorphemes. *Lexis* [online], 2. http://journals.openedition.org/lexis/688

Bryant, P.E., Bradley, L., Maclean, M. and Crossland, J. (1989) Nursery rhymes, phonological skills and reading. *Journal of Child Language*, 16(2), 407–428.

Centre for Literacy in Primary Education (CLPE) (2023) *Reflecting Realities. Survey of Ethnic Representation within UK Children's Literature 2022*. London: CLPE.

Clark, C. and Dugdale, G. (2008) *Literacy Changes Lives: The Role of Literacy in Offending Behaviour*. London: National Literacy Trust.

Clark, C. and Picton, I. (2023) *Author Visits in Schools, and Children and Young People's Reading and Writing Engagement in 2023*. London: National Literacy Trust.

Clark, C. and Poulton, L. (2011) *Book Ownership and its Relation to Reading Enjoyment, Attitudes, Behaviour and Attainment*. London: National Literacy Trust.

Clark., C., Picton, I. and Galway, M. (2023) *Children and Young People's Reading in 2023*. London: National Literacy Trust.

Clark, C. and Rumbold, K. (2006) *Reading for Pleasure: A Research Overview*. London: The National Literacy Trust.

Collins, K. and Glover, M. (2015) *I Am Reading: Nurturing Young Children's Meaning Making and Joyful Engagement with Any Book*. Portsmouth: Heinemann.

Cree, A., Kay, A. and Steward, J. (2022) *The Economic and Social Cost of Illiteracy: A Snapshot of Illiteracy in a Global Context*. World Literacy Foundation.

Cremin, T. (2019) *Reading Communities: Why, What and How?* NATE Primary Matters.

Cremin, T., Mottram, M., Collins, F., Powell, P. and Safford. K. (2009) Teachers as readers: building communities of readers. *Literacy*, 43(1), 11–19.

Crystal, D. (2005) *How language Works*. London: Penguin.

David, A. (2020) Reading to children is so powerful, so simple and yet so misunderstood. London: National Literacy Trust.

Dehaene, S. (2009) *Reading in the Brain: The Science of How We Read*. New York: Penguin Books.

Department for Education (DfE) (2011) *Teachers' Standards in England from September 2012*. London: DfE.

DfE (2013) *The National Curriculum in England*. London: DfE.

DfE (2023a) *The Reading Framework*. London: DfE.

DfE (2023b) *Development Matters: Non-Statutory Guidance for the Early Years Foundation Stage*. London: DfE.

DfE (2023c) *Economic Benefits of Effective Reception Classes*. London: DfE.

DfE (2023d) *Validation of systematic synthetic phonics programmes: supporting documentatation*. London: DfE.

DfE (2024a) *Early Years Foundation Stage Statutory Framework: For Group and School-Based Providers*. London: DfE.

DfE (2024b) *Early Years Foundation Stage Profile Handbook*. London: DfE.

Department for Education and Employment (DfEE) (1999) *Progression in Phonics: Materials for Whole Class Teaching*. London: DfEE.

Department of Education and Science (DfES) (1985) *Better Schools*, Cmnd. 9469. London: HMSO.

DfES (1987) *The National Curriculum: A Consulation Document*. London: DfES.

DfES (2007) *Letters and Sounds: Principles and Practice of High Quality Phonics: Notes of Guidance for Practitioners and Teachers*. Norwich: DfES.

Dunst, C.J., Meter, D. and Hamby, D.W. (2011) Relationship between young children's nursery rhyme experiences and knowledge and phonological and print-related abilities. *CELL Reviews*, 4(1).

Elliott, V., Nelson-Addy, L., Chantiluke, R. and Courtney, M. (2021) *Lit in Colour: Diversity in Literature in English Schools*. Research report co-commissioned by Runnymede Trust and Penguin Books.

Fox, M. (2008) *Reading Magic: Why Reading Aloud to Our Children Will Change Their Lives Forever*. New York: Houghton Mifflin Harcourt.

Fry, E. (2004) Phonics: A large phoneme-grapheme frequency count revisited. *Journal of Literacy Research*, 36, 85–98.

Gathercole, S.E., Lamont, E. and Alloway, T.P. (2006) Working memory in the classroom. In S. Pickering (ed.), *Working Memory and Education*. London: Academic Press.

Gotlieb, R., Rhinehart, L. and Wolf, M. (2022) The 'reading brain' is taught, not born: Evidence from evolving neuroscience of reading for teachers and society. *The Reading League Journal*, September/October.

Gough, P. and Tunmer, W. (1986) Decoding, reading and reading disability. *Remedical and Special Education*, 7, 6–10.

Hart, B. and Risley, T.R. (2003) The early catastrophe: The 30 million word gap by age 3. *American Educator*, 27, 4–9.

Hodges, R.E. (1966) The case for teaching sound-to-letter correspondences in spelling. *Elementary School Journal*, 66, 327–336.

Iheakanwa, J.U., Obro, S. and Akpochafo, W.P. (2021) Reading ability, study habits and students' academic performance in social studies. *Library Philosophy and Practice* (e-journal), 5675. https://digitalcommons.unl.edu/libphilprac/5675

Joliffe, W., Waugh, D. and Gill, A. (2019) *Teaching Systematic Synthetic Phonics in Primary Schools*, 3rd edition. London: Learning Matters.

Kisilevsky, B.S., Hains, S., Brown, C., Lee, C., Cowperthwaite, B., Stutzman, S., Swansburg, M., Lee, K., Xie, X., Huang, H., Ye, H.-E., Zhang, K. and Wang, Z. (2008) Fetal sensitivity to properties of maternal speech and language. *Infant Behaviour Development*, 32, 59–71.

Kozloff, M. (2002) A whole language catalogue of the grotesque (Blog post). Retrieved from http://people.uncw.edu/kozloffm/wlquotes.html

Masterson, J., Stuart, M., Dixon, M. and Lovejoy, S. (2003) Children's Printed Word Database. Economic and Social Research Council funded project, R00023406.

Milton, J. and Treffers-Daller, J. (2013) Vocabulary size revisited: the link between vocabulary size and academic achievement. *Applied Linguistics Review*, 4(1), 151–172.

Ministry of Justice (2021) *Prisoner education statistics April 2009 to March 2020*. Official Statistics Bulletin, Ministry of Justice.

Mulcahy, E., Bernardes, E. and Baars, S. (2019) The relationship between reading age, education and life outcomes. Lexonik. https://cfey.org/reports/2016/12/the-relationship-between-reading-age-education-and-life-outcomes/

National Children's Book and Literacy Alliance (2015) Kids see! Kids do! Become a literacy role model. https://thencbla.org/education/parent-handbook/kids-see-kids-do-become-a-literacy-role-model/

Neaum, S. (2017) *What Comes before Phonics?* London: Sage.

OECD (2002) *Reading for Change: Performance and Engagement across Countries: Results from PISA 2000*, PISA, OECD Publishing, Paris, https://doi.org/10.1787/9789264099289-en.

Ofsted (2023) *Education Inspection Framework*. London: Ofsted.

Ofsted (2024) *School Inspection Handbook*. London: Ofsted.

Ofsted (2009) *English at the Crossroads*. London: Ofsted.

Ofsted (2010) *Reading by Six*. Manchester: Ofsted.

Ofsted (2014) *Getting Them Reading Early*. Manchester: Ofsted.

Ofsted (2024) *Telling The Story: The English Education Subject Report*. London: Ofsted.

Open University (2024) Reading for pleasure pedagogy. https://ourfp.org/reading-for-pleasure-pedagogy

Ouellette, G.P. and Sénéchal, M. (2008) A window into early literacy: Exploring the cognitive and linguistic underpinnings of invented spelling. *Scientific Studies of Reading*, 12(2), 195–219.

Oxford Language Report (2024) *The Oxford Language Report 2023: Building Children's Vocabulary at Home and at School*. Oxford: Oxford University Press.

Partanen, E., Teija Kujala, T., Näätänen, R., Liitola, A., Sambeth, A. and Huotilainen, M. (2013) Learning-induced neural plasticity of speech processing before birth. *Proceedings of the National Academy of Sciences*, 110(37), 15145–15150.

Pegado, F., Nakamura, K. and Hannagan, T. (2014) How does literacy break mirror invariance in the visual system? *Frontiers in Psychology*, 5, 703.

Perfetti, C.A., Landi, N. and Oakhill, J. (2005) The acquisition of reading comprehension skill. In M. J. Snowling and C. Hulme (eds), *The Science of Reading: A Handbook* (pp. 227–247). Oxford: Blackwell.

Philps, D. (2012) Submorphemes: Backtracking from English 'kn- words' to the emergence of the linguistic sign. *Miranda* [online], 7. http://journals.openedition.org/miranda/4244

Rose, J. (2006) *Independent Review of the Teaching of Early Reading, Final Report*. Nottingham: DfES.

Shinabarger, N. (2017) *Literacy and Criminality. The Idea of an Essay*, Volume 4, Article 29. Cedarville University.

Snow, C.E. and Juel, C. (2005) Teaching children to read: What do we know about how to do it? In M.J. Snowling and C. Hulme (eds), *The Science of Reading: A Handbook* (pp. 501–520). Oxford: Blackwell Publishing.

Stainthorp, R. and Hughes, D. (1999) *Learning from Children who Read at an Early Age*. London: Routledge.

Standard and Testing Agency (STA) (2024) *Phonics Screening Check: 2024 Materials*. STA: Coventry.

Stebbins, R. (2013) *The Committed Reader: Reading For Utility, Pleasure, And Fulfilment In The Twenty-First Century*. Lanham, MD: Scarecrow Press.

Voegtline, K.M., Costigan, K.A., Pater, H. and DiPietro, J. (2013) Near-term fetal response to maternal spoken voice. *Infant Behaviour Development*, 36, 526–533.

Whitehead, M. (2010) *Language and Literacy in the Early Years*, 4th edition. London: Sage.

Wolf, M. (2007) *Proust and the Squid: The Story and the Science of the Reading Brain*. New York: HarperCollins.

Yeatman, J.D., Dougherty, R.F., Ben-Shachar, M. and Wandell, B.A. (2012) Development of white matter and reading skills *Proceedings of the National Academy of Sciences of the United States of America*, 109(44), E3045–53.

Zeynep, O., Pedro, J.F., Stern, C., Desmond, K., Otto, N., Talbot, C.B., Vargas-Gutierrez, P. and Waddell, S. (2023) Multisensory learning binds neurons into a cross-modal memory engram. *Nature*, 617(7692), 777–784.

INDEX

ABC rule, of phonics teaching, 215–216
accuracy, 204
adjacent consonants, 121–122, 132–133
affricatives, 61
alliteration, 13, 19, 31
alternative graphemes, 160–168
   for phonemes, 162–165
   spelling rules for, 173–175
   word bank, 182–186
   within words, 166–167
assessment for learning, 214
assimilation, 62
auditory, 13
auditory memory games, 81–82
author visits, 208
automaticity, 75, 204

best bet boards, 178
best bet decisions, 165–167
bingo game, 33
blending, 75–76
   arms, 84
   assisted, 79–80
   CVC words, 121
   difficulties, 82
   fluency, 81, 83, 85
   moving flashcards, 84
   oral, 82
   phonemes using wooden train tracks, 88
   practising, 79
   pure sounds and, 79
   and reading words, using frame, 91
   and segmenting, 93–94, 125–126
   slide, 83–84
   sound buttons, 83
   sticks, 89
   successive, 80
   techniques to stop overt segmenting and, 85
   using bulldozer toy/building blocks to practising, 87
book area checklist, 210
book care, 47
book talk, 206
building blocks
   learning high-frequency words using, 154
   practising phonemic blending, 87
bulldozer blending, 87
bumper cars, 101

CCVC and CVCC words, 122–123
choral reading, 204
chunking words, 138–139
CLL (communication, language and literacy), 45–46
closed syllables, 136, 142
CLOVER acronym, 168, 169
CLPE Reflecting Realities, 208

cluster reduction, 62
code breaking exercise, 103
cognitive load, 57
coin flip bingo, 177
communication and language, 41
   Development Matters statements for, 42–43
   early learning goals, 45–46
compound words, 135, 139–141, 144
comprehension, 46, 48
consonant casserole, 129
consonant clusters/blends. *See* adjacent consonants
consonant digraphs, 109
consonants, 107, 121
   adjacent, 121–122
   vowels and, 122–123, 170
consonant sound, 13
consonant strings, 123, 132
continuant consonants, 80–81
crayon box sorting, 56
cupcake tin activity, 127
CVC (consonant–vowel–consonant) words, 75, 78–79, 83, 92
   extending, 124–125

decodable books, 202–203
decodable compound and multisyllabic words, 146
decoding, 75, 93, 121, 147
Department for Education and Science, 6
Department for Education and Skills (DfES), 8
Development Matters, 39, 41–44
dexterity, 93
DfE (Department for Education), 9, 41, 187
digraphs, 107, 159
   activity using table to learn, 114
   bingo building game, 117
   common dilemmas, 112
   consonant, 109
   and double letters, 108–109
   introduction, 108
   naming the letters, 112
   phoneme frames, 113
   sound buttons, 112–113
   split, 161
   spotting, 111–112
   spotting game, 118
   vowel, 110–111, 137
   word list, 119
dino races, 197
diphthongs, 107, 110, 135
diversity, 207–208
double letters, initial digraphs and, 108–109
Duplo windows, 91

early language skills, importance of, 15
early learning goals (ELGs), 45–46

Early Years Foundation Stage (EYFS), 39, 40–44, 45
Early Years Foundation Stage Profile (EYFSP), 39, 45–46
echo reading, 204
Education Endowment Foundation, 203
Education Inspection Framework, 221
Education Reform Act, 6
egg box words, 90
Elkonin boxes. *See* phoneme frames
emergent literacy, 13, 14–15
encoding, 93, 94
English language, 1–2
    common words in, 148
envelope word sliders, 128
EYFS (Early Years Foundation Stage), 39, 40–44, 45
EYFSP (Early Years Foundation Stage Profile), 39, 45–46

fidelity, 211
final consonant deletion, 62
fine motor developmental milestones, 95–96
fine motor skills, 93
finger hopscotch, 73
flashcards, moving, 84
fluency
    developing, 85, 203–204
    high-frequency words to developing, 154
    pyramids, 205
    strategies to developing, 204–205
    using word ladder to practising, 130
folded paper, practising word sounds using, 142
Fox, Mem, 23
fricatives, 61
    stopping of, 62
friezes and sound mats, 65

ghost letters, 172–173
glides, 61
GPCs. *See* grapheme–phoneme correspondences (GPCs)
Gradual Release of Responsibility Model, 204
grapheme–phoneme correspondences (GPCs), 10, 57, 63–64, 81–83, 93, 101, 121, 149
graphemes, 57, 93, 114–115, 159
    alternative, 160–168
    identify, using dice and marker pen, 179
    and phonemes, 177–178
    reading, using word ladder, 180

heart words, 147, 150
high-frequency words, 147–158
    decodable words, 149
    heart words, 147, 150
    mnemonics, 151
    placing sound buttons under tricky words, 150
    spelling pyramids, 151–152
    spelling strategy, 152–153
    tricky words, 149–150, 155–158
    using building blocks, 154
    visual aids, 151
human buckeroo game, 35

illiteracy, economic cost of, 2
Independent Review of the Teaching of Early Reading (Rose), 6
inferior frontal cortex/frontal lobe, 77
interview lessons, 216–219

jigsaw puzzle, 141
jumbled jellyfish, 52

keypad-style activity, learning tricky words using, 158

language, communication and, 41–43, 45–46
language comprehension, 41
language-rich environment audit, 36–37
learning to read, 4, 77
    multiple aspects to, 5
    and spell more complex words, 159–176
    teaching phonics, 5
lesson observation template, 220
'le' syllable rule, 169
letter
    combinations of, 107–108
    confusion, 66
    and name recognition, 53–54
    phonics-based letter instruction, 65
    recognition, 69–73
    –sound knowledge, 64
    and sound palette, 72
letter names, 112
Letters and Sounds guidance, 8, 9
library visits, 208
liquid gliding, 62
liquids, 61
listening
    and attention/understanding, 45–46
    and spelling game, using casserole dish, 129
literacy, 41
    communication skills of, 8
    Development Matters statements for, 43–44
    early learning goals, 46
    importance of names as introduction to, 44
    skills, practising, 105
love of reading, developing, 201–209

Magna Doodle, 105
Matthew effect, 29
mirror invariance, 66–67
mnemonics, 151
model reading, with fluency/disfluency, 204
monster munch, 115
morphology, 121
multi-sensory phonics, 12
multi-sensory resources and activities, 213–214
multisyllabic words, 135, 136, 138–140, 169–171
multi-system interplay, during language acquisition, 66

names
    games with, 44–45
    letter and name recognition, 53–54
    practising spelling, 52, 55–56
    recognising and writing, 50–51
nasal phonemes, 61
National Curriculum, 6, 202
National Literacy Strategy, 5, 7, 8
National Literacy Trust, 27, 208
nursery rhymes, 23

occipito-temporal cortex, 77
odd one out, 116
Ofsted
    five Ws, 223–224
    inspections and reading deep dives, 221–227
    observations of phonics lessons and reading sessions, 224
    questions and potential supporting evidence, 224–226
    triangulation of evidence for, 222

onset and rime, 13, 18–19
open syllables, 136–137, 142
oracy skills, 47
oral, 13
    blending, 13, 82
    segmenting, 13
Oxford Language Report, 27

paired reading, 204
paper cuffs, practising reading difficult words
        using, 155
parents, as first teacher, 28–29
parietal temporal region, 77
passwords and pin codes, 158
pedestrian crossing, 130
phoneme frames, 97, 113, 125
phoneme-object associations, 74
phonemes, 13, 30, 35, 57, 61, 93, 159
    alternative, 161–162, 168
    framing exercise, 104
    further alternative graphemes for, 162–165
    graphemes and, 177–178
    practising, 102
phonemic awareness, 13, 20–22
    developing (activity), 21–22
    level, 19–20
    six levels of, 20–21
phonetically plausible attempt, at spelling, 99–100
phonics, 3, 57
    multi-sensory approach to, 11–12
    preparing children for, 13–38
    readiness for advanced stages, 160
    teaching into phases, 8
phonics-based letter instruction, 65
phonics lesson
    ABC rule, 215–216
    adaptations, 214
    applying knowledge, 213
    assessment for learning, 214
    data-driven, 215
    key elements of, 212–216
    multi-sensory resources and
            activities, 213–214
    pace, 213
    phonics-rich environment, 215
    planned decodable words, 214
    practising newly taught skill, 212
    reading and writing opportunities, 214
    resources, 213
    revisiting and reviewing, 212
    subject knowledge, 215
    systematic and synthetic, 212
    teaching new skills, 212
Phonics Screening Check, 9
    achieving expected standard in, 189, 190
    administration, 187–189
    criticisms, 191
    data use and reporting, 189–190
    example, 198
    follow-up after failure, 190
    preparation tips for, 190–191
    reasons for including pseudowords, 188
    scoring guidance of non-words sections, 198–199
    sections, 187
    Year 1, 187–199
phonics viewfinder, 71
phonogram, 159

phonological awareness, 13, 15–20, 48
    components of, 16
    onset and rime level, 18–19
    phonemic awareness level, 19–20
    practical activity, 15
    syllable level, 17–18
    word level, 16
poetry reading, 204
polysyllabic words, 135, 137–138, 139, 146, 169
posting letters, 70
pre-planned decodable words, 214
pre-reading skills, 11, 14, 23, 40, 79
print knowledge, 24
Progression in Phonics guidance, 7
pronunciation, 58
    guide for initial sounds, 59–60
prosody, 204
pseudowords, 187, 188, 192–193, 196, 198–199
pure sounds, 58–60, 79, 170

quadgraph, 159

r-controlled syllables, 137
reading
    building blocks of, 10–11, 14
    choice and variety, 207
    decodable books, 202–203
    developing love of, 201–209
    diversity, 207–208
    environments, creating engaging book corners, 207
    fluency, 203–205
    for just 30 minutes a week, 205
    language comprehension, 41
    longer words, 135–136
    mental process of, 76–77
    outdoors, 208
    for pleasure, 201–202, 207
    purposes to, 28–29
    pyramid, 11
    repetitive, 28, 218
    simple view of, 5–6
    social reading environments, 205–206
    beyond the bookshelf, 208
    timeline, 3–4
    word reading, 41
    and writing opportunities, 214
reading aloud, 206
    across curriculum, 208
reading brain, 77–78
reading buddies, 206
Reading Framework, 9, 206
Reading Magic (Fox), 23
Reading Wars, 4
real and non-words
    paper basketball game to identify, 193
    practising using dinosaur toys and word ladders, 197
    sorting using cereal boxes, 195
    using dog bowls and bone treats, 194
reduplication, 62
repeated reading, 205
repetitive reading, benefits of, 28, 218
retelling and imagination, 48
rhyme, tuning into, 22–23
rime, onset and, 13, 18–19
roll and read activity, 179
Rose, J., 6
Rose Review, 7–8, 187

School Inspection Handbook, 222
school-ready poem, 40
schwa, 57, 58, 159, 170–172
scooping phrases, 205
searchlights model, 5
seek and spell, 157
segmenting, 75–76, 93
    and blending, 93–94, 125–126
    and encoding, 94
    fingers, 97
    manipulatives, 96
    phoneme frames, 97
    robot technique, 98
    sound mapping, 98
    and spelling, 94, 96–99
    and spelling words, using cupcake tin, 127
    word chains, 96–97
self-review framework, 228–229
semivowel, 61
sensory name board, 50
shared reading, 27
sight word, 147
silent letters. *See* ghost letters
silly sentences, 167–168
'Silly Soup', 19
slide and spell, 131
social reading environments, 205–206
sound buttons, 83, 112–113, 150, 161
sound mapping, 98
speaking, 46
speech production, common phonological errors
        in, 61–62
spelling, 93
    development, 94–95
    phonetically plausible attempt at, 99–100
    practising, using track game, 181
    segmenting and, 96–99
    steps to, 99
spelling lines, 98–99
spelling pyramids, 151–152
spelling rules, 173–175
spelling tracks, 181
split digraphs, 161
    syllable rule, 169
stop phonemes, 61
stories, sharing, 27
story structure, 48
story time and sharing stories, 206
subject knowledge, 208, 215
submorphemes, 124, 173
successive blending, 80
swopping lines, 139
syllable deletion, 62
syllable pyramids, 139
syllables, 14, 17–18, 32–33, 135, 159
    consonant and vowel patterns to identifying, 170
    'le' syllable rule, 169
    open and closed, 136–137, 142
    segmentation of polysyllabic words, 169
    split-digraph syllable rule, 169
    types, 136–137, 168–169
    and vowel sounds, practising, 145

syllable tracks, 143
synonym, 39
synthetic phonics, 3, 4, 9, 212
systematic phonics, 3, 212
systematic, synthetic phonics (SSP)
        programmes, 7
    reasons for using, 218
    validation criteria for, 9–10

tactile letter cards, 69
Teachers as Readers project, 201
teaching early reading, 3
teaching of reading, 9
    evaluating, 224
    impact on spelling and writing, 8
    timeline of research, 4
temporal lobe, 77
there/their/they're, 151
train track blending, 88
trickier consonant strings, 123
tricky words, 147, 149–150, 155–158, 160
trigraphs, 107, 159
    introduction, 108
    phoneme frames, 113
    sound buttons, 112–113
    spotting, 111
    vowel, 137
    vowel digraphs and, 110–111
    word list, 119

University of Oregon, 15

VC (vowel and consonant), 75, 170
velar fronting, 61–62
visual aids, 151
visual perception and discrimination, 24–25
vocabulary, 14, 47–48
    development, 25–27
vowels, 14, 107, 121, 135, 159
    and consonants, 122–123, 170
    digraphs and trigraphs, 110–111
    representing schwa, 170
    and syllable types, 136–138, 168–169
vowel sounds
    discriminating between, 62
    practising syllable and, 145
vowel team syllable, 137

word building, using toy cars, 101
word chains, 96–97
word families, 19
word ladders, 130, 180
wordless books, 47–48
word puzzles, 196
word reading, 5, 41, 46
word substitution, 17
working memory, 75, 81
writing, 46
    phonetically plausible attempts at,
        99–100

Zone of Proximal Development, 204